THE CULT

&

CONSTITUTION

The Culling of our Contestations

BIJOY KRUSHNA MAHANTI

INDIA • SINGAPORE • MALAYSIA

ISBN
Hardcase 979-8-89929-665-9
Paperback 979-8-89777-298-8

Contents

Prologue

That is originally nothing in this book, but all the writings that pleased the author imputing into a computer and then compile them.

The "Cult and Constitution" is a critical concept that refers to the almost religious reverence some people have for the Constitution, treating it as an infallible and unchangeable document rather than a flexible framework meant to evolve with society. This idea is often discussed in legal and political discourse, particularly in relation to constitutional originalism, legal interpretations, and debates over civil rights.

Blind Devotion to the Constitution – Some individuals or groups treat the Constitution as sacred, resisting changes or modern interpretations even when necessary.

The idea of blind devotion to the Constitution refers to a rigid, almost religious adherence to the document, where individuals or groups resist any reinterpretation or amendment, regardless of societal changes or evolving legal and ethical standards. This mindset often manifests in several ways:

Many adherents to this view follow originalism, the belief that the Constitution should be interpreted exactly as the Founding Fathers intended. They argue that deviating from this approach risks undermining the integrity of the legal system. However, critics argue that this perspective ignores the fact that society, technology, and moral values have changed dramatically since the 18th century.

Despite the framers designing the Constitution to be amendable, some people treat it as fixed and unchangeable. This resistance can slow or block necessary reforms, such as expanding civil rights protections or addressing modern issues like digital privacy.

While some claim to uphold the "pure" Constitution, they often emphasize certain amendments—especially the First Amendment (free speech) and Second Amendment (gun rights)—while downplaying others, like the Fourth Amendment (privacy rights) or the Equal Protection Clause. This selective devotion can be used to justify specific political or ideological agendas.

When the Constitution is viewed as sacred and infallible, it discourages critical analysis and debate. This can lead to:

Inflexibility in responding to new challenges (e.g., internet regulations, climate change policies).

Legal decisions that rely more on tradition than on contemporary ethical considerations.

The dismissal of historical injustices embedded in the original document, such as compromises on slavery and voting rights.

While respect for the Constitution is essential for legal stability, treating it as an unchangeable relic rather than a living document can hinder progress. Recognizing its historical context and adaptability is crucial to ensuring it continues to serve the evolving needs of society.

Originalism vs. Living Constitution – Supporters of originalism argue that the Constitution should be interpreted strictly as intended by its framers, while critics believe in a more adaptive, evolving interpretation.

Originalism is the belief that the Constitution should be interpreted strictly based on its original meaning when it was written. Judges who follow this philosophy aim to apply the exact words and intentions of the Founding Fathers, rather than adapting the Constitution to contemporary societal values.

The Living Constitution theory argues that the document must be interpreted in the context of modern society. Courts should consider contemporary values, changing societal norms, and the practical effects of their rulings.

Impact on Rights and Governance – The "Cult and Constitution" can influence legal rulings, policies, and political decisions, sometimes leading to resistance against progressive changes in areas like free speech, gun control, and privacy rights.

The "Cult and Constitution" can significantly shape legal rulings, policies, and political decisions, particularly when strict constitutional interpretations are used to resist progressive changes. This rigid approach can create obstacles in areas like free speech, gun control, privacy rights, and civil rights expansion. The "Cult and Constitution" influences governance by prioritizing rigid interpretations over evolving societal needs. While constitutional stability is important, an unyielding devotion to original intent can block necessary reforms in free speech, gun control, privacy, and civil rights. Balancing constitutional fidelity with adaptability remains one of the greatest challenges in modern governance.

Criticism of Constitutional Fundamentalism – Legal scholars argue that treating the Constitution as an unchallengeable doctrine can hinder necessary reforms and adaptation to contemporary issues.

Constitutional fundamentalism refers to the belief that the U.S. Constitution is a fixed, unchallengeable doctrine that should not be altered or reinterpreted, even in response to modern societal changes. Many legal scholars, historians, and policymakers argue that this rigid approach creates significant obstacles to necessary legal and political reforms.

Constitutional fundamentalism, while rooted in the idea of preserving the nation's founding principles, can hinder necessary reforms, block progress on modern issues, and selectively serve political interests. Legal scholars emphasize that the Constitution must be interpreted as a living document that evolves with society, rather than a rigid, unchallengeable framework that prevents adaptation.

The term "Cult and Constitution" in the Indian context can be interpreted in several ways, reflecting the nation's complex relationship with its foundational legal document.

Reverence for the Constitution:

In India, the Constitution is often held in high esteem, symbolizing the country's commitment to democracy, secularism, and social justice.

This reverence is evident in various public demonstrations and cultural expressions. For instance, during protests against certain government policies perceived as discriminatory, citizens have been known to publicly read the Preamble to the Constitution, emphasizing its core values of justice, liberty, equality, and fraternity. Such acts underscore the deep respect and almost sacrosanct status the Constitution holds in the collective consciousness of many Indians.

Judicial Interpretation and the Basic Structure Doctrine:

The Indian judiciary has played a pivotal role in interpreting the Constitution, sometimes leading to debates about judicial overreach. The Basic Structure Doctrine, established by the Supreme Court in the landmark case of Kesavananda Bharati v. State of Kerala AIR 1973 SC 1461, posits that while the Parliament has wide-ranging powers to amend the Constitution, it cannot alter its "basic structure." This includes fundamental principles like the supremacy of the Constitution, the rule of law, and the separation of powers. This doctrine ensures that certain core values remain inviolable, reflecting a protective attitude towards the Constitution's foundational principles.

Critiques of Constitutional Fundamentalism:

While the Constitution is revered, there are critiques regarding its interpretation and application. Some scholars argue that an overly rigid or selective interpretation can lead to "constitutional fundamentalism," where certain provisions are emphasized to the detriment of others, potentially undermining the document's holistic vision. This perspective suggests that while the Constitution should be respected, it must also be interpreted in a dynamic and inclusive manner, considering the evolving needs and values of society.

In summary, the "Cult and Constitution" in India encapsulates a spectrum of attitudes—from deep reverence and protective judicial doctrines to critical analyses of its interpretation. This multifaceted relationship highlights the Constitution's central role in India's democratic ethos and the ongoing discourse on its application in contemporary society.

The Cult and Constitution[1]
[The culling of our contestations[2]][3]

The term "cult" typically refers to a social group defined by its religious, spiritual, or philosophical beliefs, practices, or rituals, often perceived as unconventional or outside the mainstream. Cults can vary widely in their beliefs and practices, but they commonly share some characteristics to illustrate[4]:

1. A central, charismatic leader who is often venerated or considered infallible.
2. Encouragement or enforcement of isolation from society, including family and friends, to maintain control over members.
3. Techniques to manipulate and control members, such as indoctrination, psychological pressure, and exploitation.
4. Belief in possessing an exclusive truth or revelation that sets them apart from others.
5. Expectation of total commitment and often significant personal sacrifice from members.

The causes behind the formation of cults and their constitutions (structures and functions) can be complex and multifaceted, here are some of their key factors:

1. Individuals may join cults to fulfill psychological needs, such as the need for belonging, purpose, or identity. Cults often provide a sense of community and meaning that some people may find lacking in their lives.
2. A charismatic leader can attract followers through persuasive communication, personal charm, and promises of either salvation or enlightenment.
3. Times of social upheaval, economic instability, or widespread disillusionment can make people more susceptible to joining cults. In such times, cults may appear either as a refuge or a solution to their problems.

4. Cults often exploit cognitive dissonance, where conflicting beliefs or behaviors lead individuals to rationalize and justify the cult's practices and beliefs.
5. Cults often use psychological techniques, such as love bombing[5] (excessive positive attention), information control, and fear tactics, to indoctrinate and retain members.

Cults typically possess a hierarchical structure with a central, charismatic leader at the top. This leader often holds ultimate authority and may be seen either as infallible or divine. Below the leader, there may be a hierarchy of lieutenants or inner circle members or a kitchen cabinet, who help maintain control and enforce the leader's directives.

The belief system of a cult is usually highly defined and rigid, often presenting an exclusive truth or revelation. This belief system may include apocalyptic predictions, unique religious doctrines, or philosophies that set the group apart from mainstream society.

Membership in a cult is typically characterized by high levels of commitment and loyalty. Members may be required to undergo significant personal sacrifice, including financial contributions, relinquishment of personal autonomy, and severing ties with non-members, including family and friends.

Cults often have unique rituals and practices that reinforce the group's beliefs and foster a sense of community. These practices can range from daily routines and communal living to elaborate ceremonies and rites of passage.

Cults employ various control mechanisms to maintain order and loyalty among members. These can include information control (restricting access to outside information), emotional manipulation (love bombing, guilt, and fear), and behavioral control (regulating daily activities and personal choices).

The economic structure of a cult often involves members contributing financially to the group, sometimes to the point of economic exploitation. The leader or leadership group usually controls these resources, further solidifying their power and influence.

To illustrate these points, one considers a few well-known examples of cults and their structures:

1. Heaven's Gate: Led by Marshall Applewhite[6], this cult believed in an impending apocalypse and the need to leave Earth to reach a higher plane of existence. Members were highly committed, following strict lifestyle regulations and ultimately participating in a mass suicide.

2. The People's Temple: Founded by Jim Jones[7], this cult started as a progressive, inclusive community but evolved into a highly controlling environment. Jones exerted immense psychological control over his followers, leading to the mass suicide/murder event at Jonestown.

3. Scientology: Founded by L. Ron Hubbard[8], presents a hierarchical structure with advanced levels of spiritual enlightenment. The church employs intense information control, isolation tactics, and significant financial demands on its members.

Understanding the dynamics and causes behind cults provides insights into how individuals can become deeply involved in such groups, often to the detriment of their personal autonomy and well-being. Cults remain a fascinating and concerning phenomenon, highlighting the complex interplay between psychological needs, social influences, and charismatic leadership.

The phrase "The Cult and Constitution" could be interpreted in various context depending on the presenting dialogue. Without additional context, here are a few potential angles, such as;

Historical and political context could refer to historical periods when cults or religious groups have significantly influenced political and constitutional developments. For instance, during the French Revolution, the Cult of the Supreme Being was established by Maximilien Robespierre, which played a role in shaping the revolutionary government's policies and constitutional alteration.

Legal and religious studies pertain to the intersection of cult (or new and few religious movements) and constitutional law. Many countries have constitutions that guarantee freedom of religion, and the legal system often has to balance this freedom against concerns about potentially harmful practices within certain cults. Discussions in this context would involve how constitutions protect religious freedom while also ensuring public safety and individual rights.

Sociological perspective examining how cults or tightly knit religious group interact with societal norms and legal format and frameworks, particularly constitutional rights and freedoms. This includes the tension between collective religious practices and individual constitutional rights.

Literature or cultural analysis a more metaphorical or literary sense, the Cult and Constitution might explore themes in literature or cultural discourse where ideologies or belief systems (cult) clash with or influence foundational societal principles (Constitutions).

Historical and Political Context

French Revolution: The Cult of the Supreme being was an attempt to create a civic religion that would replace Christianity and unify the republic. It was part of a broader effort to de-Christianize France and promote enlightenment values through a state-sanctioned belief system.

Legal and Religious studies

US Constitution: The first amendment guarantees freedom of religion, which has led to numerous legal battles over the rights of religious groups versus state interests. So also the Indian Constitution guarantees the freedom of religion under Articles 25-28[9], which ensures that all individuals in India have the right to freely profess, practice, and propagate their religion, This fundamental right is crucial in maintaining India's secular fabric and ensuring religious harmony among its diverse population. Cases involving groups like the Branch Davidians or Scientology often bring these issues to the forefront.

Sociological Perspective

Freedom Vrs. Regulation: Sociologists suggest how societies regulate new religious movements and the implications for personal freedoms. This includes the role of governments in intervening when cults are accused of illegal or harmful activities.

Literature or Cultural analysis

Dystopian Fiction: Books like George Orwell's "1984"[10] or Aldous Huxley's "Brave New World"[11] often explore how ideological cults (Totalitarian Regimes) impose their will on populations, challenging the very idea of constitutional freedoms.

Specific Examples

France: An artificial religion created during the French Revolution that was meant to promote republican values to replace Christianity. This attempt at a State imposed belief system had significant political and constitutional implications.

United States: The 1993 Waco Siege involving the Branch Davidians raised questions about religious freedom and government intervention. The Constitutional implications of the government's action s were widely debated.

Legal battles over the Church of Scientology's practices and its recognition as a religion have tested the boundaries of religious freedom under the first amendment.

These angles provide a broad understanding how "the Cult and Constitution" could be analysed and understood in various disciplines.

Happiness

Astavakra Rishi says in Astavakra Gita that, "Rare is he who, observing his own ways, gives up the desires of pleasures and knowledge. Nothing quiet[12].

Not so quiet, but for my happiness, what everyone loves to live happily ever after, forever, was unbegotten, like many of my peers, found myself mostly disquiet, and disturbed many a times, for most of my disturbing mundanities. Mundane happenings, made one and one's life, a struggle, most of times, we find no meaning and purpose in those moments of struggle, to happen with all.

I being born and, living in a Hindu house hold, but not a very staunch one, happiness was always what my fate had ordained, what God had designed for me as illustratively, like preaching of Swami Sivananda Saraswati a Hindu spiritual, and a proponent of Vedanta, himself a practicing physician for several years before taking up monasticism of, शान्तिः पृथिवीतले विकसतु शान्तिरावातु द्विपदे शान्तिर्विश्वमानवे। शान्तिर्ब्रह्मणि सर्वभूतानि शान्तिः सर्वभूतेषु चेतना, transliterated, as to whether happiness is by one's peace, as a concept of societal association, and harmony, sans hostility, avoiding violence, what in a social sense, having peace as common, in it's use to mean lack of conflict and freedom from fear of violence between individuals or groups, as the most covetable possession on the earth, that the greatest of treasures in all the universe, the most important and indispensable factor for all of one's growth and development as from a tiny acorn to a mighty oak.

It is in the tranquility and the quiet of the night that the seed slowly sprouts from under the soil. The bud opens in the depth of the most silent hours, and also, in a state of peace and love, people evolve, grow in their distinctive culture, to develop perfect civilization, or to find it be simpler, than that, happiness was or might have been with you all along—or you just may not have taken the time to realize it much more complicated than you ever imagined, that you probably knew well that it's not about driving the latest model car, or like a child fidgeting with a mechanical toy, what after a time, the begotten happiness denudes.

In essence, the reflection interweaves ancient wisdom with personal insights, underscoring that peace and happiness are intrinsic to our being and can be cultivated through inner awareness and societal harmony.

The traditions, of the elders, to bless the young to live with happiness ever after are based on their religion. In Hinduism, it is varied but the Sanatana Dharma[13] updated, about religious rituals, the intervening festivals, daily chants and yoga's, in the developments related to Hindu religion, says Rajendran, a freelancer, who studied Sanatana Dharma, writing the most important concept of happiness in Hinduism is that when the source of our happiness bases on an external or internal factors, ends up in none sufferance. Happiness is never outside but is within what you have. The happiness provided by a sense object perishes like dew underfoot in the early dawn. Aim for one's bliss which cannot be wiped away by any external force. There can be no happiness when there is either any attachment or fear. To be happy many people try to avoid problems but the best option to deal with problems is to confront them rather than to evade. In Hindu tradition, blessings for a life time of happiness often stem from religious practices and rituals that are deeply ingrained in the culture. However, the core understanding of happiness transcends mere external or internal factors; it lies within the individual's capacity to find contentment regardless of circumstances. The impermanence of happiness derived from material objects is likened to dew that evaporates at dawn, emphasising the fleeting nature of worldly pleasures. True happiness, as espoused in Hindu philosophy, is rooted in discovering one's inner bliss, immune to external forces. This bliss arises from transcending attachments and fears, confronting life's challenges rather than avoiding them. The narrative of Gautama Buddha's renunciation of his princely comforts underscores the idea that enduring happiness arises from seeking something deeper within oneself, beyond transient pleasures. Confronting the inevitabilities of life-disease, old age, and death-with wisdom and equanimity leads to a state of lasting bliss. Rajendran's reflection echoes the fundamental tenet of Hinduism; to attain happiness through self awareness, spiritual growth, and the pursuit of true knowledge. By recognizing the impermanence of external sources of happiness and cultivating inner contentment, individuals can achieve a state of bliss that transcends worldly fluctuations.

The concept of happiness varies significantly across different cultures and philosophies. In Western contexts, the word "happy" is derived from the Icelandic word "happ," to mean luck or chance. This etymology suggests that in Western thought, happiness is often seen as something transient and dependent on external circumstances. It's perceived as a fleeting state, influenced by luck or fortune, making it elusive and difficult to grasp permanently.

In contrast, Hindu philosophy offers a deeper, more intrinsic understanding of happiness. Here, the term "bliss" (Ananda) is used to describe a state of profound and enduring contentment that is not contingent on external factors. This bliss is considered far more substantial and worthwhile than the Western concept of happiness. It is something to be discovered and realized through spiritual practice and self-awareness, rather than something to be stumbled upon by chance.

Key Differences: Dependence on External Factors: Western Happiness: Often linked to external circumstances such as success, relationships, or material possessions. It's seen as something that can come and go based on luck or external events. Often pursued through achieving goals, acquiring possessions, and fulfilling desires.

Hindu Bliss (Ananda): Seen as an intrinsic state that can be cultivated through inner growth and spiritual practice. It is not dependent on external conditions but rather on one's own state of mind and spiritual realization. Attained through self-realization, understanding the true nature of the self, and aligning with spiritual truths. Practices such as meditation, selfless service (Seva), and devotion (Bhakti) are paths to this bliss.

Hindu Bliss: Brings about a profound sense of peace, flexibility, creativity, sociability, love, and forgiveness. It provides the energy to tolerate and overcome life's daily frustrations, leading to a more resilient and harmonious life.

Hindu Perspective on Bliss

In Hinduism, true happiness or bliss is realized when an individual understands and reaches the truth about their own nature and the nature of reality. This realization is often described as Moksha or liberation, which is the freeing of oneself from the cycle of birth and rebirth (Samsara) and the suffering that comes with it. Achieving this state of enlightenment allows one to experience a constant state of Ananda, a deep, abiding joy and peace.

Practical Implications:

Realizing this state of bliss has practical implications for daily life: Flexibility: Becoming adaptable and resilient in the face of change. Creativity: Tapping into a deeper source of inspiration and innovation. Sociability: Building more genuine and compassionate relationships. Loving and Forgiving: Cultivating a heart full of love and the ability to forgive easily. Energy and Tolerance: Gaining the strength to endure life's challenges without becoming overwhelmed. Effects on Life: Western Happiness: Can lead to temporary pleasure and satisfaction but is often accompanied by anxiety and the fear of loss.

In summary, while the Western concept of happiness is often seen as elusive and based on chance, Hindu philosophy offers a more profound and attainable state of bliss that can be realized through spiritual practice and self-discovery. This bliss leads to a more enriched, balanced, and resilient life.

It's indeed fascinating to observe the resurgence and growing relevance of ancient philosophies in the modern, digital age. This renewed interest, particularly in Eastern traditions like Hindu philosophy and practices such as Yoga, underscores a global search for deeper meaning and sustainable well-being in an increasingly fast-paced and technology-driven world.

The Cyclical Nature of Time:

Ancient philosophies, especially those from India, view time as cyclical rather than linear. This contrasts sharply with the Gregorian calendar system, which measures time in a linear, progressive manner. According to Hindu philosophy, life operates in cycles (Yugas), encompassing both good and bad periods. This cyclical perspective fosters a more accepting and resilient mindset, recognizing that challenges are temporary and part of a larger, repeating pattern.

Yoga and Self-Awareness:

Yoga has become a ubiquitous practice, transcending cultural boundaries to be embraced globally. It is not just a physical exercise but a comprehensive system for mental, emotional, and spiritual well-being. Yoga and related practices like meditation are prominently featured in self-help and self-awareness literature in the West. They are promoted for their ability to reduce stress, increase mindfulness, and enhance overall quality of life.

Ancient Traditions in Modern Contexts:

The teachings of ancient gurus and mythologists have found new relevance in contemporary settings:

Corporate Environments: Spiritual and philosophical teachings are being integrated into corporate culture. Techniques derived from Yoga and mindfulness are used to improve leadership skills, enhance employee well-being, and foster a more cohesive and productive work environment. Gurus and motivational speakers often attract corporate leaders, offering insights that help in navigating the complexities of modern business.

Boardrooms and Work Spaces: Stories and lessons from ancient myths are used to address modern challenges. Mythologists for instance, use traditional narratives to provide insights into management, ethics, and leadership. These stories offer timeless wisdom that can be applied to contemporary issues, making them highly relevant for today's audiences.

The Quest for Happiness

The universal question of how to achieve happiness and minimize suffering remains central to human desire. Ancient philosophies provide several pathways to this, like Inner Peace and Resilience: Practices like meditation and mindfulness cultivate inner peace and resilience, helping individuals navigate life's ups and downs more effectively. Balanced Perspective: Understanding the cyclical nature of time and life helps individuals maintain a balanced perspective, reducing the impact of negative experiences and enhancing appreciation of positive ones. Holistic Well-Being: Emphasizing holistic well-being, ancient traditions advocate for a balance between physical health, mental clarity, and spiritual fulfillment. This comprehensive approach to health is increasingly being adopted in the West.

The Role of Modern Gurus and Teachers:

Modern spiritual teachers and gurus play a pivotal role in bridging ancient wisdom and contemporary needs. They adapt traditional teachings to modern contexts, making them accessible and relevant. Their influence extends beyond personal spirituality to areas like corporate leadership, personal development, and holistic health.

In summary, the revival of ancient philosophies and practices in the digital age reflects a growing recognition of their enduring relevance. By integrating these timeless teachings into modern life, individuals and organizations alike are finding new ways to achieve happiness, resilience, and holistic well-being. This blending of ancient wisdom with contemporary life offers a profound and enriching approach to navigating the complexities of the modern world.

Your question about achieving happiness and having your life play out as desired is a profound one, especially in an era where we're inundated with information and opinions from various sources. Here's a structured approach to navigating this complex question:

Understanding the Nature of Happiness

Happiness is a deeply personal and multifaceted experience. It's important to distinguish between fleeting pleasures and lasting fulfillment. Fleeting pleasures are often tied to external events and material possessions, while lasting fulfillment typically arises from internal states of being and meaningful experiences.

Cultivating Inner Peace and Resilience

Ancient philosophies, including those from Hinduism, emphasize cultivating inner peace and resilience as key to enduring happiness. Practices such as mindfulness, meditation, and yoga can help: Mindfulness and Meditation: These practices train your mind to stay present, reduce anxiety, and enhance your capacity to handle stress. Yoga: Beyond physical benefits, yoga promotes mental clarity and emotional balance. Embracing the cyclical nature of life. Accepting that life is cyclical and that both good and bad times are inevitable can help you maintain a balanced perspective:

Perspective: Understanding that challenges are temporary and part of a larger cycle can reduce the impact of negative experiences. Resilience: Building resilience helps you recover from setbacks and continue moving forward with a positive outlook.

Aligning with Your Values and Purpose

The public goods ought to be the object of the legislator; general utility ought to be the foundation of his reasoning. To know the true good of the community is what constitutes the science of legislation; the art consists in finding the means to realize that good[14].

The principle of utility, vaguely announced, is seldom contradicted; it is even looked upon as a sort of commonplace both in politics and morals. But this almost universal assent is only apparent. The same ideas are not attached to this principle; the same value is not given to it; no uniform and logical manner of reasoning results from it.

To give it all the efficacy which it ought to have, that is to make it the foundation of a system of reasoning, three conditions are necessary. First to attach clear and precise ideas to the word utility, exactly the same with all who employ it. Second to establish the unity and the sovereignty of this principle, by rigorously excluding very other. It is nothing to subscribe to it in general; it must be admitted without an exception. Third to find the processes of a moral arithmetic by which uniform results may be arrived at.

The cause of dissent from the doctrine of utility may all be referred to two false principles, which exercise an influence, sometimes open and sometimes secret, upon the judgments of men. If these can be pointed out and excluded, the true principle will remain in purity and strength.

These three principles are like three roads which often cross each other, but of which only one leads to the wished for destination. The traveller turns often from one into another, and loses in these wanderings more than half his time and strength. The true route is however the easiest, it has mile stones which cannot be shifted, if has inscriptions, in a universal language, which cannot be effaced; while the two false routes have only contradictory directions in enigmatical characters. But without abusing the language of allegory, let us seek to give a clear idea of the true principle, and of its two adversaries.

Nature has placed man under the empire of pleasure and of pain. We owe to them all our ideas; we refer to them all our judgments, and all the determinations of our life. He who pretends to withdraw himself from this subjection knows not what he says. His only object is to seek pleasure and to shun pain, even at the very instant that he rejects the greatest pleasures or embraceing pain the most acute. These eternal and irresistible sentiments ought to be the great study of the moralist and the legislator. The principle of utility subjects everything to these two motives.

Utility is an abstract term. It expresses the property or tendency of a thing to prevent some evil or to procure some good. Evil is pain, or its cause. Good is pleasure, or the cause of pleasure. That which is conformable to the utility, or the interest of an individual, is what tends to augment the total sum of his happiness. That which is conformable to the utility, or the interest of a community, is what tends to augment the total sum of the happiness of the individuals that compose it.

A principle is a first idea, which is made the beginning or basis of a system of reasoning. To illustrate it by a sensible image, it is a fixed point to which the first link of a chain is attached. Such a principle must be clearly evident-to illustrate and to explain it must secure its acknowledgement. Such are the axioms of mathematics; they do not provide directly; it is enough to show that they cannot be rejected without falling into absurdity.

The logic of utility consists in setting out, in all the operations of the judgement from the calculation or comparison of pains and pleasures, and in not allowing the interference of any other idea.

I am a partisan of the principle of utility when I measure my approbation or disapprobation of a public or private act by its tendency to produce pleasure or pain; when I employ the words just, unjust, moral, immoral, good, bad, simply as collective terms including the ideas of certain pains or pleasures; it being always understood that I use the words pain and pleasure in their ordinary signification, without inventing any arbitrary definition for the sake of excluding certain pleasures or denying the existence of certain pains. In this matter, we want no refinement, no metaphysics. It is not necessary to consult Plato, nor Aristotle. Pain and Pleasure are what everybody feels to be such-the peasant and the prince, the unlearned as well as the philosopher.

He who adopts the principles of utility esteems virtue to be a good only on account of the pleasures which results from it; he regards vice as an evil only because of the pains, it produces. Moral good is good only by its tendency to produce physical good. Moral evil is evil only by its tendency to produce physical evil, but when I say physical, I mean the pains and pleasures of the soul as well as the pains and pleasures of sense. I have in view a man, such as he is, in his actual constitution.

If the partisan of the principle of utility finds in the common list of virtues an action from which there results more pain than pleasure, he does not hesitate to regard that pretended virtue as a vice, he will not suffer himself to be imposed upon by the general error, he will not lightly believe in the policy of employing false virtues to maintain the true.

If he finds in the common list of offence some indifferent action, some innocent pleasure, he will not hesitate to transport this pretended offence into the class of lawful actions, he will pity the pretended criminals, and will reserve his indignation for their persecutors.

Living a life aligned with your core values and purpose brings deeper satisfaction: Identify Your Values: Reflect on what truly matters to you. What are your core beliefs and principles? Purpose: Seek activities and goals that align with your values. This alignment fosters a sense of fulfillment and direction. Practicing Self-Compassion and Acceptance; Being kind to yourself and accepting your imperfections is crucial: Self-Compassion: Treat yourself with the same kindness and understanding you would offer to a friend. Acceptance: Recognize and accept your current situation without harsh judgment, which allows for personal growth and transformation. Connecting with others; Meaningful connections and relationships significantly contribute to happiness: Quality Relationships: Foster relationships that provide support, understanding, and companionship. Community: Engage with communities that share your interests and values, which can offer a sense of belonging and support. Balancing Information Intake; In the digital age, managing the flow of information is essential to avoid overwhelm: Digital Detox: Set boundaries for your social media and information consumption to prevent overload. Selective Engagement: Engage with content that adds value and aligns with your goals and values. Practical Steps for Daily Life; Morning Routine: Start your day with practices that grounds you, such as meditation or reading something inspirational. Set Intentions: Define clear intentions for your day to stay focused on what matters most to you.

Mindful Breaks: Take regular breaks to practice mindfulness, even for a few minutes, to maintain balance and clarity. Reflection: End your day with reflection. Consider what went well, what you're grateful for, and what you learned. Integrating Wisdom from Various Sources. Sacred Texts and Teachings: Reflect on the teachings of spiritual leaders and sacred texts. Apply their wisdom to your daily life in practical ways.

Life Experiences: Learn from the experiences of others, but tailor advice to fit your unique context and circumstances. Community Support: Engage with groups that offer constructive and supportive interactions, both online and offline.

By taking these steps, you can create a life plan that aligns with your desires and fosters true happiness. Remember, the journey to happiness is continuous and requires patience, self-compassion, and a willingness to adapt and grow.

The people would really love to have a simple formula, that helps them sort out the quotes, learn lessons, images and video clips in a way one can easily understand and apply when their bosses' yell at them, for no fault of their, when they have to console colleagues who feels unfairly treated or when a candidate to whom offers are made, to change her mind at the last minute on joining the team. At these times, it's hard to recall the lovely quotes, stories and dictums. You want to tear the little hair one has, fling things around and scream.

It's true that in moments of high stress, it's challenging to recall the wisdom from quotes, lessons, and inspirational content. Simplifying these teachings into an easily accessible formula can help. Here's a straightforward approach that can be used in stressful situations to regain composure and respond effectively:

Breathe (Pause and breathe)

Action: Take a deep breath. Inhale slowly for a count of four, hold for a count of four, and exhale slowly for a count of four. Repeat this a few times. Why: Deep breathing helps calm the nervous system, reducing the immediate stress response. Recognize (Identify the emotion) Action: Acknowledge what you're feeling without judgment. Label the emotion (e.g., anger, frustration, sadness). Why: Naming the emotion can help to diffuse its intensity and give you a moment of clarity. Evaluate (Assess the situation) Action: Quickly evaluate the situation. Ask yourself, "What's really happening here? What is within my control?" Why: Understanding the specifics of the situation can help you respond more rationally and effectively.

Accept (Embrace imperfection)

Action: Accept that some situations are beyond your control and that perfection is not always attainable. Why: Acceptance can reduce feelings of frustration and helplessness, allowing you to focus on what you can change. Think (Consider your response) Action: Before reacting, take a moment to think. What's the best way to respond? Consider the long-term impact of your actions. Why: Thoughtful responses are more constructive and lead to better outcomes than impulsive reactions. Help (Act with compassion) Action: Offer support to yourself and others involved. This could mean speaking calmly, offering a solution, or simply being present. Why: Compassionate actions can de-escalate tension and foster a positive environment.

Empower (Move forward positively) Action: Empower yourself by focusing on what you can do next. Set a small, manageable action to improve the situation. Why: Taking proactive steps helps regain a sense of control and moves you towards resolution.

Practical Application Scenarios

When Your Boss Yells at You Breathe: Take a deep breath to calm yourself. Recognize: Identify your emotions—fear, frustration, or anger. Evaluate: Assess if there's any constructive feedback or just a release of tension. Accept: Understand that everyone has bad days and it might not be personal. Think: Plan a measured response. "How can I address the issue calmly?" Help: Show compassion by listening and responding politely. Empower: Set a goal to discuss any misunderstandings later when emotions have cooled.

Consoling a Colleague

Breathe: Before speaking, take a deep breath to center yourself. Recognize: Acknowledge their feelings of unfair treatment. Evaluate: Understand the facts of what happened. Accept: Accept that you might not be able to change the situation immediately. Think: Consider how you can best support them. Help: Offer a listening ear, kind words, or practical advice. Empower: Encourage them to speak up or seek solutions constructively. By breaking down complex teachings into this simple, actionable formula, you can effectively manage stress and respond constructively, even in challenging situations.

Spiritual and philosophic traditions have been around since Hinduism started, to focus on knowledge, existence and what is real all around. Surely, then, some bright spark in the old days would have thought of an answer to basic question: How can we be happy? Indeed, they did, and offered a simple four-level model that in turn can be translated into a three-step action process recognise the model in your life and you can easily put into practice all the stories and quotes, and since it is not connected directly to any one religion, it's universal.

It sounds like you're referring to a framework that distills the essence of ancient spiritual and philosophical traditions into a practical model for achieving happiness. One such model that aligns with the descriptions and has universal applicability is the Four Purusharthas of Hindu philosophy, which can be translated into a three-step action process for modern application. The Purusharthas outline the four goals of a human life: Dharma (duty), Artha (prosperity), Kama (pleasure), and Moksha (liberation). Here's how they can be simplified and applied:

The Four-Level Model: The Purusharthas

Dharma (Duty/Ethical Living)

Concept: Living a life of righteousness, duty, and moral values. Purpose: Provides a framework for ethical living and fulfilling one's responsibilities to oneself and others.

Artha (Prosperity/Wealth) Concept: Pursuit of wealth and material success to support a stable and comfortable life. Purpose: Ensures financial security and the means to support oneself and family.

Kama (Pleasure/Desire)

Concept: Enjoyment of life's pleasures, including love, art, and culture. Purpose: Allows for emotional and sensory fulfillment, contributing to a well-rounded life.

Moksha (Liberation/Enlightenment)

Concept: Spiritual liberation and self-realization.

Purpose: The ultimate goal of life, freeing oneself from the cycle of rebirth and achieving eternal peace.

Three-Step Action Process

To apply this model in a practical, modern context, you can translate it into a three-step action process: Recognize, Balance, and Integrate.

Recognize

Action: Identify which aspects of the four Purusharthas are currently present or lacking in your life. Application: Reflect on your daily activities and priorities. Are you fulfilling your duties (Dharma)?

Are you pursuing your financial and material goals (Artha)? Are you allowing yourself to enjoy life's pleasures (Kama)? Are you on a path towards spiritual growth (Moksha)?

Balance-Action: Aim to create a balance among all four aspects. Application: Adjust your life to ensure that you are not overly focused on one area at the expense of others. For example, if you are working excessively (Artha) and neglecting your personal relationships or health (Kama), make time for relaxation and social connections. If you are caught up in sensory pleasures (Kama) and ignoring your responsibilities (Dharma), prioritize your duties. Integrate-Action: Integrate the principles of the Purusharthas into your daily routines and decision-making processes. Application: Use the insights from the Purusharthas to guide your actions and choices. When faced with a decision, consider how it aligns with your ethical values (Dharma), how it affects your financial stability (Artha), how it contributes to your happiness (Kama), and whether it supports your long-term spiritual goals (Moksha).

Practical Scenarios

At Work-Recognize: Identify if your job is fulfilling your need for financial security (Artha) and if it aligns with your ethical values (Dharma).

Balance: Ensure you are not neglecting your family and personal life (Kama) due to work pressures. Integrate: Make decisions that uphold your moral values, contribute to your financial goals, and allow time for personal fulfillment.

Personal Relationships

Recognize: Acknowledge the importance of nurturing relationships (Kama) and fulfilling your duties towards loved ones (Dharma). Balance: Find a balance between work (Artha) and spending quality time with family and friends (Kama).

Integrate: Make efforts to be present in your relationships, express love and appreciation, and ensure your interactions are ethical and meaningful.

Personal Growth

Recognize: Identify areas where you need spiritual growth (Moksha) and self-improvement (Dharma). Balance: Allocate time for spiritual practices and self-reflection without neglecting your material needs (Artha) and enjoyment of life (Kama). Integrate: Regularly practice mindfulness, meditation, or other spiritual activities that contribute to your overall well-being and enlightenment.

By recognizing the elements of the Purusharthas in your life, balancing your attention and efforts among them, and integrating their principles into your daily actions, you can create a holistic approach to happiness and fulfillment. This model, being universal and not tied to any one religion, provides a practical framework for addressing life's challenges and finding lasting happiness.

Doxography[15]

It is within the context of ancient philosophy, is that the great majority of Greek (and Roman) as well as other cultures philosophical writings have been irretrievably lost. But this loss is made good to some extent not only by quotations from lost works recorded by later writers, but also by the varieties of ancient reportage that are extant. The modern name for these forms of reportage is 'doxography', which could be translated as 'tenet-writing'[16]. Broadly speaking, doxography encompasses those writings, or parts of them, in which later author presents philosophical views of some or other of the ancient philosophers or schools, in some or other areas, or on some or other topics of philosophy, whether with or without presentation of the argumentation or analysis through which they offered philosophical support or provide reasons in favor of their 'tenets', and whether or not they also include critical evaluations and comments of the author's own. In other words, these are works (or part of them) taking as their subject matter, the tenets or doctrines of the philosophers, rather than independent works of philosophy in which the author addresses in the first instance issues or topics of philosophy, with ancillary discussion along the way of the opinions of other philosophers. The terms for tenets, or views, in ancient Greek are *doxai* or *dogmata*, in Latin *opiniones*; those for doctrines are, in Greek, *areskonta*, translated into Latin as *placita*.

The term "doxography" was coined by the German scholar Hermann Diels in his seminal work "Doxographi Graeci" (1879), which focused on writings related to natural philosophy. Diels' research primarily examined fragments and summaries of philosophical doctrines concerning cosmology, physics, and other natural sciences. His methodology involved tracing these fragments back to their sources, often through multiple intermediary stages, to reconstruct the original ideas. One of the earliest figures in the tradition of doxography is Theophrastus, a student and successor of Aristotle. Theophrastus' work, particularly the "Physikai Doxai" (Physical Tenets), is foundational in this tradition. This treatise, as indicated by the fragments preserved mainly through the Neoplatonist commentator Simplicius, dealt with the principles of natural philosophy, discussing the views of pre-Socratic philosophers such as Thales and Heraclitus.

The term 'doxography' has come to be applied in a much larger sense than seems to have been intended by its creator Hermann Diels[17]. This name for the genre, if we may misleadingly call it, that derives from the Latin neologism 'doxographi' used by Diels to indicate the authors of a rather strictly specified type of literature studied and edited in his 1879 monumental *Doxographi Graeci* ('Greek Doxographers'). His researches were focused on writings concerned with the *physical* part of philosophy (includes principles, theology, cosmology, astronomy, meteorology, biology and even a part of medicine). But today overviews in the field of ethics are also called doxographical. And scholars describe of 'doxographies' to be found in the dialogues of Plato and the treatises of Aristotle, although these were works in which issues of philosophy are addressed, with only ancillary discussion of the views of others.

The tradition of authors of their works in the doxography of physics begins with Aristotle's pupil and successor Theophrastus[18]. In the catalogue of his oeuvre preserved in his *Life in Diogenes Laertius*[19] a treatise is listed of '*Physikôn Doxôn*, sixteen books'. For the Greek title in the nominative one has a choice between *Physikôn Doxai* ('Tenets of the Natural Philosophers') and *Physikai Doxai* ('Tenets in Natural Philosophy'). Usener[20] and Diels[21] opted for the first alternative, but in the opinion of many scholars today the second option is much more plausible. To this treatise they attributed a number of fragments dealing with the principles (*archai*: Thales' water, Heraclitus' fire, etc.) transmitted for the most part by Simplicius[22], a Neoplatonist[23] commentator on Aristotle of the 6th c. CE.

That Simplicius and others explicitly quote from Theophrastus' *Physics*, a different treatise, did not bother them. They further posited that a short monograph of Theophrastus, the *De Sensibus*, dealing with theories concerning the senses and their objects from Parmenides to Democritus and to Plato, is a fragment of this treatise as well. The simple fact however that Plato, not first and foremost a philosopher of nature, is treated here on the same level as Democritus and the other natural philosophers (as is also the case in the fragments dealing with the principles) should have made them more hesitant, even within the scope of their own hypothesis, as to the interpretation of the title of the foundational treatise in sixteen books.

The method employed by Theophrastus and his successors often involved organizing philosophical doctrines according to subjects, a technique rooted in the dialectical method of Aristotle. Aristotle's approach to philosophy included the collection and evaluation of the opinions (doxai) of his predecessors, which he categorized and scrutinized to build his own arguments. This method of organizing knowledge into categories and analyzing differing viewpoints became a template for doxographical works.

Modern scholarship acknowledges the necessity of doxography in reconstructing lost philosophical works but also emphasizes the potential distortions introduced through successive transmissions. Comparisons between the surviving works of philosophers like Plato and Aristotle and their representation in doxographical texts reveal inconsistencies and adaptations, suggesting that later authors often modified the original doctrines to suit their contexts or purposes.

In summary, doxography provides a critical link to the philosophical ideas of antiquity, enabling contemporary scholars to piece together the intellectual heritage of lost works. Despite the challenges in ensuring the accuracy of these reconstructions, the contributions of doxographers like Theophrastus and the methodological framework established by Diels remain central to the study of ancient philosophy.

The *Metarsiology*[24] attributed to Theophrastus[25], extant in Syrian and Arabic translation, was discovered and published too late to be taken into account by Diels. Doubts about the attribution are formulated by Bakker 2016. For the text, and for the relation to the *Placita*[26].

According to Diels' revision of the hypothesis[27] a number of extant writings (as well as sections of writings) concerned with doctrines in the fields of natural philosophy ultimately derive from the *Physikôn Doxai* (as he called the work), via several intermediary stages, which are as follows:

The *Placita* of an otherwise unknown Aëtius[28], who is mentioned several times by Theodoret[29]; to be dated to the late 1st or perhaps early 2nd CE. Theodoret as source was for the first time adduced by Diels. This Aëtian work, he thought, may be reconstructed (a) from the *Placita* of ps-Plutarch, (b) from quotations in the *Anthology* of Stobaeus[30], and (c) from echoes in the *Therapy of Greek Diseases* of Theodoret. Ps-Plutarch is an epitome of Aëtius. Stobaeus as a rule quotes verbatim, but has a different systematic lay-out. The *Anthology*, moreover, has been much abridged and damaged in the course of transmission, so in a number of cases Stobaean parallels for ps-Plutarch are no longer extant. Aëtius will also have been used by other authors. Diels indeed proved that the second part of ps-Galen *Philosophical History* is an epitome of a version of ps-Plutarch. In his turn, Aëtius would for the most part derive from a postulated treatise to which Diels gave the name *Vetusta Placita* ('Older Tenets'), which would have been used by Cicero[31], Varro[32] and others. Its latest possible date, accordingly, is the early 1st c. BCE.

The Aëtius[33] hypothesis was new; it has proved to be tenable, though it has been shown to be in need of revision. Before Diels, scholars believed in the existence of a single early source, parts of which would have been taken over and adapted by Cicero as well as much later by, for instance, ps-Galen. The *Vetusta Placita* hypothesis, on the other hand, is dubious, and the way back to Theophrastus was more complicated to be uncertain, if only because hard evidence is so scarce, than Diels, who just stuck to Usener's point of view about Theophrastus, wished to consider.

Diels next posited that Theophrastus' treatise, the *Vetusta Placita*, and Aëtius had the same kind of systematic lay-out as the extant *Placita* of ps-Plutarch, viz. according to subject. The individual books and sections of books of this tract are indeed concerned with specific themes, such as for instance book two, which deals with the cosmos and the heavenly bodies. Within the framework of a section devoted to a particular subject, e.g., the sun, or the moon, the individual chapters may be concerned with various specific issues pertaining to the sun, or the moon, and so on.

Diels further argued that other reports, in other authors, should also be connected with Theophrastus' foundational treatise. The passages dealing with the tenets of Presocratic [34]philosophers in the history of philosophy by Diogenes Laërtius[35], which is arranged according to schools and individuals, rather than subjects, as well as similar sections of the first book of Hippolytus' *Refutation of All Heresies* and of the *Stromateis* ('Patchworks') of another ps-Plutarch, what in Diels' view also went back, ultimately, to the *Tenets of the Natural Philosophers*. He failed to take the difference between treatment according to subject and that according to person, or school, succinctly into account. His argumentation was also dubious in other respects. From the undeniable fact that there are striking resemblances between Theophrastus' fragments concerned with the principles on the one hand, and what is found on that score in Aëtius, Diogenes Laërtius, and Hippolytus on the other, it does not follow that corresponding passages in these later authors for which we have no Theophrastean parallels derive from Theophrastus. This is source criticism, or *Quellenforschung*[36], at its most vulnerable. Diels moreover preferred to overlook the equally undeniable fact that Aristotle's treatment of the principles in the first book of the *Metaphysics* exhibits equally striking correspondences with Theophrastus' fragments, and so with the later tradition as well, which could therefore go back ultimately to Aristotle, and not to Theophrastus.

Diels saw the development from Theophrastus to these later and (in his view) dependent authors as a decline, and a progressive obfuscation and deterioration. His cladistic reconstruction of the doxographical tradition is clearly related to the famous so-called 'Lachmannian[37]' stemma of a group of manuscripts, from later copies to the lost common ancestor, or archetype, the text of which (as scholars believed at the time) may be reconstructed in a virtually mechanical way. Diels was very much aware of this analogy, which surely was an important factor in convincing him and others that the splendid results of his investigations were irrefutable. In the 19th century the method attributed to Lachmann was assumed to be beyond criticism.

By thus (spoken automatically) tracing back these mutually corresponding passages in later authors to the, as he assumed, faithful reporter Theophrastus, Diels believed he gained access to reliable information about Presocratic philosophy. The stemmatic method back to the archetype it became possible to bestow upon a passage (a brief lemma in, for instance, Aëtius) dealing with a tenet of a Presocratic philosopher, the conditional status of being an attestation which, though still at second hand, should be early and therefore the more to be trusted. It is with the importance meted out to such so-called 'fragments' that these lemmata, removed by Diels' scissors from Aëtian chapters dealing with *subjects*, figure in the chronological series of chapters devoted to *persons* in two fundamental works he published.

These are the *Poetarum Philosophorum Fragmenta*[38], and the famous, several times revised (in later editions by Diels' collaborator Kranz), and often reprinted *Fragmente der Vorsokratiker*[39]. Scholars indeed still tend to view these Aëtian lemmata as a sort of Theophrastean fragments, and Theophrastus is believed to be a bona fide source. This also holds for those passages in Hippolytus, Diogenes Laërtius[40] and other authors in D.-K., which had been traced back to Theophrastus hypothetically.

However, when one compares Aëtian lemmata concerned with tenets of extant authors, like Plato or Aristotle, with the doctrines found in the original texts, it becomes clear to what extent these *doxai* have been adapted and distorted, or 'modernized', in some sense of the word. This consequently should also hold for lemmata dealing with lost authors, as Xylander [41]already pointed out in his 16th century edition of Plutarch, which included the *Epitome* of ps-Plutarch.

The role of Theodoret as a source for Aëtius has been questioned and doubted. However, no one doubts that there must be a source PS shared by ps.Plutarch and Stobaeus. One can also prove that there must be such a source shared by Theodoret and Stobaeus. As a final step one can prove that the PS source and the TS source cannot be distinguished from each other so are identical. Thus Diels' original intuition is vindicated.

Usener's influence[42] is also the cause of a fatal blind spot in Diels. He failed to acknowledge that Theophrastus, too, had a sort of *Doktorvater*, namely Aristotle. Aristotle, in his treatises, as a rule lists and discusses the opinions (*doxai*) of men in general and of the experts (who often are philosophers) in particular, concerning an issue in metaphysics, or physics, or psychology, and sometimes ethics, before embarking on his own investigations. These opinions are ordered according to the method of *diaeresis*, or division: a classification according to sets, sub-sets and sub-sub-sets with specific differences. Aristotle checks to what extent these opinions are in agreement among themselves or contradict each other, and then tries to establish to what extent one of the available options may prove acceptable, at least as the starting-point for further inquiry, or whether some option may be available which others have failed to consider. We call these exegetical and evaluative overviews 'dialectical', in the Aristotelian sense of the word of course. An overview of this nature should establish which *genus*, or set, is at issue, that is to say whether we are faced with a theoretical discipline, such as physics (and then with what *species*, or sub-set, e.g., zoology), or with a non-theoretical discipline such as poetics. This approach should also be applied to the sub-sets, or particular objects of inquiry, embraced by a particular sub-set. According to *Posterior Analytics* [43]various aspects should (or may) be treated separately, viz.: (1) does the object of the inquiry possess a particular property or attribute, or not; (2) the reason why it does possess this attribute; (3) the existence or non-existence of the object (for instance: do gods exist?—a question one does not need to ask when humans, or the sun, are at issue); and (4), the substance or definition of the object. Here an important part is played by the Aristotelian so-called categories and other kinds of predicates, because it is of major importance to establish to what category (viz. substance, or quality, or quantity, or place, or doing and being-affected etc.) a given object of inquiry and/or its attributes belong, or whether and in what sense for instance motion (or rest) may be predicated of it. These four different primary questions, or types of questions, may moreover be formulated in respect of each category (viz., not only of substance, but also of quality, etc.). Take the objects of mathematics. According to Aristotle these do not belong to the category of substance but to that of quantity. But within this latter category one may formulate questions about properties, or attributes, which may belong to them; enquire whether they exist, and if so, in what way; ask whether they move or not; and so on.

Aristotle in his treatise on dialectic and its methods, its *Topics*, provides instructions on how to select and classify propositions (*protaseis*) and problems (*problêmata*):

We should also make selections from the literature and include these in separate lists for each set, with separate headings, for instance 'On the Good', or 'On the Living Being'—that is to say the Good as a whole, starting with (the question) 'what is it?' One should cite the *doxai* [opinions, tenets] of individual thinkers, e.g., that Empedocles said that the elements of bodies are four in number of propositions and problems there are—to comprehend the matter in outline—three sets: some are ethical, others physical, others again logical. Ethical: for instance (the problem) whether one should obey one's parents or the law, when these disagree with each other. Logical: for instance (the problem) whether the knowledge of opposites is the same, or not. Physical: for instance (the problem) whether the cosmos is eternal or not.

Consequently, propositions and problems can be, and therefore in some cases should be, elucidated by means of tenets, or opinions: *doxai*. As there are three sets of propositions, so there are three sets of *doxai*: physical, ethical, and 'logical' (i.e., general). An example of such a diaeresis, or division, of a sub-set which is of fundamental importance for Aristotle is found at the beginning of his *Physics*. This division pertains to two categories and one predicate of a different sort: the number (category of quantity), nature (category of substance) and motion vs. rest (category of doing and being-affected) of the principles (*archai*) and elements (*stoicheia*) posited by Aristotle's predecessors in the field of natural philosophy. In line with the rule formulated in the

Topics names of philosophers are added to some of the *doxai*. Numerous other examples of this ingredient of the dialectical method are to be found in Aristotle's writings.

The passage from the *Topics*, and Aristotle's general practice, help to determine and explain the title of the Theophrastean treatise Diels believed to be foundational: it should be *Physikai Doxai*, i.e., 'Tenets in [the various fields of] Natural Philosophy'. And one of the rare extant fragments of this treatise not only proves (because of the formulation in Greek of the title as quoted) that this title really is 'Physical Tenets', also demonstrates that such tenets were criticized according to the rules of dialectic[44]. Theophrastus, we are informed, cited a tenet of Plato's and then formulated 'the objections' against it. The Greek word for 'objections' found in this fragment, *enstaseis*[45], is a technical term in Aristotle's *Topics*. Physical tenets are tenets, or theses, in the fields of natural philosophy in the largest sense, ranging from the principles, via cosmology, astronomy and meteorology etc., to human psychology (including philosophy of mind), biology, and even nosology or the theory of diseases. Physical tenets are not only formulated by *physikoi*, natural philosophers, but also by physicians and astronomers. Aëtius indeed contains a number of medical and astronomical *doxai*, the oldest of which may derive from sources that can perhaps be attributed to some of Aristotle's collaborators. (For further reading on this topic[46].

Theophrastus applies the diaeretic method [47]in his treatise *De Sensibus*. The chief division—already found in corresponding passages in Aristotle—is between those who posit that knowledge is to be ascribed to similarity ('like knows like') and those who posit that it is to be ascribed to contrast ('unlike knows unlike'). Another division, not paralleled in Aristotle, also plays an important part in classifying and dialectically discussing the tenets, viz. between those who assume that there is a difference between thinking and sense-perception, and those who do not. Finally, within each class the philosophers are treated in a sequence determined by the number of senses that are posited (category of quantity). The last philosopher to be discussed is Democritus[48], not Plato. This is because Democritus according to Theophrastus assumes that knowledge comes about through both similarity and contrast.

This presentation, viz. a division, or divisions, of contrasting tenets (names included) dealing with specific issues, followed by an exceptional (or compromise) view, which fails to fit this division, is *not* a standard feature of Aristotle's dialectical overviews. However we do find partial anticipations of this methodology in Aristotle, e.g. in the second chapter of *De Anima* I he opposes three views concerned with the principles that constitute the soul: some hold that these are corporeal, others that they are incorporeal, while a third group posits a blend of corporeal and incorporeal principles. In Aristotle however, we do not find the strings of detailed sortings of individual tenets followed by a compromise or maverick opinion typical of numerous *Placita* chapters, while Theophrastus' presentation in the *De Sensibus* is in this respect close to the *Placita* routine. Consequently, we may submit that it is Aristotle's dialectical methodology, as revised by Theophrastus, which determines the structure of large sections of the *Placita*. It should be noted, moreover, that the introduction of ps-Plutarch's *Placita*, that 'according to Aristotle and Theophrastus and almost all the Peripatetics says a perfect human being should devote himself to *problems* in the fields of natural philosophy and ethics'.

Theophrastus *and* Aristotle, then, were used in this way. An example: The chapters in Aëtius and Cicero (*Academics* 2.122) dealing with a number of various and occasionally even bizarre views concerning the position, motion, shape, etc. of the earth in the last resort patently derive, as to their main themes and oppositions and even as to some telling details, from a chapter in Aristotle's *On the Heavens*. Cicero here mentions Theophrastus by name; he therefore may well be involved too, as an intermediary source. But we have no further evidence concerning his contribution in this particular instance. It is rather amazing that the great Diels, who clearly was aware of the importance of the diaeretic method in Aristotle's writings and in Theophrastus' *De Sensibus*, failed to apply this insight to the *Placita* literature. The diaphonic organization, moreover, of chapters containing tenets that are listed according to criteria determined by various divisions obviously determines not only the presentation but also, to some extent, the contents of the material.

It would seem that, just as is the case for Aristotle, also in that of Theophrastus more than one treatise provided material that ultimately found a home in the *Placita*, namely at the very least the *Physikai Doxai*, the *Physics*, the *De sensibus*, and the *Metarsiology*.

When we inquire into the way ancient authors have used the information provided by Aëtius' *Placita*, by its progeny, and by its post-Theophrastean predecessors, we often find that the function of these collections of *doxai* is not much different from the functions of similar overviews in the context of Aristotle's dialectical discussions. The main objective of these authors, who are in a position to base themselves on evidence that has already been provided with a definite structure, is to ascertain whether a given *doxa* may eventually prove to be useful, and which *doxai* should be rejected—depending, naturally, on the point of view of the user (who may be a physician or a philosopher, a Stoic or an Epicurean, a Platonist or an Aristotelian, a pagan or a Christian). Sometimes all the *doxai* belonging to a specific sub-set, or dealing with a specific theme, may turn out to be unacceptable, or useless, under certain circumstances or to somebody in particular. The fact should never be lost from view that the *Placita* merely provides a *status quaestionis*[49]: material for instruction, discussion and reflection on, say, the shape of the moon, or the size of the sun, or the causes of earthquakes, or of the flooding of the Nile, or the various explanations of visual perception. Neither a suspension of judgement, in the manner of the Skeptics, nor a positive outcome, in the manner of Aristotle or the Stoics, is ever formulated, no explicit advice ever given either way. Only very rarely is there a critical note.

Furthermore, there is a significant difference between Aristotle's overviews (which we know much better than those of Theophrastus, so for the sake of clarity one may restrict oneself to Aristotle) and the corresponding passages and sections in Aëtius and his family. Aristotle's purpose was to make a choice and to find a solution, and many later authors also wanted this. But numerous chapters in the *Placita* literature when taken at face-value seem to make a decision impossible, because the bald diaeretic contrast between the tenets listed in the lemmata results in a logjam, or *diaphonia* ('discordance'), as the ancient Skeptics called it. It might be concluded from this stalemate that the only remaining option is to suspend one's judgment. It was at the time impossible, for instance, to find out whether there is one cosmic system, or more. It is an attractive idea that at least part of the material (in the course of time naturally updated by the inclusion of post-Aristotelian tenets) was adapted by Academic Skeptics to induce the tranquillity of mind which follows upon suspension of judgment.

Consequently, doxography in the narrower sense (derived from the nature of the majority of the sources discussed and edited by Diels in the *Doxographi Graeci*), can be defined as: the normally very brief presentation according to theme, or subject, of contrasting (or even bizarre, or compromise) tenets in natural philosophy (or science, if you wish), which in itself does not provide a decisive answer to the issue involved although it may assist you to find a solution. The application of the term 'doxography' to what one finds in Aristotle (or, on a much more limited scale, in Plato, who occasionally quotes the views of others to further a discussion) can therefore be misleading.

Turning now to doxography in the broad sense, we observe that Cicero's leisured and extensive presentations, e.g., in his *On the Nature of the Gods* of the Epicurean and Stoic doctrines in the field of theology-cum-physics—presentations followed by Academic-Skeptical refutations—may be, and have been, called by the name of doxography. But there are obvious differences from doxographies of the Aëtian type. To be sure, one might perhaps, with some hesitation, maintain that what we have here is a sort of blow-up of the dialectical scheme one also finds in the *Placita* literature, with the skeptical component made explicit: contrasting doctrines which turn out to be improvable. Such a move however, is less valid for Diogenes Laërtius, in spite of the fact that this author several times makes a distinction between the life (*bios*) of a person (Plato; the Stoic Zeno of Citium) and the *areskonta* or *dogmata* of this person, or of his school. It is therefore perhaps better to classify these overviews in Cicero and Diogenes Laërtius as belonging with an ancient genre which we may view as a sub-species of doxography, namely the (largely lost) literature *Peri Haireseôn* ('On Schools'), which deals with philosophical, or medical, schools and eventually may include arguments against the position of a particular *hairesis* ('school'). Philodemus[50], and Arius Didymus [51](on ethics), belong here as well.

Scholars, one notices, also speak of ethical doxographies. One could justify this usage by submitting that this is going beyond Diels, and back to Aristotle. We have seen that Aristotle advised his pupils (and himself) also to construct lists of ethical propositions and problems. In his ethical treatises we actually find dialectical overviews concerning problems in ethics, though on a much more modest scale than in the physical treatises. But a doxographical literature in the field of ethics, which as to scale and taxonomy would be even remotely comparable to physical doxography, never existed. Yet one occasionally encounters short lists and overviews of ethical tenets in some later authors. It is therefore possible that modest doxographical collections of ethical views did circulate, and we may have some evidence concerned with the circulation (and adaptation) of a diaeretical overview of tenets about the End, or Highest Good.

A text of Aëtius in a single column has now been published[52] superseding Diels' text in two columns. The evidence of the primary and secondary sources for the reconstruction of each individual chapter is cited in full, though for Plutarch and Stobaeus only in the positive apparatus criticus. For each chapter its reconstruction from the witnesses is explained, its position in the context of the *Placita* and sometimes of the wider tradition determined, its contents and structure analyzed, such parallel evidence as is available, both earlier and later to much later, analyzed, and problems of interpretation raised by the text and contents of individual tenets are often separately discussed. Each chapter ends with a generous collection of further related texts to widen the horizon and place the topic of the chapter in the context of the history of ancient philosophy from beginning to end. These commentaries and collections of texts situate the *Placita* at a key point in the development over the centuries of Greek philosophy, looking backwards as well as forward. The existing remains amount to about six-sevenths of the original.

Finally, it should be pointed out that doxographic works are tools of a sort. They constitute a type of secondary literature of a fluid and unstable character, both as to form and as to contents. Shorter and longer versions may be available alongside each other; in fact, for all the losses sustained by ancient literature, some still are. Materials may be added, or lost, or added again in a continuous process of epitomizing and enlarging and updating—and it remained possible, of course, to inspect and excerpt original sources at least in some cases.

In order the better to understand the value of the available evidence pertaining to lost philosophical works from Antiquity one therefore should attempt to understand the traditions and transmissions that are involved as a whole. One should take the rationale of the extant overviews into account, and try to discover the intentions of authors who made use of doxographies. A naïve use of the available collections of philosophical fragments, implying the putting on the same level of reliability of most of the evidence that remains, does not always produce good results.

Hindu or Vedic philosophy[53] is the set of Indian philosophical systems developing alongside the religion of Hinduism and emerging in the Iron[54] and Classical[55] periods, which consists of six orthodox schools of thought (*shad-darshana*[56]): Samkhya Yoga[57], Nyaya[58], Vaisheshika[59], Mimamsa[60] and Vedanta[61]. In Indian tradition, the word used for philosophy is Darshana, the view point or perspective, from the Sanskrit root *drish* ('to see, to experience').

It is the *āstika* philosophical traditions: those that accept the Vedas as an authoritative, important source of knowledge. Indian philosophy during the ancient and medieval periods of India also yielded philosophies that share philosophical concepts with these *āstika* philosophies to reject the Vedas, and have been called *nāstika* Indian philosophies[62].

Nyāya Sūtras[63]

Mimamsa[64] the Indian system of interpretation Mimamsa, to the legal fraternity as it has immense relevance and importance in application to modern legal interpretation. Mimamsa means reflection, consideration, profound through, investigation, examination, discussion in short, interpretation; and sutras (or shlokas) may be understood as aphorisms. Vedic texts used such a complex language in classic Sanskriti that common man could not understand them and perform the rituals correctly. For the average educated common man to understand and follow the Vedas it was necessary to lay down rules to interpret the Vedas. Rishi Jaimini[65] took it upon himself to accomplish this task by composing Mimamsa Sutras over 2500 years ago.

At the outset it is important to note some of the salient features of the Mimamsa Sutras. First, the methodology and approach of the sutras is very scientific and logical. It is in the form of logical discussion arriving at a conclusion like in modern adjudication. A topic in the Vedas which is not clear and requiring interpretation is stated (proposition), objections to the proposition are recorded and considered and conclusion arrived at resolving the issue. The logic of Mimamsa is the logic of law. Secondly, if Vedas are taken to be suprema lex, which they are in Indian religious philosophy, and likened to the Constitution, it explains the hierarchy of law. According to Mimamsa Vedas are supreme being divine revelation and therefore no name is attached to it (called Sruti-heard). They were handed down from generation to generation by word of mouth, Smrti (remembrance) on the other hand are Sruti heard, recollected and retold. These are attributed to some author or the other like Yajnavalka Smrti[66], Manu Smrti[67] etc. Mimamsa Sutras lay down rules for interpretation of the Sruti and Smrti. Even the Smrtis required interpretation which was provided by Commentaries. It is interesting to note that applying the same Mimamsa Sutras two commentators-Vijnanesvara[68] and

Jimultavahana[69] interpreted the Yajnavalkya Smrti[70] and came up with two schools of Hindu law-Mitakshara[71] and Dayabhaga[72] incorporating customary laws.

Mimamsa sets hierarchy of these texts and lays down that in case of conflict vedas will have prevalence over Smrti and Smrti running contrary to Vedas will be invalid. In other words, Smrtis must conform to and be consistent with the Vedas. In modern perspective it translates to the principle that all enacted law must conform to and be consistent with the Constitution. Likewise Mimamsa defines substantive provision (called Vidhi) and proviso, exception etc. (Arthavada) and lays down that in case of a conflict the Vidhi shall prevail over Arthavada and the latter cannot control the former.

The position in modern times has not changed - a substantive provision (section) cannot be controlled by proviso, exception etc.

With these introductory remarks we now proceed on our deliberations starting with historical overview of legal jurisprudence and interpretation of law the world over.

In a historical overview, need for interpretation is not a phenomenon special or peculiar to any age (including the modern age), region or country. All ancient scriptures and even modern philosophical and literary works use such language as to pack deep meanings in short texts.

This creates a nightmare for common man who finds himself totally lost in understanding the true meaning of those texts. Use of such language is natural to such scholars. But in law such language is used to avoid the law becoming unnecessarily lengthy and cumbersome. But this results in the law also becoming incomprehensible for the common man for whom the law is made and he needs a lawyer to tell him, in his language (common parlance), the meaning or sense of the law. Even the law recognizes that the words in a provision should be assigned their common parlance meaning.

In ancient times throughout the world law and state- craft were all rolled into one. Moral wrong (sin) and legal wrong were not distinguishable. Therefore all expertise and skills of interpretation were directed towards interpreting and explaining the religious texts which incorporated all wrongs and penances (punishments) therefor. India was no exception.

It is astonishing that in spite of lack of modes of communication and travel, all civilizations grew on parallel lines. Some parallels involving Indian scriptures and ancient western laws are remarkable.

The oldest known exposition on law dates back to 3000 BC (ancient Egyptian law) which was characterized by rhetoric speech, social equality and impartiality. Then we have the code of Ur-Nammu[73] (ca 2050 BC) followed by Laws of Eshnunna[74] (ca 1930 BC), Codex Lipit-Ishtar of Isin[75] (ca 1870 BC), and Codex Hammurabi[76] (1796-1750 BC). All these texts were not strictly legal provisions but contained a lot of social norms based on accepted behaviour. They prescribed punishments for violation of those accepted norms.

The contemporary time in India was known as the Vedic period (4000-1000 BC). This period in India is remarkably different from the western countries. While this period witnessed development of social norms or quasi-legal provisions in the west, India basked in its glory of spiritual, religious and philosophical excellence. During this long period scriptures like Vedas[77], Smrtis[78], Upnishads[79] etc. were composed. Vedas, believed to be words of the divine, are called Śruti - heard. These were remembered, recollected and retold by different sages and such works are known as Smrti - remembrance. Dharmaśāstra[80] comprehends both Śruti and Smrti but is often used to designate the Smrtis alone. Smrtis were interpreted and explained in commentaries. These commentaries professing to interpret law in the Śruti and Smrtis incorporated the customs and usages in vogue as wells and form customary source of Hindu law. Commentaries are also known as Nibandhas[81] and Upanishads which were comparatively easy to understand. Smrtis, Upanishads etc. prescribed rules for conducting Yagas[82] for obtaining material gains, power, children and attaining salvation (moksha); and stated of divine punishment for violation of those rules as well as humanly penances for absolving one of his sins. They were more in the nature of guidelines than law but had social sanction and applied to everybody, although people were sometimes treated differently in accordance with their social status.

The next important milestone can be noted in the form of Biblical law (the Torah or the holy scripture of Judaism written in Hebrew) which is dated between 539-334 BC. Like the Vedas which is believed to be divine teaching Torah is also stated to be God's teachings to Moses. The forerunners of western laws were the Greek laws propounded by the great philosophers like Socrates, his disciple Plato and his disciple Aristotle. Socrates never reduced his teachings and theories into writing. It was his disciple Plato (429-348 BC) and his disciple Aristotle (384-322 BC) who laid foundation of Greek laws. Similarly the earliest code of Roman law also known as the Twelve Tables came to be adopted in 451-450 BC. Contemporary Indian thinker was Kautilya (4th Century BCE) who composed or rather compiled the Arthasāstra[83]. Thus the period of 6th to 4th Century BCE was a global golden period giving the world laws for making and keeping the society decent by disciplined and very orderly. Sanctions, prescriptions and injunctions were provided for unacceptable behavior. The King was expected to ensure compliance of these laws. In India this period is remarkable not only for development of law and establishment of justice delivery system, it saw the intellect and wisdom reaching its pinnacle.

The three beacon lights of this period were Panini in the field of grammar and linguistics, Jaiminî in the field of interpretation and Kautilya the law-giver. Panini was a grammarian, master of Sanskrit morphology, syntax and semantics and is known for his largest extant Sanskrit grammar known as Aṣtadhyayi[84]. He is considered father of linguistics. Jaimini, on the other hand, was aware of and seized with limitations of the not so educated or illiterate common man in understanding the Vedas and thereby his failure to perform the rituals correctly.

Jaiminî[85] took it upon himself to formulate rules for interpretation of the Vedic texts and in the process formulated 2668 Sutras. These aphorisms[86] interpreting and explaining the language of the Vedas are applicable to any text - religious, philosophical, poetic, literary and legal. These would therefore be eternally relevant. The Mimâmsa Sutras were thus employed to interpret the Smrtis - which are Śruti having been remembered, recollected and retold by different sages by their very nature inherited the language style of the Śruti - which required interpretation for the benefit of the common man. As stated above, these Sutras were applied for interpreting Yajñavalkya Smrti by the commentators like Vijñâneśvara[87] and Jimutavahana[88] to give us the Hindu law. The application of the Mimâmsa Sutras to Hindu law was discussed by Kishori Lal Sarkar in his Tagore Law Lectures in 1905.

Kautilya was a great economist, politician, teacher, tactician, jurist and administrator - all rolled into one. He was the greatest law-giver India ever had. His Arthaśāstra is a practical treatise on secular law, economics, and state-craft all in one place. He is considered to be the first to propound tort law and his theories on tort law are relevant even today. Similarly, he was the first to propound and put in place separate civil and criminal law in India clearly defining offences and prescribing punishments and establishing the machinery for administration of the justice delivery system.

It may be noted that while development of legal jurisprudence continued in the West marked by the classic epoch of Roman law (3rd to 1st Century BC) led by Cicero (106-43 BC), there was a lull in India or at least nothing has come to notice to fill the gap till Manu (200 BC-100 AD). Many more books and treatise may be waiting in oblivion to be discovered.

It is of importance to note here that while laws were laid down everywhere no system was developed in the West to interpret those laws. A glaring example is that of the Codex Hammurabi. His law "if a man puts out the eye of another man, his eye shall be put out" had all along been quoted as "an eye for an eye" considered barbaric. It was believed that these grim retaliatory punishments took no note of excuses or explanations, but only of the fact. However later authors explained that these punishments varied with status of the offender qua the victim. For example, "if a man has destroyed the eye of a man of the gentleman class, they shall destroy his eye If he has destroyed the eye of a commoner he shall pay one mina of silver[89]. If he has destroyed the eye of a gentleman's slave...he shall pay half the slave's price." Still later authors like Joshua Dressler opined that "an eye for an eye" should be interpreted as prescribing correspondence between crime and punishment (or proportionality)[90]. He opined that "properly read as 'no more than an eye for an eye' it also significantly limited the excess of private revenge in an attempt to reduce the consequences of the blood feuds." This underlines the importance and significance of proper interpretation. Scholars are still struggling for properly interpreting certain texts of Plato and Aristotle.

In India, way back in 500-200 BC Jaiminî proposed a system of interpretation which came to be known as Mîmâmsâ or Purva Mimâmsâ[91] consisting of rules or Sutras of interpretation. It was Jaiminî in India who propounded not only the rules of interpretation but a system thereof. It is true that these rules were propounded for interpreting the Vedas but that does not lessen their importance for legal interpretation because it is not the context but the principle, not the form but the substance that matters. The aim was to interpret the Vedic rules for yāgas but the principles, at least relating to linguistic (lexical and syntactical) and logical interpretation are valid and applicable to any text, legal texts not excluded. In this book we shall discuss the rules propounded by Jaiminî (these have been brought out by eminent authors and Judges like Madan Lal Sandal, N.V. Thadani, Kishori Lal Sarkar, P.V. Kane and Justice Markandey Katju) as regards the principles derived from Mimâmsa Sutras to the extent they can be applied to modern legal interpretation.

Jaimini's Mîmâmsâ though written about 2500 years ago was discovered much later and translated into English still later. An attempt to properly project the same as rules or principles of interpretation (even though restricted to their application to Hindu Law) was made only in 1905 by Kishori Lal Sarkar in his Tagore Law Lectures (published in 1909). This had been the unfortunate fate of the ancient Indian wisdom. For example the Kautilya's Arthaśāstra went into oblivion after Emperor

Ashoka's reign and was re-discovered and translated only in 1912 by Prof. R.Samasastry[92]. These and such other masterpieces could not regain their due recognition and acceptance because of the unfortunate turns of historical events.

In the result, as we are painfully aware, we always turn to the West for wisdom and guidance. Nevertheless the richness of our ancient texts written in Sanskrit has always been recognized and appreciated. Sir Henry Sumner Maine in his Ancient Laws wrote:

"...until philology has effected a complete analysis of Sanskrit literature, our best sources of knowledge are undoubtedly the Greek Homeric poems..."

Similar views were expressed by Prof. F. Max Müller:

"...how imperfect our knowledge of universal history, our insight into the development of the human intellect, must always remain, if we narrow our horizon to the history of Greeks and Romans, Saxons and Celts, with a dim background of Palestine, Egypt, and Babylon, and leave out of sight our nearest intellectual relatives, the Aryans of India, the framers of the most wonderful language, the Sanskrit, the fellow-workers in the construction of our fundamental concepts, the fathers of the most natural of natural religions, the makers of the most transparent of mythologies, the inventors of the most subtle philosophy, and the givers of the most elaborate laws."

What is intriguing, however, is the fact that while the British appreciated the Mimâmsâ rules of interpretation and recognized the Mitakshara[93] and Dayabhaga[94] schools of Hindu law derived by application of the Mimâmsâ rules to the Smrtis as valid and acceptable law; they put the Mimâmsâ rules in the category of philosophy, and out of legal spheres. Although it has not so far been examined from this angle, it appears probable that while the British did not have anything in their legal system similar to the personal laws of the Hindus or Muslims and per force had to apply them; they did have a well compiled rules of statutory interpretation handed down by Maxwell and did not want or need any interference or modification with that. Thus the Mîmâmsâ rules, though very logical, were played down as being relevant only for interpretation of the Vedas and not legal texts, except of course to Hindu law.

History cannot be overturned, but time has come when we objectively analyse and evaluate the prevailing British imposed legal system vis-a-vis our own ancient wisdom and apply the same to the extent feasible and desirable.

It is in this context that the Mîmâmsâ Rules of Interpretation assume importance with regard to legal interpretation.

Ancient Indian systems

In Indian systems the Vedas are believed to be eternal, self existent, not composed by any author human or divine, and infallible. They codify Dharma (duties and virtues - individual and collective, ruler and the ruled do's and don'ts for accepted behaviour). They form and explain the Hindu philosophy, accepted and revered by every Hindu believer.

These treatise or repositories of knowledge inter alia contain procedural guidelines for sacrificial fire and offering, sacrifices (yaga), to attain salvation, peace and prosperity (may be by pleasing the Vedic deities; but the Mimamsakas do not believe that reward of the sacrifices are given by the deities. They believe that the sacrifices endow the believers with capacities to achieve their aim). These deities were different from today's for reasons discussed below.

Vedas being the revealed (heard) knowledge are called Śruti. These were matter of speech and admitted of no change. The knowledge of the Vedas was further explained and dissipated by teachings of the sages and these collections of teachings were called Upanishads. These form the basis for the Hindu religion and are also called Vedanta (end of Veda). Literally Upanishad means 'to sit down close to'. Thus these were teachings to disciples sitting around the teacher. Bhagavad Gita is the classic devotional Upanishad delivered by the Lord Krishna to the disciple Arjuna. Though Upanishads are treatise on Vedas, they are considered their part. More often the Upanishads are included in the category of Śruti. The Upanishads are thus digests on the Vedas. The revelation was heard, contemplated and delivered in the form of laws for general observance incorporating customs and practice. These were matter of memory and hence are called Smrti. Vedas do not contain any law. The Hindu Law is contained in Smrtis. Puranas on the other hand are texts eulogizing various deities, through divine stories like Vishnu Purana, Garud Purana etc.

The ancient Indian religious beliefs, rituals practices differed vastly in form and content from today. The reason and logic for such variance was highlighted by Maine as under:

"…in the infancy of the race, men could only account for sustained or periodically recurring action by supposing a personal agent. Thus the wind blowing was a person and of course a divine person; the sun rising, culminating and setting was a person and a divine person; the earth yielding her increase was a person and divine."

Max Müller also noted that the Vedas classified the deities in three groups, terrestrial, aerial, and celestial:

"…who admitted three deities only, viz. Agni or fire, whose place is on the earth; Vayu or Indra, the wind and the God of the thunderstorm, whose place is in the air; and Surya, the sun, whose place is in the sky.

A very useful division of the Vedic Gods has been made by Yaksha, into terrestrial, aerial, and celestial, and if the old Hindu theologians meant no more than that all the manifestations of divine power in nature might be traced back to three centres of force, one in the sky, the other in the air, and the last on the earth, he deserves great credit for his sagacity.

Thus in India the wind, rains, sun, earth etc. which affected and controlled the peoples' daily life were treated as Gods and Goddesses (Pawan, Indra, Surya, Bhoomi etc.). For peaceful living and prosperity it was considered necessary to keep them pleased and the only way to please them was by offering sacrifices (yaga). The Vedas, particularly Rig Veda, provide rules and procedures for the sacrificial fire and yaga in the form of richas or shlokas. However these were not easily comprehendible not only to the common man who was mostly illiterate but even to the common priests performing the yaga (in any event every person was not entitled to read Vedas) and needed to be interpreted so that there should not be any mistake in observance of the rituals.

The Vedas needed to be contemplated and explained. Thus the Indian philosophy was developed around Vedas. Two such systems are particularly important in the context of the present legal system: the Nyayaśāstra or Nyaya theory and the Mîmâmsâ rules of interpretation. However, as we shall see Mimâmsâ is also influenced by the Nyaya theory.

Nyayaśāstra or Nyaya-Vaisesika

The Nyayaśāstra or Nyaya-Vaisesika theory of knowledge (ascribed to Gautam and developed by Gangesa[95]; and Buddhist philosophy - 600-300 BC) may be described as the science of the methods and conditions of valid thought and true knowledge of objects. It is a useful tool for ascertaining truthfulness or falsity of facts or knowledge under procedural law. The Nyayaśāstra employs the methodology of inference which involves a combination of inductive and deductive logic. The logic, as understood therein, means: "the science of right reasoning or the science of discussion." The accepted and recognised manner of resolving disputes or adjudication was to put questions and counter questions to petitioner and respondent and arrive at a conclusion: "Vivaade pruchhati pprasnam pratiprasnam tathaiva cha Nyayapurvancha vadati pradvivaaka iti smrutah." The adjudicator or the Judge was called 'Pradvivaakah'. The system is very much akin to present day adversarial adjudication process.

According to the Nyāyaśāstra "knowledge means a true belief that carries with it an assurance of its truth" and "knowledge cognizes objects that are distinct from and outside of itself. It cannot turn back on itself and cognize its own existence, far less its validity." Similarly validity of a knowledge cannot be tested by some other knowledge. For doing so the second knowledge has to be proved.

The Nyaya theory by now has developed into a formal logic of relations between concepts and their determinants. Accordingly knowledge means awareness or apprehension of objects. It includes all cognitions that have a more or less determinate objective reference. The knowledge and the objects of knowledge are categorically distinguished.

Knowledge is based on the behaviour or conduct of a living being. Knowledge has been classified, in the first instance, into presentation (anubhava) which is primary, and memory (Smrti) which is secondary.

Presentation is necessarily personal experience present or past. Memory on the other hand has to be of past event and may be of self experience or of some other person's experience.

Concept of valid knowledge implies three necessary factors: the subject (the one who knows or the person stating knowledge of an object or fact, pramâtâ), the object (the proposition, prameya) and the method of (proving the) knowledge (pramâna). Thus for presenting a knowledge there has to be a subject or the one who knows (the primary witness proving an object or fact claiming personal knowledge); an object or fact knowledge of which is claimed, it may be a living being, a material object, an event, or a happening; and method of testing truthfulness of the knowledge.

The Nyaya theory recognizes five means of testing the truth or validity of knowledge: perception, inference, comparison, testimony and argument. All these are recognized as valid tests under Law of evidence the world over. This has been explained by the example of 'fire'. If one goes to the place from where smoke issues forth, he will have the perception of fire. Existence of fire at a distant place may also be known from the testimony of another person. Existence of fire can also be inferred from the observed smoke. While the knowledge from testimony and inference requires confirmation by perception (other's), the perceptual knowledge of the thing does not need further confirmation. In other words perception is the most primary and fundamental of all sources of knowledge. The Nyaya theory however cautions that "that perception is the final test of all other knowledge does not mean that the truth of perception is self- evident or that it cannot but be true". So perception also may have to be proved. For example dying declaration or prosecutrix's evidence may in certain circumstances need corroboration. Similarly a school leaving certificate adduced in evidence in support of date of birth has to be proved.

Perception can be of material things, attributes [Nyaya theory recognizes 24 kinds of attributes or Guna: colour (rüpa), taste (rasa), smell (gandha), touch (sparśa), sound (sabda), number (sankhya), magnitude (partimana), differential (prthaktva), conjunction (samyoga), disjunction (vibhaga), remoteness (paratva), nearness (aparatva), fluidity (dravatva), viscidity (sneha), knowledge (buddhi), pleasure (sukha), pain (dukkha), desire (ichhā), aversion (dvesa), effort (prayatna), heaviness (gurutva), merit (dharma), demerit (adharma), and faculty (samskāra)]; and actions. Perception is also an important aspect in Mimâmsa.

Inference (anumana) means such knowledge as follows some other knowledge. It has been defined in the Nyaya theory as the knowledge of an object, not by direct observation, but by means of the knowledge of a sign or mark (linga) and that of its universal relation with the inferred object. Determination of this relation is elaborately discussed in the Nyaya theory. Accordingly an inference is a combined deductive-inductive reasoning. Inferences have been classified on the basis of (i) purpose; (ii) nature of the universal relation between the object and the sign or mark; and (iii) nature of induction by which we get the knowledge of the universal proposition involved in the inference. For example the relation between fire and smoke is universal. Hence by observing smoke, existence of fire can safely be inferred. The theory also talks about the fallacies of inference. For example by observing the direction of smoke, direction of the wind can be inferred but in case where the wind direction is frequently changing, the inference may be fallacious.

Upmana (comparison) is another tool of inference and is generally defined as the ground of our knowledge of a thing from its similarity or dissimilarity to another thing previously well-known. But the knowledge of similarity or dissimilarity is of accidental character of this or that kind of upmana. The knowledge of denotative relation between a word and a certain class of objects is common to all cases of upmana. Hence upmana is defined as the process of reasoning by which we know that the word denotes a certain class of objects on the basis of some authoritative statements. For example if the post-mortem report says that death occurred due to injury by some sharp edged weapon but does not specify the weapon then the butcher's knife produced as exhibit can be compared with this description and description of the injuries like size and depth of the injury to fasten the liability.

Sabda or testimony is verbal knowledge. All verbal testimony (Oral evidence) is not valid. The Nyaya theory accepts only those verbal testimonies which are valid. Elements of śabda are (i) perception (auditory, in case of spoken sentences; or visual in case of written ones), (ii) understanding of the meaning of the sentences perceived, and (iii) nature of the source of knowledge in testimony. For example, the testimony flowing from trustworthy persons is valid. Further, testimony must always be personal. Hearsay evidence is not valid and therefore not admissible. The validity of verbal (oral) testimony is tested by examination and cross-examination of the witnesses.

Last of the method of proof, but not the least, is argument or tarka. The process of reasoning in tarka consists in the deduction of an untenable proposition from a certain position. This has the logical effect of exposing the invalidity of that position and thereby lending support to the counter-position. This method assumes immense importance in cases based on circumstantial evidence.

In common legal language the principles of Nyaya theory can be summarized as follows:

A person making a grievance, complaint or petition (the subject); states facts and circumstances and raises pleas or contentions (the object); which he seeks to support or prove by pleadings, affidavits, evidence, witnesses, documents etc. (methods of knowledge).

An object cannot be proved by pleadings, averments or assertions.

No fact can be proved by another unverified fact. Object can be proved by perception, inference, comparison, testimony and arguments.

Evidence of a Trustworthy Witness Proves the Fact

These propositions, very much part of the modern Law of Evidence and the Codes of Civil and Criminal Procedures, were given more than 25 centuries ago (during 600-300 BC) and are still valid and in use but without due credit to our ancient wisdom.

Mimâmsâ Sútras[96] are rules of interpretation evolved for interpretation of the Vedic texts. The Vedas have been held to be eternal and having no known author (human or divine). Therefore there was no body to explain or clarify the meaning or intentions of these texts. The authors of Mîmâmsâ (Mîmâmsâkas) were basically concerned with the resolution of conflicts, ambiguities and contradictions noted in the Śrutivakyas (Vedic sentences) because these created hurdles for the common man in performing the yagas correctly. The Mîmâmsakas therefore evolved hyperfine doctrines for ascertaining the meaning of these texts developing an elaborate system of interpretation. These were finally formalized in the form of aphorisms by Jaimini. This was necessary so as to alleviate chances of mistakes while performing yaga. These aphorisms[97] though evolved for interpreting Vedic texts, were later applied to Smrtis, texts of which applied to religion as well as Hindu personal law like adoption, inheritance etc. Mimamsa was used to interpret Smrtis not only by commentators but also the courts prior to codification of Hindu law in 1955- 56. These rules adopt interdisciplinary and converging approach applying principles of grammar, exegesis and logic and therefore are relevant to this day and can be applied to legal texts to a great extent because, as stated above, the principles or rules of interpretation broadly remain the same for all types of texts, legal texts included. They can be applied to any text with circumspection and caution. It is in this background that the Mîmâmsâ rules of interpretation are discussed in this book and an attempt has been made to apply them for interpreting modern legal texts as far as feasible and practicable.

Mimâmsâ is in two parts: practical and theological (theology - study of Gods). The practical part is ascribed to Jaiminî and is commonly called Purva Mîmâmsâ. Jaimini was an Indian rishi (sage), a disciple of the great rishi Parashar. The other part, Uttar Mîmâmsâ, is ascribed to Shankaracharya) and is called Védánta. The Purva Mimâmsâ deals with the practical aspects of karma or religious observance to be taken for specific ends and hence is also sometimes called Karma Mimamsa. The Vedanta or Uttar Mimamsâ on the other hand deals exclusively with theological aspects and is also called Brahma Mimamsa. Here we are concerned with the Purva Mimamsa or simply Mimamsa.

The object of the Mimamsa is the interpretation of the Vedic texts which ordain the duty (dharma) of the people in the form of injunction or command. Mimamsa has been defined as the process of 'investigation into a topic of discussion and coming to a conclusion thereon'.

The Mîmâmsâ rules of interpretation are in form of Sutras or aphorisms under different chapters, sections and topics (adhikaranas). Thus the work consists of 12 Adhyayas (chapters) spread over 2668 Sutras under 731 Adhikaranas. Each topic is treated in five logical step establishing a system of interpretation and this is the strength and beauty of Mîmâmsâ rules of interpretation:

1. Statement of the subject or matter to be explained (vishaya). the proposition or the principle.
2. Inviting/considering the objections, doubt or question arising out of that matter - objections or counter to the proposition (samasya).
3. Statement of prima facie argument in support of the objections (purvapaksha).
4. Stating the answer to the objections or demonstrated conclusion (siddhanta).
5. Giving the connection, or reasoning (sangati).

Like Nyāyaśāstra the Mimâmsa Sutras acknowledge and use five sources of knowledge or modes of proof viz. perception, inference (anumana), comparison (upamana), presumption (arthapatti), and evidence (documents and verbal communication). The Mîmâmsâ principles ensure that every interpretation will be based on sound logic and cogent reasoning.

The nature of Jaiminî's Mîmâmsâ cannot be better described than what Colebrooke, one of the most accurate and level-headed of Western scholars of Sanskrit, wrote:

The disquisitions of the Mimâmsâ bear, therefore, a certain resemblance to juridical questions; and, in fact, the Hindu Law being blended with the religion of the people, the same modes of reasoning are applicable, and are applied to the one as to the other. The logic of the Mimamsa is the logic of the law, the rule of interpretation of civil and religious ordinances. Each case is examined and determined upon general principles; and from the cases decided the principles may be collected. A well-ordered arrangement of them would constitute the philosophy of law: and this is, in truth, what has been attempted in Mîmâmsa. Jaimini's arrangement, however, is not philosophical; and I am not acquainted with any elementary work of this school in which a better distribution has been achieved.

Similarly Professor Max Müller also appreciated the practical investigative procedures of Mîmâmsâ and expressed his reservation on regarding it as a system of (Indian) Philosophy:

We may wonder why it should ever have been raised to the rank of a philosophical system by the side of the Uttara-Mîmâmsâ or the Vedanta, but it is its method rather than the matter to which it is applied, that seems to have invested it with a certain importance. This Mimâmsâ method of discussing questions has been adopted in other branches of learning also, for instance, by the highest legal authorities in trying to settle contested questions of law. We meet with it in other systems of philosophy also as recognized method of discussing various opinions before arriving at a final conclusion. (Emphasis supplied by author)

It is surprising that despite thus opining Max Müller has placed Purva Mimâmsâ as one of the six systems of Indian philosophy, more so when he admired the richness of the Sanskrit language. He wrote:

And if I were to ask myself from what literature we, here in Europe, we who have been nurtured almost exclusively on the thoughts of Greeks and Romans, and of one Semitic race, the Jewish, may draw that corrective which is most wanted in order to make our inner life more perfect, more comprehensive, more universal, in fact more truly human, a life, not for this life only, but a transfigured and eternal life-again I should point to India.

Thus Mimâmsâ is a practical "process of 'investigation' into a topic of discussion and coming to a conclusion thereon"; and the logic of the Mîmâmsâ principles of interpretation is the logic of law. Despite the inherent practical qualities of the Mîmâmsâ principles these are not applied by the Indian Courts. Lamenting on this state of affairs and recognizing the ignorance of the legal fraternity about the Mîmâmsâ principles the Supreme Court observed:It is deeply regrettable that in our Courts of law lawyers quote Maxwell and Craies but nobody refers to the Mimamsa Principles of Interpretation. Most lawyers would not have even heard of their existence. Today our so-called educated people are largely ignorant about the great intellectual achievements of our ancestors and the intellectual treasury which they have bequeathed us. The Mimamsa Principles of Interpretation is part of that great intellectual treasury, but it is distressing to note that apart from the reference to these principles in the judgment of Sir John Edge, the then Chief Justice of Allahabad High Court in Beni Prasad v Hardai Bibi 1892 ILR 14 All 67 (FB), a hundred years ago and in some judgments of (M. Katju, J.) there has been almost no utilization of these principles even in our own country.

On these premises we shall now describe these principles in brief. Some of the fundamental doctrines (principles) of Mîmâmsâ put forward by Jaimini, and explained by Sabara, Kumārila Bhatt and others; as discussed by P.V. Kane are:

(a) Vedas are eternal, self existent, not composed by any author, human or divine, and are infallible.

(b) The connection between word and sense is eternal. The Mîmâmsakas hold that the 'Word, the denotation and the relation of these two are eternal'.

(c) There is no real creation or dissolution of the whole universe. The constituent parts may come and go but the universe as a whole has no beginning and no end.

This proposition, though not very relevant to legal matters, is a very scientific proposition universally accepted as "conservation of matter".

(d) Veda says 'one desirous of heaven should perform a sacrifice' (svargakamo yajeta). It has been interpreted as meaning that a person has no capacity or potency to achieve svarga (heaven). For this he has to perform yāga, but then unless he performs all the prescribed rites main and subordinate - he will not achieve the result or the potency or capacity to achieve the result: the svarga. This has been called the doctrine of Apurva. This doctrine further postulates that the whole rites performed as prescribed make the performer capable of or entitled to the result, but each subordinate rite (anga) therein also gives certain capacities for achieving part of the whole result. The rules for performing the rites are termed Vidhi.

This may be understood in modern terms as laying down that an act ordained by law to be done must be done in the manner as prescribed by the law.

(e) Svatah pramanya (self-validity of cognition): postulates that all cognitions (knowledge including perception as distinguished from emotion), are intrinsically valid in themselves. They do not require any extraneous help to establish their validity, but invalidity of cognitions is (paratah) established extraneously by showing that there was defect in the organ that produced the cognition or it is established later on that a particular cognition was wrong.

On these fundamental principles the Mîmâmsakas proceeded to interpret the Vedic texts. At the outset it is to be noted that Mîmâmsâ is broadly arranged in three parts; Theory of words; Theory of sentences and the Order or sequence.

For interpreting the Vedas the Mîmâmsakas consider the texts as composed of six parts as are contained in any modern enacted law. These are: definition (clause) or 'sangya'; key to interpretation or 'paribhasha' (defining words according to the special context of their use); statement of general rule or 'vidhi' (substantive provision); restrictive rule or 'niyam' (proviso); heading, to which a number of rules belong (like Parts or Chapters containing more than one section/provision); rules or 'adhikar' (section, sub-section, clause etc.); and general application of a rule or 'atidesh' (applicability of the provision or exception, analogy if any).

The foremost thing to be reckoned is that the Mimamsakas hold that no part of the Vedas, even a word, is useless irrelevant or meaningless. Although this is the well accepted rule against redundancy, an erroneous impression has gained ground that the Vedic texts contain only vidhis and therefore any word or passage not conforming to the requirements of vidhi are useless superfluous and irrelevant. In fact such passages, as a rule, follow the vidhi and are clearly distinguishable from vidhi. These are in the nature of qualifier, explanation, exception etc. attached to the vidhi and have been termed Arthavadas but are not redundant.

The rules of interpretation are drawn from the general scope and intention of the codified legislation. Besides this, the nature of the transactions and the situation also affects the interpretation of those legislation. Interpretation is the process which is adopted for determination of the meaning of a writing and is the most important aid to determine its true meaning or the intent of the framers of the documents. It is the art of finding out the true sense of words written in those legislation the sense which their author intended to convey. It is not a science but an art to find out the meaning of words in the context of a given situation. Maxwell is the name who has greater position in the scope of Interpretation of Statutes.

In this course of time, the discussion of the other prevalent important rules of interpretation that existed prior to Maxwell are left apart and are hardly used in the present time. Especially, in the Eastern part of the world where there is wide influence of Hinduism. There exist many scriptures which played important role in the interpretation of the Hindu Texts. These scriptures consisted of the elaborate rules for finding the actual meaning of the words and phrases used in the Vedas and Purans. Among all those scriptures, the most important scripture which consisted the rules for such interpretation is the Mimangsa.

Elaborate rules of interpretation were evolved even at a very early stage of Hindu civilization and culture. The rules given by 'Jaimini', the author of Mimamsat Sutras, originally meant for srutis were employed for the interpretation of Smrities also. Mimangsa can be called as the stepping stone to Dharmasasthras.

During the post-Buddhist era, Jaimini attempted the work of systematizing the rules of Mimamsa, which had evolved since the earliest times of Vedic civilization, and establishing their validity in his work.

The aim of the Purva Mimamsa is to examine the nature of dharma. Its interest is more practical than speculative, and therefore the philosophical speculations found in it are subordinate to the ritualistic purpose. Thus the scriptures governing the Hindu life need basically to be interpreted in accordance with the Mimamsa rules.

Dharma is the scheme of right living. Jaimini defines dharma as an ordinance or command. Dharma is what is enjoined, and it leads to happiness. Activities which result in loss or pain (anartha) are not dharma. Thus the lack of observing the commands leads not only to missing the happiness but becoming subject to suffering also.

There is a greater scope of use of Mimangsa Principles of interpretation in the present context in the interpretation of statutes. However, if the practice of its application is concerned, it is not up to the expected level. Yet some remarkable attempts are made in this regard to ensure that the rules of interpretation under Mimangsa have the validity and applicability in the present context too.

"Mimangsa" (or Mimansa) is a scripture related to Hindu Religion and is considered the most important tool for the interpretation of other Hindu Scriptures. The meaning of Mimangsa refers to the act of taking serious concern over the religious matters stated in the Vedas. It provides particular methods for interpreting the matters stated in the scriptures like 'Vedas', 'Smirities' etc. In the course of interpretation, there can be found many methods of interpretation given by Manu, Yagyabalkya, Narad, Vyas, Bhrihaspati and others but no concrete method of interpretation is given by them as given by Jaimini in Mimangsa. The Mimansa Principles were the traditional system of interpretation of legal texts. Although originally they were created for interpreting religious texts [pertaining to the Yagya sacrifice], gradually they came to be utilized for interpreting legal texts and also for interpreting texts on philosophy, grammar, etc. i.e. they became of universal application. Thus, Shankaracharya has used the Mimansa adhikaranas in his bhashya on the Vedanta sutras. There were hundreds of books [all in Sanskrit] written on the subject, though only a few dozens have survived the ravages of time.

Mimangsa is divided into two parts the first one is the Eastern Mimansa (Purvi Mimangsa) which is propounded by Jaimini while the other is the Northern Mimansa (Uttar Mimansa or Vrahma Mimangsa). The Purvi Mimangsa is decides about the proper intrepretation rules of the Karmakandaparak Mantras and Vedas while the Uttar Mimangsa (also known as Vedanta consists of the situation of the eternity. In the course of interpretation, the Purvi Mimangsa is the main reference.

In ancient and medieval India there was tremendous development not only in the fields of Science and Philosophy, but also in the field of law. However, the advent of British rule denied us the benefits of these developments as the alien rulers made it a policy to demoralise and denigrate us by propagating the idea that Indians were a race with no worthwhile achievement to their credit.

As is well known, the principles of interpretation of statutes mainly relied on in our law courts are those dealt with in the works of Western jurists like Maxwell and Craies. However, in our country we had developed from very early times a scientific system of interpretation known as the Mimansa Principles and these were regularly followed by our renowned jurists like Vijnaneshwara (author of *Mitakshara)*,

Jimutvahana (author of *Dayabhag)*, Nanda Pandit (author of *Dattak Mimansa)* etc. Whenever there was any conflict between the Smritis e.g. Manusmriti and Yagnavalkya Smriti, or ambiguity in a Shruti or Smriti, the Mimansa Principles were applied. Most of these principles are rational and scientific, and in some respects superior to the principles obtaining in Western Law. At present there is no reason why we should not apply them in appropriate cases.

In a recent case, *Tribhuwannath* v. *D.I.O.S.,* Writ Petition No. 17544 of 1990 decided on 30-3-1992[98] one of these principles was applied. In this case the petitioner, who was the seniormost teacher in an Intermediate College, had filed a writ petition in the Allahabad High Court claiming that he should have been appointed ad hoc Principal on the retirement of the previous Principal, but the management had superseded him. In the course of hearing two Division Bench decisions apparently conflicting with each other, were cited. While the Division Bench ruling written by Hon'ble R.M. Sahai, J. had held that the seniormost teacher should be appointed ad hoc Principal the Division Bench ruling delivered by Hon'ble V.N. Khare, J. had held that it is the discretion of the Management as to who is to be appointed. By way of employing the *Samanjasya* principle of Mimansa it was easy to reconcile the conflicting decisions by holding that the former decision should be interpreted to mean that *ordinarily* the seniormost teacher should be appointed Principal, while the latter decision should be interpreted to mean that in exceptional cases, viz., if there are grave charges against him, he can be superseded by a reasoned order, though only after giving him a show-cause notice.

The Mimansa or the Purva Mimansa Rules to be exact, were laid down by Jaimini in his *Sutras* written around 600 B.C. That they are very ancient is proved by the fact that they are referred to in many Smritis which themselves are very old. Thus, the Apastamba Sutras copiously refer to Jaimini's principles. Since these Sutras are written in very concise form it became necessary to explain them. Many commentaries were written on them, the main ones being of Sabara, who lived around

Second Century A.D., and Kumarila Bhatta and Prabhakara, who lived around the Eighth Century A.D.

Before mentioning some of the Mimansa Principles it is necessary to give a short background. Classical Hindu Philosophy has six schools (shatdarshan) all of which aim at Moksha (liberation). Purva Mimansa is one of these schools, and according to it one can achieve Moksha by performing Yagya (sacrifice) in accordance with the Shastras. The Shastras consist of Shruti and Smriti, the former being superior to the latter. Shruti consists of the four Vedas, the Brahmanas, the Aranyaks and the Upanishads. Brahmanas are treatises written in prose which prescribe methods of performing various Yagyas. To every Veda one or more Brahmanas are attached. Thus, the Aitareya Brahmana is attached to the Rig Veda, the Taitareya Brahmana to the Black Yajur Veda, the Shatapatha Brahmana to the White Yajur Veda, and the Tandya Brahmana to the Sama Veda.

After Shankaracharya's renowned victory over Mandan Misra, Purva Mimansa, as a philosophic system, declined in importance. Shankaracharya was a proponent of Uttar Mimansa (also known as Vedanta), according to which Moksha can be achieved by knowledge of Brahma. Shankaracharya preached that Jnanakanda (the Vedantic Path) is superior to Karmakanda (the performance of Yagya). He shifted the emphasis in the Shrutis from the Brahmanas to the Upanishads, and his view was accepted, and ever since Vedanta became the dominant school of Hindu philosophy.

However, though Purva Mimansa lost prominence to Vedanta in Philosophy, its importance remained as paramount as before in the legal sphere. It must however be clarified that the Mimansaks were not jurists. Their aim was to perform the Yagya properly, for they sincerely believed that this was the means to achieve moksha. For the conduct of Yagyas in accordance with the rules they had to devise a system of interpretation to resolve the conflicts, ambiguities, etc. in the Shrutis, which were aggravated by the archaic, pre-Panini Sanskrit employed in the Vedic texts. No doubt the principles of interpretation were initially evolved to resolve conflicts that arose in connection with the meaning of rules governing performance of the Yagya, but gradually these principles came to be accepted for interpreting legal texts also which were mixed up with religious rules in the Smritis. It was therefore natural that our great commentators like Vijnaneshwara, Jimutvahana, etc. had utilised these Mimansa principles whenever faced with any ambiguity or conflict in the various Shastras.

Unfortunately, there has not been much effort to explain these principles. The advent of Anglo-Saxon Law must have been responsible for this lack of study.

The Mimansa principles are in two respects superior to Maxwell's principles of interpretation, viz.: (1) They can be utilised not only for interpreting statutes but also judgments, whereas Maxwell's principles can only be used for interpreting statutory law, (2) They are more detailed and systematic.

The Mimansa Principles distinguish between obligatory statements and non-obligatory statements. The main obligatory rule is called a Vidhi (or a Pratishedh, if it is in negative form). Vidhis are of 4 types, (1) Utpatti Vidhi, or a substantive injunction (e.g. 'perform the agnihotra'), (2) Viniyoga Vidhi, or applicatory rules (e.g. 'with curdled milk perform the agnihotra'), (3) Prayog Vidhi, or rules of procedure, and (4) Adhikara Vidhis (rules regarding rights and personal competence). Apart from these Vidhis proper (mentioned above) there are also certain quasi Vidhis called niyamas and parishankhyas, but it is not necessary to go into details here. Vidhis are found in Brahmanas.

The main non-obligatory statement is known as an Arthavada. An Arthavada is a statement of praise or explanation. Most of the Vedas proper consist of Arthavadas as much of the Vedic hymns are in praise of some god, and do not lay down any injunction. Arthavada is like the preamble or statement of objects in a statute. An Arthavada has no legal force by itself, but it is not entirely useless since like a statement of objects or preamble it can help to clarify an ambiguous Vidhi, or give the reason for it. Sometimes a Vidhi is also seen couched in the form of Arthavada. This situation has necessitated the need for evolving a system of interpretation. Six axioms of interpretation have therefore been developed for the interpretation of shastras They are:

(1) The Sarthakyata axiom, which means that every word and sentence must have some meaning.

(2) The Laghava axiom (Gauravah doshah), which states that that construction which makes the meaning simpler and shorter is to be preferred.

(3) The Arthaikatva axiom, which states that a double meaning should not be attached to a word or sentence occurring at one and the same place. Such a double meaning is known as a Vakyabheda, and is a fault (dosh).

(4) The Gunapradhan axiom, which states that if a word or sentence purporting to express a subordinate idea clashes with the principal idea the former must be adjusted to the latter, or must be disregarded altogether.

(5) The Samanjasya axiom[99] which states that all attempts should be made at reconciliation of apparently conflicting texts. Jimutvahana has applied this principle for reconciling conflicting texts of Manu and Yajnavalkya on the right of succession.

(6) The Vikalpa axiom, which states that if there is a real and irreconcilable contradiction between two legal rules having equal force, the rule more in accordance with equity and usage should be adopted at one's option. Thus where one of the rules is a higher legal norm as compared to the other, e.g. a Shruti in relation to Smriti, by the Badha principle[100] the former prevails.

It may be mentioned here that the Mimansaks made every effort to reconcile conflicts, and held that Vikalpa was to be resorted to only if all other means of reconciliation failed, for Vikalpa had eight faults (dosh).

Apart from the above mentioned axioms of interpretation there are the four well-known general principles of interpretation in Mimansa, viz.:

(1) The Shruti Principle, or the literal rule. This is illustrated by the well-known Garhapatya maxim. There is the Vedic verse "Aindra garhapatyam Upatishthate" (with the Indra verse one should worship Garhapatya). Now this Vidhi can have several meanings e.g. (1) One should worship Garhapatya (the household fire) with a verse addressed to Indra, (2) One should worship both Indra as well as Garhapatya, (3) One should worship either of the two. The correct interpretation, according to the Shruti principle, is the first interpretation.

(2) The Linga principle (also called Lakshana artha) or the suggestive power of words or expressions. This principle can be illustrated by the decision of the Supreme Court in *U.P. Bhoodan Yagna Samiti* v. *Brij Kishore*[101], where the words "landless person" were held to refer to landless peasants only and not to landless businessmen.

(3) The Vakya Principle, or syntactical arrangement, and

(4) Prakarana, which permits construction by referring to some other text in order to make the meaning clear.

The first principle (Shruti) is to be resorted to if (1) the meaning of the text is clear, and (2) it accords with the intention. But there are texts whose meaning seems to be clear, but to give that literal meaning would totally undermine its intention. For example, if a literal meaning is to be given to the English law which forbade a layman to 'lay hands' on a priest, the layman who wounded a priest with a weapon would not be doing anything illegal. Similarly on a literal construction when the Turkish Sultan Mohammed II sawed the Venetian Governor's body in two it was no breach of his promise to spare his head, and Tamarlane's burying alive a garrison was no violation of his pledge to shed no blood.

We see therefore that the literal rule will sometimes lead to absurdity and totally efface the intention of the law. In fact, as Lord Denning[102] has pointed out, the modern method of interpretation is to seek the intention rather than to follow the literal rule. This is signified in the decision of the Supreme Court of India in *Charan Lal Sahu* v. *Union of India*[103] The Mimansaks were great intention seekers, and the

Linga, Vakya and Prakarana principles all aim at finding the intention of the law.

Only the broad outlines have been indicated above, but it has to be noted that the Mimansa Principles go into minute details and systematically arrange the principles of interpretation into categories and sub-categories with all their ramifications. For example, the Vakya principle (mentioned above) include adhayahara and anusanga (supplying of missing words and expressions), upakarsha and apakarsha (transference of clauses up or down in the sentence), etc.

To give an illustration of the anusanga principle[104] (elliptical extension) it is interesting to see how Jimutavahana interpreted the text of Manu which states "Of a woman married according to the Brahma, Daiva, Arsha, Gandharvaand Prajapatya form, the property shall go to her husband, if she dies without issue. But her wealth, given to her on her marriage in the form called Asura, Rakshas and Paisacha, on her death without issue shall become the property of her parents". Jimutavahana employing the anusanga principle interpreted this text to the effect that the words "wealth given to her on her marriage" should also be inserted in the first sentence after the words "the property".

The difference between the Linga principle and the Vakya principle may also be noticed. In the former no violence is done to the wording of the text, but the words or expressions are construed differently from the literal sense, and hence Linga is really construction by context. In Vakya, however, some violence is done to the text e.g., by connecting two separate sentences, or by adding words or expressions, or by transferring words or expressions up or down a sentence. This violence may sometimes become necessary to save the text from becoming meaningless or absurd, just as the surgeon may have to do violence to the body (by operation) to save the patient's life. For this purpose the Uha principle (use of reason) is employed.[105] In this connection it may be mentioned that Maxwell also permits doing violence to the statute in exceptional situations. He says "where the language of a statute, in its ordinary meaning and grammatical construction, leads to a manifest contradiction of the apparent purpose of the enactment, or to some inconvenience or absurdity, hardship or injustice, presumably not intended, a construction may be put upon it which modifies the meaning of the words, and even the structure of the sentence. This may be done by departing from the rules of grammar, by giving an unusual meaning to particular words, by altering their collocation, by rejecting them altogether, or by interpolating other words, under the influence, no doubt, of an irresistible conviction that the legislature could not possibly have intended what the words signify, and that the modifications thus made are mere corrections of careless language and really give the true intention". This approach seems to have been followed by the Supreme Court in *S.S. Kalra* v. *Union of India*[106], wherein it has observed that sometimes courts can supply words which have been accidentally omitted.

Apart from the above mentioned principles of interpretation there are also a large number of popular maxims (nyayas) which are in essence illustrations of the above principles. Thus, in the *Tribhuwannath case* [1] (supra) the maxim of the lost horses and burnt chariot (Nashtashvadagdharatha nyaya) was applied for harmonising two apparently conflicting decisions of the Allahabad High Court. Similarly, there is the maxim 'the popular sense prevails over the etymological sense' which is illustrated by the word 'Pankaj'. This word literally means anything born in mud and therefore can refer to dozens of things. But by usage it has come to mean only lotus.

There are various other such maxims (nyayas) e.g., the Aruni, holika, barhi, shodashi, garhapatya, the maxim of the wooden sword (sphadi nyaya) the partridge (kapijjala) maxim, the maxim of the two monsters (sundopsunda nyaya), the maxim of the larger fish eating the smaller fish (matsya nyaya) etc.[107] Nyayas are extremely useful in understanding the principles of interpretation. In fact many of these maxims have been used by our commentators.[108]

Application of Mimansa principles sometimes lead to different results. For example, there is a text of Vasishta which says "a woman should not give or take a son in adoption except with the assent of her husband". This has been interpreted in 4 different ways by our commentators. (1) The Dattak Mimansa holds that no widow can adopt a son because the assent required is assent at the time of adoption, and the husband being dead no assent of his can be had at the time of adoption. Vachaspati, of the Mithila School of Mitakshara, is of the same opinion, but for a different reason. According to him, adoption can only be resorted to after performing the homa, and since a woman cannot perform the homa with Vedic mantras, she cannot adopt. (2) The Dayabhaga view is that the husband's assent is not required at the time of actual adoption, and hence if the husband had given assent in his lifetime his widow can adopt after his death. (3) The view of the Dravida School of Mitakshara is that the words "except with the assent of the husband" are only illustrative, and hence assent of her husband's agnates or father-in-law's agnates is sufficient. (4) The Vyavaharmayukha and Nirnayasindhu hold that assent is required only for the woman whose husband is living and hence a widow can freely adopt unless she had been expressly forbidden by her late husband. To give another example, both the Mitakshara and Dayabhaga use mimansa principles in interpreting the Smritis but with different results. For example, the word 'sapinda' has been interpreted differently in Dayabhaga and Mitakshara. Both these systems lay down that the nearest Sapinda has the right to inherit, but according to Dayabhaga 'Sapinda' means the person who has the right to offer the pinda (rice balls) in the shraddha ceremony to the deceased, while the Mitakshara interprets the word 'pinda' to mean particles of the body, and not rice balls, and hence sapinda means one having the same particles as the deceased (i.e. nearer in blood).

The fact that Mimansa principles sometimes lead to different results however does not diminish their utility. Maxwell's principles also lead to different results. This only shows that principles of interpretation should not be applied blindly. Principles of interpretation are good servants but bad masters, as observed by the Supreme Court in *Keshavji Ravji and Co.* v. *C.I.*[109] They are to be utilised for discovering the meaning of the legal text, but they are not to be applied without having regard to the context and commonsense and reason. They are, after all, not rules of law but a methodology for resolving certain difficulties.

It is also pertinent to mention the mimansa principles were originally evolved for interpreting the religious texts pertaining to the Yagyas, and hence all of them may not be relevant for interpreting legal texts.

In conclusion I would like to clarify that it is not my opinion that we should not use the sound and useful ideas of Western jurists like Maxwell. It would be foolhardy to discard the good ideas of Western jurists. It has never been the Indian tradition to reject foreign ideas, merely because they are foreign. There are many good things we have to learn from Westerners. But at the same time we should not blindly ape the Westerners and discard our own traditional ideas if they are found still useful and relevant. After all we too have produced great thinkers, and we can utilise their sound ideas wherever appropriate after making suitable adaptations to suit the prevailing conditions.

Utilization of Mimansa Principles

Knowledge of Mimansa Principles enables one to creatively develop the law. A few examples of utilization of Mimansa Principles in some of my judgments is given below:

1. In *Sardar Mohammad Ansar Khan* v. *State of U.P.*[110] the controversy was as to which of two clerks appointed on the same day in an Intermediate College would be senior, and hence entitled to promotion as Head Clerk. Now there is no rule to cater to this situation. However, Chapter 2, Regulation 3 of the U.P. Intermediate Education Regulations states that where 2 teachers are appointed on the same day, the senior in age will be senior. Using the atidesh Principle of mimansa it was held that the same principle which applies to teachers should be also applied to clerks, and hence the senior in age would be senior. The atidesh principle originated in the practical difficulty of performing certain yagyas. There are some yagyas (e.g. agnihotra, darshapurnamani, etc.) whose method of performance is given in detail in the Brahmanas. These are known as prakriti yagyas. However, there are other yagyas whose rules are not given any where, and these are known as vikriti yagyas. The question arose how these latter are to be performed? The atidesh principle was created to resolve this difficulty, and according to this principle the vikriti yagya is to be performed according to the rules of the prakriti yagya belonging to the same genus.

2. In *Tribhuwan Misra* v. *D.I.O.S.* (*supra*) the Samanjasya principle was used to reconcile 2 apparently conflicting Division Bench rulings. This technique avoided reference to a Full Bench which would have tied up 3 or more Judges for several days in resolving the conflict. No doubt this decision

(as a Single Judge) curtailed the full effect of the 2 Division Bench decisions, but that was done on the authority of the maxim of the lost horse; and burnt chariot (Nasrhtashva Dagdharatha Nyaya). This is based on the story of two men travelling in their respective chariots. One of them lost his horses and the other's chariot was burnt through the out break of fire inn the in where they were spending the night. The horses that were left were harnessed to the remaining chariot, and the two men pursued their journey together. Its teaching is union for mutual advantage, which has been quoted in the 16th Vartika to Panini, and is explained by Patanjali. It is referred to in Kumarila Bhatta's 'Tantravartika'.

3. The Anusanga Principle of Mimansa has been used in *Mahabir Prasad Dwivedi* v. *State*[111] The principle has been explained in great detail in this decision, which may be seen in the aforesaid journal. The conclusion reached in this decision could not have been reacted by any principle of Western Jurisprudence, and this illustrates the great use which can be made of Mimansa Principles to make the statute more democratic and equitable.

The Laghava Principle has been used in *Vinay Khare* v. *State of U.P.*[112] The controversy in this case was that if in a competitive examination two candidates got equal marks whether the candidate who got more marks in the oral interview should be placed higher in the select list or the candidate who got more marks in the written test. It was held in this case that the candidate who got more marks in the written test should be placed higher because to interpret general suitability on the basis of marks in the written test is a short and simple interpretation and provides a clear objective test, whereas the criteria in the oral interview involves consideration of the candidate's personality, dress, physique, etc. which is complicated and in which there are more chances of favouritism and arbitrariness.

Applicability of Mimangsa Rules of Interpretation

The application of Mimangsa Rules of Interpretation although is primarily focused with the interpretation of many Hindu Scriptures like Vedas, Smirities, Shrutis etc, its application in modern times also cannot be ignored.

There are two reasons for the application of Mimansa principles to law: (1) The Mimansa Rules deal with the Brahmana portions of the shruti, i.e., the portion which laid down injunctions, and the law, too, being largely in the form of injunctions was attracted to them; (2) Mimansa is a practical subject, and the law, too, being practical was inclined to incorporate them. The great commentators like Vijnaneshwara (author of the Mitakshara), Jimutvahana (author of the Dayabhaga), Nanda Pandit (author of Dattak Mimansa), Vachaspati, Neelkanth, etc., were all profound scholars of Mimansa, and they regularly used the Mimansa Principles when confronted with any difficulty regarding interpretation of the Smrities (which contained the law in those times).

Talking about the application of Mimangsa Rules of Interpretation in the interpretation of the statutes and laws of Nepal, it is not found so much used. But in the context of India, the use of Mimangsa Rules of Interpretation has been used for exploring the meaning of the legal provisions.

The Supreme Court applied one of these principle after quoting a 'Shloka'. In this regard, the Supreme Court of India in the case of UP Bhoodan Yagna Samiti, UP V. Braj Kishore, observed:

"In this country, we have a heritage of rich literature, it is interesting to note that literature of interpretation also is very well known. The principles of interpretation have been enunciated in various Shlokas which have been known for hundreds of years."

Sir John Edge, the then Chief Justice of Allahabad High Court, has referred to the Mimamsa principle in Beni Prasad v Hardai Bibi FA No. 35 Of 1888.

Similarly, Gunapradhan Axiom of the Mimamsa principle was applied for interpretation of section 419 of UP Sales Tax Act in Amit Plastic Industry, Ghaziabad v Divisional Level Committee, Meerut CMWP No.312 OF 1989.

In the case of Tribhuwan Mishra v Distt. Inspector of Schools, Azamgarh (1992) 1 UPLBEC 716 'Samajasya Axiom' was applied.

Supreme Court has recognized the value of the Mimansa Rules of Interpretation in the case of M/s Ispat Industries Ltd vs Commissioner of Customs AIR Online 2006 SC 69, M/s Craft Interiors Pvt. Ltd vs. Commissioner of Central Excise 2006 AIR SCW 5546.

It can be shown how Mimansa principles can be a powerful tool in the hands of the Judge in molding the law to make it more rational, equitable and democratic. Use of Mimansa Principles gives a flexibility which Western principles of interpretation totally lack. Knowledge of the great achievements of our ancestors will inspire us and give us the confidence and strength to solve our present problems.

If the aforementioned rules under Mimangsa Principles of Interpretation are analyzed, the Laghav and Shruti Principle signifies what the Literal Rule of Interpretation signifies.

Again, if the Linga Principle under Mimangsa is concerned, it is similar to what Section 12 of Nepal Kanoon Byakhya Sambandhi Ain 2010.

The Vakya Rule of Interpretation is quite similar to the Mischief Rule of Interpretation.

Similarly, the General Principles Regarding the Application of Texts has been able to segregate the rules that are mandatory in nature and those which are not mandatory in nature.

Knowledge of the Mimansa principles enables one to infuse equity and the democratic spirit into the law in a manner unknown to western techniques of interpretation.

"An example of this is the decision in Mahavir Prasad Dwivedi v. State of U.P. AIR 1992 ALL 351 In that case the facts were that the petitioner had been elected Chairman of a Town Area in U.P. He was removed by the Collector after giving him a hearing, and the Collector's order was confirmed by the State Government. But the State Government had not given an opportunity of hearing to the petitioner. The question before the court was whether the State Government, too, had to give an opportunity of hearing before it confirmed the order of the Collector. After a great deal of consideration the present writer answered it in the affirmative, utilizing the Anusunga principle of Mimansa."

The use of Mimangsa Rules of Interpretation is not so far been found implemented in Nepal. There is also an ongoing debate about whether or not these rules of Mimamsa be incorporated in the legislative form. Some say that these rules cannot be incorporated in the legislative form. It is because, according to them, the rules present in the Mimangsa is obviously the rules of extrinsic aid and if rules of extrinsic aid and construction are codified then it may be that some radical sources are kept out of purview of interpretation unknowingly. Besides, Mimangsa gives its much priority to Hindu Religion. In the case if the Economics stand contrary to the Dharmasasthras, Mimangsa rules prefers Dharmasasthras to Economics. This might look contemporary to be used efficiently in the Hindu Laws in particular but looks conservative if used in a general sense.

Mimangsa principles of interpretation gave the rules of exegesis which though primarily intended as aids for the interpretation of rules contained in the Vedas and other Dharmasasthras relating to ceremonial observances and sacrifices, were applied, though not with uniformly, in construction of texts of municipal law as well. Rules for interpretation in the form of a scientific system were developed since very early times known as Mimamsa Principles of Interpretation. These principles were regularly used by the renowned jurists like Vijnaneshwara (author of Mitakshra), Jimutvahana (author of Dayabagh), Nanda Pandit (author of Dattak Mimamsa), etc. Whenever there was any conflict between two Smrities, eg.,

Manusmriti and Yagnavlkya Smriti, or ambiguity in a Shruti or Smriti, the Mimamsa Principles were utilized. These Mimamsa rules were laid down by Jaimini in his Sutras written abound 500 B.C. No doubt, these principles of interpretation were initially laid down for interpreting religious texts pertaining to 'Yagya' (sacrifice), but gradually the same principles came to be used for interpreting legal texts also, particularly since in the Smrities the religious texts and legal texts are mixed up in the same treatises.

From the various court decisions given by the judiciary of India in different context, it is clear that the Mimangsa Principles of Interpretation are still suitable at present context as it also contains a scientific basis for the interpretation. If the Mimangsa rules of Interpretation are also used along with other rules of interpretations like Maxwell's or Craies', the legal system can find it easy in the interpretation of statutes because rich and scientific methods of interpretation are also prevalent in Mimangsa which can be effective aid for interpretation of statutes in mostly India and Nepal where there is the larger influence of Hindu Religion.

Sibling Tradition of Hindu Philosophy

They are diverse, united by shared history and concepts, same textual resources, similar ontological and soteriological focus, and cosmology. While Buddhism and Jainism are considered distinct philosophies and religions, some heterodox (nāstika) traditions such as Cārvāka are often considered as distinct schools within Hindu philosophy because the word *Hindu* is also an exonym and historically, the term has also been used as a geographical and cultural identifier for people living in the Indian subcontinent.

Epistemology is pramana, has been a key, much debated field of study in Hinduism since ancient times. *Pramāṇa* is a Hindu theory of knowledge and discusses the valid means by which human beings can gain accurate knowledge. The focus of *pramāṇa* is how correct knowledge can be acquired, how one knows, how one does not, and to what extent knowledge pertinent about someone or something can be acquired.

Ancient and medieval Hindu texts identify six *pramāṇas* as correct means of accurate knowledge and truths:

Pratyakṣa – Direct perception; *Anumāna* – Inference or indirect perception; *Upamāna* – Comparison and analogy; *Arthāpatti* – Postulation, derivation from circumstances; *Anupalabdi* – Non-perception, absence of proof; and *Shabda* – Word, testimony of past or present reliable experts.

Each of these are further categorized in terms of conditionality, completeness, confidence and possibility of error, by the different schools. The schools vary on how many of these six are valid paths of knowledge. For example, the Cārvāka nāstika philosophy holds that only one (perception) is an epistemically reliable means of knowledge, the Samkhya school holds that three are (perception, inference and testimony), while the Mīmāṃsā and Advaita schools hold that all six are epistemically useful and reliable means to knowledge.

Samkhya[113] is the oldest of the orthodox philosophical systems in Hinduism, with origins in the 1st millennium BCE. It is a rationalist school of Indian philosophy, and had a strong influence on other schools of Indian philosophies.

Samkhya school espouses dualism between witness-consciousness and 'nature' (mind, perception, matter). It regards the universe as consisting of two: *Puruṣa* (witness-consciousness) And *prakriti* ('nature'). *Jiva* (a living being) is that state in which *puruṣa* is bonded to *prakriti* in some form. This fusion, state the Samkhya scholars, led to the emergence of *buddhi* (awareness, intellect) and *ahankara* (individualized ego consciousness, "I-maker"). The universe is described by this school as one created by Purusa-Prakriti entities infused with various permutations and combinations of variously enumerated elements, senses, feelings, activity and mind.

It's philosophy includes a theory of *gunas* (qualities, innate tendencies, psyche). *Guna*, it states, are of three types: *Sattva* being good, compassionate, illuminating, positive, and constructive; *Rajas guna* is one of activity, chaotic, passion, impulsive, potentially good or bad; and *Tamas* being the quality of darkness, ignorance, destructive, lethargic, negative. Everything, all life forms and human beings, state Samkhya scholars, have these three *gunas*, but in different proportions. The interplay of these *gunas* defines the character of someone or something, of nature and determines the progress of life. Samkhya theorises a pluralism of Selfs (*Jeevatmas*) who possess consciousness. Samkhya has historically been theistic or non-theistic, and there has been debate about its specific view on God.

The *Samkhya karika*, one of the key texts of this school of Hindu philosophy, opens by stating its goal to be "three kinds of human suffering" and means to prevent them. The text then presents a distillation of its theories on epistemology, metaphysics, axiology and soteriology. For example, it states, from the triad of suffering, arises this inquiry into the means of preventing it. That is useless – if you say so, I say: No, because suffering is not absolute and final.

The Guṇas (qualities) respectively consist in pleasure, pain and dullness, are adapted to manifestation, activity and restraint; mutually domineer, rest on each other, produce each other, consort together, and are reciprocally present.

Goodness is considered to be alleviating and enlightening; foulness, urgent and persisting; darkness, heavy and enveloping. Like a lamp, they cooperate for a purpose by union of contraries.

There is a general cause, which is diffuse. It operates by means of the three qualities, by mixture, by modification; for different objects are diversified by influence of the several qualities respectively.

Since the assemblage of perceivable objects is for use (by man); Since the converse of that which has the three qualities with other properties must exist (in man); Since there must be superintendence (within man); Since there must be some entity that enjoys (within man); Since there is a tendency to abstraction (in man), therefore soul is.

The soteriology in Samkhya aims at the realization of Puruṣa as distinct from Prakriti; this knowledge of the Self is held to end transmigration and lead to absolute freedom (kaivalya).

Yoga[114] is among other things, the name of one of the six *āstika* philosophical schools. The Yoga philosophical system aligns closely with the dualist premises of the Samkhya school. The Yoga school accepts Samkhya psychology and metaphysics, but is considered theistic because it accepts the concept of personal god (Ishvara), unlike Samkhya. The epistemology of the Yoga school, like the Sāmkhya school, relies on three of six *prāmaṇas* as the means of gaining reliable knowledge;*pratyakṣa* (perception), *anumāṇa* (inference)and *śabda* (*āptavacana* and word/testimony of reliable sources).

The universe is conceptualized as a duality in Yoga school: puruṣa (witness-consciousness) and prakṛti (mind, perception, matter); however, the Yoga school discusses this concept more generically as "seer, experiencer" and "seen, experienced" than the Samkhya school.

A key text of the Yoga school is the *Yoga Sutras of Patanjali*. Patanjali may have been, as Max Müller explains, "the author or representative of the Yoga-philosophy without being necessarily the author of the Sutras." Hindu philosophy recognizes many types of Yoga, such as rāja yoga, jñāna yoga, karma yoga, bhakti yoga, tantra yoga, mantra yoga, laya yoga, and hatha yoga.

The Yoga school builds on the Samkhya school theory that jñāna (knowledge) is a sufficient means to moksha. It suggests that systematic techniques/practice (personal experimentation) combined with Samkhya's approach to knowledge is the path to moksha. Yoga shares several central ideas with Advaita Vedanta, with the difference that Yoga is a form of experimental mysticism while Advaita Vedanta is a form of monistic personalism. Like Advaita Vedanta, the Yoga school of Hindu philosophy holds that liberation/freedom in this life is achievable, and that this occurs when an individual fully understands and realizes the equivalence of Atman (Self) and Brahman.

Vaisesika[115] philosophy is a naturalist school. It is a form of atomism in natural philosophy. It postulates that all objects in the physical universe are reducible to *paramāṇu* (atoms), and that one's experiences are derived from the interplay of substance (a function of atoms, their number and their spatial arrangements), quality, activity, commonness, particularity and inherence. Knowledge and liberation are achievable by complete understanding of the world of experience, according to Vaiśeṣika school. The Vaiśeṣika *darśana* is credited to Kaṇāda Kaśyapa from the second half of the first millennium BCE. The foundational text, the *Vaiśeṣika Sūtra*, opens as follows:

Dharma is that from which results the accomplishment of Exaltation and of the Supreme Good. The authoritativeness of the Veda arises from its being an exposition of *dharma*. The Supreme Good results from knowledge, produced from a particular *dharma*, of the essence of the Predicables, Substance, Attribute, Action, Genus, Species and Combination, by means of their resemblances and differences.

Vaiśeṣika Sūtra[116], the school is related to the Nyāya school but features differences in its epistemology, metaphysics and ontology. The epistemology of the Vaiśeṣika school, like Buddhism, accepted only two means to knowledge as reliable – perception and inference. The Vaiśeṣika school and Buddhism both consider their respective scriptures as indisputable and valid means to knowledge, the difference being that the scriptures held to be a valid and reliable source by Vaiśeṣikas were the Vedas.

Vaiśeṣika metaphysical premises are founded on a form of atomism, that reality is composed of four substances (earth, water, air, and fire). Each of these four are of two types: atomic (*paramāṇu*) and composite. An atom is, according to Vaiśeṣika scholars, that which is indestructible (*anitya*), indivisible, and has a special kind of dimension, called "small" (*aṇu*). A composite, in this philosophy, is defined to be anything which is divisible into atoms. Whatever human beings perceive is composite[117].

Nyaya[118] is a realist āstika philosophy. The school's most significant contributions to Indian philosophy were its systematic development of the theory of logic, methodology, and its treatises on epistemology. The foundational text of the Nyāya school is the *Nyāya Sūtras* of the first millennium BCE. The text is credited to Aksapada Gautama and its composition is variously dated between the sixth and second centuries BCE.

Nyāya epistemology accepts four out of six *prāmaṇas* as reliable means of gaining knowledge; *pratyakṣa* (perception), *anumāṇa* (inference), *upamāṇa* (comparison and analogy) and *śabda* (word, testimony of past or present reliable experts).

In its metaphysics, the Nyāya school is closer to the Vaiśeṣika school than the others. It holds that human suffering results from mistakes/defects produced by activity under wrong knowledge (notions and ignorance). Moksha (liberation), it states, is gained through right knowledge. This premise led Nyāya to concern itself with epistemology, that is, the reliable means to gain correct knowledge and to remove wrong notions. False knowledge is not merely ignorance to Naiyayikas; it includes delusion. Correct knowledge is discovering and overcoming one's delusions, and understanding the true nature of the soul, self and reality. The Nyāya Sūtras begin: Perception, Inference, Comparison and Word – these are the means of right knowledge. Perception is that knowledge which arises from the contact of a sense with its object and which is determinate, unnameable and non-erratic. Inference is knowledge which is preceded by perception, and is of three kinds: a priori, a posteriori, and commonly seen.

Comparison is the knowledge of a thing through its similarity to another thing previously well known. Word is the instructive assertion of a reliable person. It [knowledge] is of two kinds: that which is seen, and that which is not seen. Soul, body, senses, objects of senses, intellect, mind, activity, fault, transmigration, fruit, suffering and release – are the objects of right knowledge.

Vedanta

The Vedanta school built upon the teachings of the Upanishads and Brahma Sutras from the first millennium BCE and is the most developed and best-known of the Hindu schools[119].

The emergence of the Vedanta school represented a period in which a more knowledge-centered understanding began to emerge, focusing on *jnana* (knowledge) driven aspects of the Vedic religion and the Upanishads. These included metaphysical concepts such as ātman and Brahman, and an emphasis on meditation, self-discipline, self-knowledge and abstract spirituality, rather than ritualism. The Upanishads were variously interpreted by ancient- and medieval-era Vedanta scholars. Consequently, the Vedanta separated into many sub-schools, ranging from theistic dualism to non-theistic monism, each interpreting the texts in its own way and producing its own series of sub-commentaries.

Advaita literally means "not two, sole, unity". It is a sub-school of Vedanta, and asserts spiritual and universal non-dualism. Its metaphysics is a form of absolute monism, that is all ultimate reality is interconnected oneness. This is the oldest and most widely acknowledged Vedantic school. The foundational texts of this school are the Brahma Sutras and the early Upanishads from the 1st millennium BCE. Its first great consolidator was the 8th century scholar Adi Shankara, who continued the line of thought of the Upanishadic teachers, and that of his teacher's teacher Gaudapada. He wrote extensive commentaries on the major Vedantic scriptures and is celebrated as one of the major Hindu philosophers from whose doctrines the main currents of modern Indian thought are derived.

According to this school of Vedanta, all reality is Brahman, and there exists nothing whatsoever which is not *Brahman*. Its metaphysics includes the concept of māyā and ātman. *Māyā* connotes "that which exists, but is constantly changing and thus is spiritually unreal". The empirical reality is considered as always changing and therefore "transitory, incomplete, misleading and not what it appears to be". The concept of *ātman* is of one Atman, with the light of Atman reflected within each person as *jivatman*. Advaita Vedantins assert that ātman is same as Brahman, and this Brahman is reflected within each human being and all life, all living beings are spiritually interconnected, and there is oneness in all of existence. They hold that dualities and misunderstanding of *māyā* as the spiritual reality that matters is caused by ignorance, and are the cause of sorrow, suffering. *Jīvanmukti* (liberation during life) can be achieved through Self-knowledge, the understanding that ātman within is same as *ātman* in another person and all of Brahman – the eternal, unchanging, entirety of cosmic principles and true reality.

Some believe that Shankara is a "closet Buddhist," suggesting as evidence his positions that selfhood is illusory and an experience of it disappears after one attains enlightenment. However, Shankara does believe that there is an enduring reality that is ultimately real. He specifically rejects Buddhist propositions in his commentary on Brahma Sutras 2.2.18, 2.2.19, 2.2.20, 2.2.25, among others.

Viśiṣṭādvaita

Ramanuja (c. 1037–1137) was the foremost proponent of the philosophy of viśiṣṭādvaita or qualified non-dualism. viśiṣṭādvaita advocated the concept of a supreme being with essential qualities or attributes. viśiṣṭādvaitins argued against the advaitin conception of brahman as an impersonal empty oneness. they saw brahman as an eternal oneness, but also as the source of all creation, which was omnipresent and actively involved in existence. to them the sense of subject-object perception was illusory and a sign of ignorance. however, the individual's sense of self was not a complete illusion since it was derived from the universal beingness that is brahman. ramanuja saw vishnu as a personification of brahman.

The Viśiṣṭādvaita sub-school also disagrees with the Advaita claim that misconception (*avidyā*) is indescribable as either real or unreal (*anirvacanīya*). It sees this as a contradiction, and argues that *avidyā* must either be non-different from Brahman or different from Brahman. If it is different from Brahman, the non-dualist position of Shankara is given up, but if it is non-different, it must exist ultimately as Brahman. Ramanuja claims that *avidyā* cannot be identical with Brahman because Brahman is pure knowledge, and *avidyā* is absence of knowledge. Ramanuja also argues that the Advaita position cannot coherently maintain that Brahman is non-intentional consciousness (consciousness that does not have an object), because all cognitions are necessarily about something.

Dvaita

Dvaita refers to a theistic sub-school in Vedanta tradition of Hindu philosophy.

Also called *Tattvavāda* and *Bimbapratibimbavāda*, the Dvaita sub-school was founded by the 13th-century scholar Madhvacharya. The Dvaita Vedanta school believes that God (Vishnu, Paramatman) and the individual Selfs (Atman) (jīvātman) exist as independent realities, and these are distinct.

Dvaita Vedanta is a dualistic interpretation of the Vedas; it espouses dualism by theorizing the existence of two separate realities. The first and the only independent reality, states the Dvaita school, is that of Vishnu or Brahman. Vishnu is the Paramatman, in a manner similar to monotheistic God in other major religions. The distinguishing factor of Dvaita philosophy, as opposed to monistic Advaita Vedanta, is that God takes on a personal role and is seen as a real eternal entity that governs and controls the universe. Like Vishishtadvaita Vedanta sub-school, Dvaita philosophy also embraced Vaishnavism, with the metaphysical concept of Brahman in the Vedas identified with Vishnu and the one and only Supreme Being. However, unlike Vishishtadvaita which envisions ultimate qualified nondualism, the dualism of Dvaita was permanent. Dvaita sub-school disagrees with the Vishishtadvaita claim that Brahman is linked with the individual self and the world in the way that a soul is with its body. Madhvacharya argues that

Brahman cannot be the material cause of the world. Salvation, in Dvaita, is achievable only through the grace of God Vishnu.

Dvaitādvaita (Bhedabheda) was proposed by Nimbarka, a 13th-century Vaishnava philosopher from the Andhra region. According to this philosophy there are three categories of existence: Brahman, Self, and matter. Self and matter are different from Brahman in that they have attributes and capacities different from Brahman. Brahman exists independently, while Self and matter are dependent. Thus Self and matter have an existence that is separate yet dependent. Further, Brahman is a controller, the Self is the enjoyer, and matter the thing enjoyed. Also, the highest object of worship is Krishna and his consort Radha, attended by thousands of *gopis*; of the Vrindavan; and devotion consists in self-surrender.

Śuddhādvaita is the "purely non-dual" philosophy propounded by Vallabha Acharya (1479–1531). The founding philosopher was also the guru of the Vallabhā sampradāya ("tradition of Vallabh") or *Puṣṭimārga*, a Vaishnava tradition focused on the worship of Krishna. Vallabhacharya enunciates that Brahman has created the world without connection with any external agency such as Māyā (which itself is His power) and manifests Himself through the world. That is why Shuddhadvaita is known as "Unmodified transformation" or "Avikṛta Pariṇāmavāda". Brahman or Ishvara desired to become many, and he became the multitude of individual Selfs and the world. The Jagat or Maya is not false or illusionary, the physical material world is. Vallabha recognises Brahman as the whole and the individual as a "part" (but devoid of bliss) like sparks and fire. This sub-school thus denies the Advaita conception of Maya because the world is considered to be real insofar as it is non-different from Brahman, who is believed to be Krishna.

Acintya Bheda Abheda[120]

Chaitanya Mahaprabhu (1486–1534), stated that the Self or energy of God is both distinct and non-distinct from God, whom he identified as Krishna, Govinda, and that this, although unthinkable, may be experienced through a process of loving devotion (*bhakti*).

He followed the Dvaita concept of Madhvacharya. In accordance with the Vishnu Purana, this sub-school ascribes six virtues to God (Bhagavan): power (*aishvarya*), potency (*virya*), fame (*yasha*), prosperity (*shri*), knowledge (*jnana*), and renunciation (*vairagya*). The potency of Bhagavan, which is transcendental, is not conceivable to humans and its relationship to Bhagwan is characterized as one in which there is "inconceivable difference in non-difference" (*acintya-bhedabheda*). This potency has divisions that are described within Jiva Gosvami's *Bhagavat Sandarbha*, which comments on the internal potency, and *Paramatma Sandarbha*, which elaborates the marginal and external potencies of Bhagavan. Maya, which is central to *advaita*, is the external potency of Bhagavan, which is controlled by *Paramatma*, an expansion of Bhagavan. And, brahman is included within Bhagavan, who is the object of meditation and realization for bhakti-yogis.

Akshar Purushottam Darshan [121]

Charvaka

The Cārvāka school is one of the nāstika or "heterodox" philosophies. It rejects supernaturalism, emphasizes materialism and philosophical skepticism, holding empiricism, perception and conditional inference as the proper source of knowledge Cārvāka is an atheistic school of thought. It holds that there is neither afterlife nor rebirth, all existence is mere combination of atoms and substances, feelings and mind are an epiphenomenon, and free will exists.

Bṛhaspati is sometimes referred to as the founder of Cārvāka (also called Lokayata) philosophy. Much of the primary literature of Carvaka, the Barhaspatya sutras (ca. 600 BCE), however, are missing or lost. Its theories and development has been compiled from historic secondary literature such as those found in the shastras, sutras and the Indian epic poetry as well as from the texts of Buddhism and from Jain literature. The *Tattvôpaplava-siṁha* by the skeptic philosopher Jayarāśi Bhaṭṭa has been considered by many scholars to be an unorthodox Cārvāka text.

One of the widely studied principles of Cārvāka philosophy was its rejection of inference as a means to establish valid, universal knowledge, and metaphysical truths. In other words, the Cārvāka epistemology states that whenever one infers a truth from a set of observations or truths, one must acknowledge doubt; inferred knowledge is conditional.

Shaivaism[122]

Early history of Shaivism is difficult to determine.

However, the *Śvetāśvatara Upanishad* (400 – 200 BCE) is considered to be the earliest textual exposition of a systematic philosophy of Shaivism. Shaivism is represented by various philosophical schools, including non-dualist (*abheda*), dualist (*bheda*), and non-dualist-with-dualist (*bhedābheda*) perspectives. Vidyaranya in his works mentions three major schools of Shaiva thought: Pashupata Shaivism, Shaiva Siddhanta and Pratyabhijña (Kashmir Shaivism).

Pasupata Shaivism[123]

Pāśupata Shaivism (*Pāśupata*, 'of Paśupati') is the oldest of the major Shaiva schools. The philosophy of Pashupata sect was systematized by *Lakulish* in the 2nd century CE. *Paśu* in Paśupati refers to the effect (or created world), the word designates that which is dependent on something ulterior. Whereas, Pati means the cause (or *principium*), the word designates the Lord, who is the cause of the universe, the *pati*, or the ruler. Pashupatas disapproved of Vaishnava theology, known for its doctrine servitude of Selfs to the Supreme Being, on the grounds that dependence upon anything could not be the means of cessation of pain and other desired ends. They recognised that those depending upon another and longing for independence will not be emancipated because they still depend upon something other than themselves. According to Pāśupatas, Self possesses the attributes of the Supreme Deity when it becomes liberated from the 'germ of every pain'.

Pāśupatas divided the created world into the insentient and the sentient. The insentient was the unconscious and thus dependent on the sentient or conscious. The insentient was further divided into effects and causes. The effects were of ten kinds, the earth, four elements and their qualities, colour etc. The causes were of thirteen kinds, the five organs of cognition, the five organs of action, the three internal organs, intellect, the ego principle and the cognising principle. These insentient causes were held responsible for the illusive identification of Self with non-Self. Salvation in Pāśupata involved the union of the Self with God through the intellect.

Shaiva Siddhanta[124]

Considered normative Tantric Shaivism, Shaiva Siddhanta provides the normative rites, cosmology and theological categories of Tantric Shaivism. Being a dualistic philosophy, the goal of Shaiva Siddhanta is to become an ontologically distinct Shiva (through Shiva's grace). This tradition later merged with the Tamil Saiva movement and expression of concepts of Shaiva Siddhanta can be seen in the bhakti poetry of the Nayanars.

Kashmir Shaivism[125]

Kashmir Shaivism arose during the eighth or ninth century CE in Kashmir and made significant strides, both philosophical and theological, until the end of the twelfth century CE. It is categorised by various scholars as monistic idealism (absolute idealism, theistic monism, realistic idealism, transcendental physicalism or concrete monism. It is a school of Śaivism consisting of Trika and its philosophical articulation Pratyabhijña.

Even though, both Kashmir Shaivism and Advaita Vedanta are non-dual philosophies which give primacy to Universal Consciousness (*Chit* or *Brahman*), in Kashmir Shavisim, as opposed to Advaita, all things are a manifestation of this Consciousness. This implies that from the point of view of Kashmir Shavisim, the phenomenal world (*Śakti*) is real, and it exists and has its being in Consciousness (*Chit*). However, Advaita holds that Brahman is the reality (pure consciousness) and it is inactive (*niṣkriya*) and the phenomenal world is an appearance (*māyā*). The objective of human life, according to Kashmir Shaivism, is to merge in Shiva or Universal Consciousness, or to realize one's already existing identity with Shiva, by means of wisdom, yoga and grace.

Then I internalise this into my heart and body by looking at what parts of my body are affected. Mind and stomach are affected when I am tense about the money angle, head and ears with the noise, stomach with the overall tension. Soured relationships also affect my heart. Eventually, I commit to a different action: of listing down what my long-term financial goals, so that there is a greater understanding of what I need. I look for things that soothe me in the garden, or begin my morning with music and asanas for the body to remind me to enjoy life. I eat slowly and relish food more than hurriedly gobbling it. With my every action or thought, I consider if I am being consistent and truly improving relationships. Of course, this all sounds quite simple, but bhakti and karma are not easy and need practice. They also need frequent reminders and discipline and that's where rituals and puja come in. Puja is a way for us to hit the pause button and ask ourselves if we are working towards moksha by centering our thoughts on our mind, heart and body. Puja also appeals to our different senses, makes us feel good, think happy thoughts and hopefully translate them into actions as well.

Sadly, instead of becoming opportunities for looking within, puja has now diluted to transactions with the gods outside rather than going within to recognise how one cannot be happy all the time, and the ups and downs of life are inevitable.

The model is deceptively simple but if you have a regular checking system like a puja or a meditation practice, and constantly ask yourself if you are following dharma and surrounding yourself with similar minded folks, it will slowly become practice. You may always need a reminder, but in reminding yourself that you can't always be happy, you will recognise that you can extract every little ounce of happiness from every situation in life.

It was the Buddha researched and preached by a westerner[126], that happiness is one of the seven factors of enlightenment, in western philosophy, as picked up from the Stanford Encyclopedia of philosophy, trace back to the heart of the eighteenth century enlightenment, as loosely organized activity of prominent French thinkers of the mid-decades of the eighteenth century, called to constitute an informal society of men of letters collaborating on a loosely defined project of Enlightenment exemplified by the project of the noteworthy centers of Enlightenment outside of France as well. There is a renowned Scottish Enlightenment, the philosophes, (who were four French philosophers like Voltaire, D'Alembert, Diderot, and Montesquieu). Frances Hutcheson, Adam Smith, David Hume, Thomas Reid, a German Enlightenment (*die Aufklärung*, whose key figures of which include four other scholars, like, Christian Wolff, Moses Mendelssohn, Gotfried Ephraim Lessing and Immanuel Kant, with other hubs of Enlightenment and the then Enlightenment thinkers scattered throughout Europe and America in the eighteenth century. European politics, philosophy, science and communications were radically reoriented during the course of the "long 18th century" (1685-1815) as part of a movement referred to by its participants as the Age of Reason, or simply the Enlightenment. Enlightenment thinkers in Britain, in France and throughout Europe questioned traditional authority and embraced the notion that humanity could be improved through rational change.

The Enlightenment produced numerous books, essays, inventions, scientific discoveries, laws, wars and revolutions. The American and French Revolutions were directly inspired by Enlightenment ideals and respectively marked the peak of its influence and the beginning of its decline. The Enlightenment ultimately gave way to 19th-century Romanticism, to use your own reason!

There was no single, unified Enlightenment. Instead, it is possible to speak of the French Enlightenment, the Scottish Enlightenment and the English, German, Swiss or American Enlightenment. Individual Enlightenment thinkers often had very different approaches. Locke differed from David Hume, Jean-Jacques Rousseau from Voltaire, Thomas Jefferson from Frederick the Great. Their differences and disagreements, though, emerged out of the common Enlightenment themes of rational questioning and belief in progress through dialogue.

Centered on the dialogues and publications of the French "philosophes" (Voltaire, Rousseau, Montesquieu, Buffon and Denis

Diderot), the High Enlightenment might best be summed up by one historian's summary of Voltaire's "Philosophical Dictionary": "a chaos of clear ideas." Foremost among these was the notion that everything in the universe could be rationally demystified and cataloged. The signature publication of the period was Diderot's "Encyclopédie" (1751-77), which brought together leading authors to produce an ambitious compilation of human knowledge.

Jefferson's Pursuit of Knowledge

It was an age of enlightened despots like Frederick the Great, who unified, rationalized and modernized Prussia in between brutal multi-year wars with Austria, and of enlightened would-be revolutionaries like Thomas Paine and Thomas Jefferson, whose "Declaration of Independence" (1776) framed the American Revolution in terms taken from of Locke's essays.

It was also a time of religious (and anti-religious) innovation, as Christians sought to reposition their faith along rational lines and deists and materialists argued that the universe seemed to determine its own course without God's intervention. Locke, along with French philosopher Pierre Bayle, began to champion the idea of the separation of Church and State. Secret societies—like the Freemasons, the Bavarian Illuminati and the Rosicrucians—flourished, offering European men (and a few women) new modes of fellowship, esoteric ritual and mutual assistance. Coffeehouses, newspapers and literary salons emerged as new venues for ideas to circulate

We quest as to what makes for the unity of such tremendously diverse thinkers under the idea or label of "Enlightenment". The Enlightenment is conceived broadly. D'Alembert, a leading figure of the French Enlightenment, characterizes his eighteenth century, in the midst of it, as "the century of philosophy par excellence", as because of the tremendous intellectual and scientific progress of the age, as well as because of the expectation of the age that philosophy (in the broad sense of the time, which includes the natural and social sciences) would dramatically improve human life. Guided by D'Alembert's characterization of his century, the Enlightenment is conceived here as having its primary origin in the scientific revolution of the 16th and 17th centuries. The rise of the new science progressively undermines not only the ancient geocentric conception of the cosmos, but also the set of presuppositions that had served to constrain and guide philosophical inquiry in the earlier times. The New Science (Italian: *La Scienza Nuova* pronounced is the major work of Italian philosopher Giambattista Vico. It was first published in 1725 to little success, but has gone on to be highly regarded and influential in the philosophy of history, sociology, and anthropology. The central concepts were highly original and prefigured the Age of Enlightenment.

The full title of the 1725 edition was *Principj di una Scienza Nuova Intorno alla Natura delle Nazioni per la Quale si Ritruovano i Principj di Altro Sistema del Diritto Naturale delle Genti*, ending with a dedication to Cardinal Lorenzo Corsini, the future Pope Clement XII. *Principj* and *ritruovano* being archaic spellings of *principi* and *ritrovano*, the title may be loosely translated "Principles of a New Science Concerning the Nature of Nations, through Which Are Recovered the Principles of Another System of the Natural Law of Peoples".

The 1730 edition was titled *Cinque Libri di Giambattista Vico de' Principj d' una Scienza Nuova d'Intorno alla Comune Natura della Nazion* ("Giambattista Vico's Five Books on the Principles of a New Science Concerning Nations' Shared Nature"), ending with a dedication to Clement XII.

The 1744 edition was slightly emended to *Principj di Scienza Nuova di Giambattista Vico d'Intorno alla Comune Natura delle Nazioni* ("Giambattista Vico's Principles of New Science Concerning Nations' Shared Nature"), without a title page dedication. Clement had died in 1740 and Vico in 1744, before the edition's publication.

Creation

In 1720, Vico began work on the *Scienza Nuova* as part of a treatise on universal rights. Although it was originally supposed to be sponsored by Cardinal Corsini, Vico was forced to finance the publication himself after the cardinal pleaded financial difficulty and withdrew his patronage. It was the first work by Vico to be written in Italian, since his previous ones had been in Latin.

The first edition of the *New Science* appeared in 1725. Vico worked on two heavily revised editions. The first was published in 1730, the second posthumously in 1744.

Approach, Style And Tone

In its first section, titled "Idea of the Work" (*Idea dell'Opera*), the 1730 and 1744 editions of *The New Science* explicitly present themselves as a "science of reasoning" (*scienza di ragionare*). The work (especially the section "Of the Elements") includes a dialectic between axioms (authoritative maxims or *degnità*) and "reasonings" (*ragionamenti*) linking and clarifying the axioms.

Vico began the third edition with a detailed close reading of a front piece portrait, examining the place of Gentile nations within the providential guidance of the Hebrew God. This portrait contains a number of images that are symbolically ascribed to the flow of human history. A triangle with the Eye of Providence appears in the top left. A beam of light from the eye shines upon a brooch attached to the breastplate of "the lady with the winged temples who surmounts the celestial globe or world of nature" (center right), which represents metaphysics. The beam reflects off the brooch onto the back of a robed character standing upon a pedestal (bottom left), representing the poet Homer. All around these main characters resides a variety of objects that represent the stages of human history which Vico categorizes into three epochs: the age of the gods "in which the gentiles believed they lived under divine governments, and everything was commanded them by auspices and oracles, which are the oldest institutions in profane history; the age of the heroes "in which they reigned everywhere in aristocratic commonwealths, on account of a certain superiority of nature which they held themselves to have over the plebs (or peasants);" and the age of men "in which all men recognized themselves as equal in human nature, and therefore there were established first the popular commonwealths and then the monarchies, both of which are forms of human government." By viewing these principles as universal phenomena which combined nature and government with language and philology, Vico could insert the history of the Gentile nations into the supreme guidance by divine providence. According to Vico, the proper end for government resulted with society entering into a state of universal equity: "The last type of jurisprudence was that of natural equity, which reigns naturally in the free commonwealths, in which the people, each for his own particular good (without understanding that it is the same for all), are led to command universal laws. They naturally desire these laws to bend benignly to the least details of matters calling for equal unity."

Vico specifies that his "science" reasons primarily about the function of religion in the human world ("Idea of the Work"), and in this respect the work "comes to be a civil theology reasoned from divine providence" (*vien ad essere una teologia civile ragionata della provvidenza divina*). Reconsidering divine providence within a human or political context, Vico unearths the "poetic theologians" (*poeti teologi*) of pagan antiquity, exposing the poetic character of theology independently of Christianity's sacred history and thus of Biblical authority. Vico's use of poetic theology, anticipated in his 1710 work *De Antiquissima Italorum Sapientia* ("On the Ancient Wisdom of the Italians"), confirms his ties to the Italian Renaissance and its own appeals to *theologia poetica*. With the early Renaissance, Vico shares the call for recovering a "pagan" or "vulgar" horizon for philosophy's providential agency or for recognizing the providence of our human "metaphysical" minds (*menti*) in the world of our "political" wills (*animi*). "Poetic theology" would serve as stage for an "ascent" to recognize the inherence or latency of rational agency in our actions, even when these are brutal. This way, the particular providence of the Bible's "true God" would not be required for the thriving of properly human life. All that would be needed was (A) false religions and gods and (B) the covert work of the *conatus* (the rational principle of a constitution of experience rooted in its proper infinite form), which was examined at length in *De Antiquissima Italorum Sapientia* and evoked again in the section "Of the Method" in the 1730 and 1744 editions of *The New Science.*

Vico is often seen as espousing a cyclical philosophy of history where human history is created by man, although Vico never speaks of "history without attributes" (Paolo Cristofolini, *Vice Pagano e Barbaro*), but of a "world of nations". Which is more, in the 1744 *Scienza Nuova* (esp. the "Conclusion of the Work") Vico stresses that "the world of nations" is made by men merely with respect to their sense of certainty (*certamente*), though not fundamentally, insofar as the world is guided by the human mind "metaphysically" independent of its makings (compare opening paragraph of the *Scienza Nuova*). Furthermore, although Vico is often attributed the expression "*corsi e ricorsi*" (cycles and counter cycles of growth and decay) of "history", he never speaks in the plural of "the cycle" or of "the counter-cycle" (*ricorso*) of "human things", suggesting that political life and order, or human creations, are oriented "backward," as it were, or called back to their constitutive "metaphysical" principle.

On present day "constructivist" readings, Vico is supposed to have promoted a vision of man and society as moving in parallel from barbarism to civilization.

As societies become more developed socially, human nature also develops, and both manifest their development in changes in language, myth, folklore, economy, etc.; in short, social change produces cultural change.

Vico would therefore be using an original organic idea that culture is a system of socially produced and structured elements. Hence, knowledge of any society would come from the social structure of that society, explicable, therefore, only in terms of its own language. As such, one may find a dialectical relationship between language, knowledge and social structure.

Relying on a complex etymology, Vico argues in the *Scienza Nuova* that civilization develops in a recurring cycle (*ricorso*) of three ages: the divine, the heroic, and the human. Each age exhibits distinct political and social features and can be characterized by master tropes or figures of language. The *giganti* of the divine age rely on metaphor to compare, and thus comprehend, human and natural phenomena.

In the heroic age, metonymy and synecdoche support the development of feudal or monarchic institutions embodied by idealized figures. The final age is characterized by popular democracy and reflection via irony; in this epoch, the rise of rationality leads to *barbarie della reflessione* or barbarism of reflection, and civilization descends once more into the poetic era. Taken together, the recurring cycle of three ages – common to every nation – constitutes for Vico a *storia ideale eterna* or ideal eternal history. Therefore, it can be said that all history is the history of the rise and fall of civilizations, for which Vico provides evidence (up until, and including the Graeco-Roman historians).

Going further, David Gauthier argues in his book Morals by Agreement, writes Is morality rational? In this book Gauthier argues that moral principles are principles of rational choice. He proposes a principle whereby choice is made on an agreed basis of cooperation, rather than according to what would give an individual the greatest expectation of value. He shows that such a principle not only ensures mutual benefit and fairness, thus satisfying the standards of morality, but also that each person may actually expect greater utility by adhering to morality, even though the choice did not have that end primarily in view. In resolving what may appear to be a paradox, the author establishes morals on the firm foundation of reason. Gauthier's argument includes an account of value, linking it to preference and utility; a discussion of the circumstances in which morality is unnecessary; and an application of morals by agreement to relations between peoples at different levels of development and different generations. Finally, he reflects on the assumptions about individuality and community made by his account of rationality and morality.

That any system of moral constraints must be justified to those to whom it is meant to apply. "What theory of morals," Gauthier asks, "can ever serve any useful purpose unless it can show that all the duties it recommends are truly endorsed in each individual's reason?" (1986, 1).

The ultimate goal, then, of social contract theories is to show, in the most general sense, that social (moral, political, legal, etc.) rules can be rationally justified. This alone does not, however, distinguish the social contract from other approaches in moral and political philosophy, all of which attempt to show that moral and political rules are rationally justifiable in some sense. The true distinctiveness of the social contract approach is that justification does not rely, for its foundation, on some exogenous reason or truth. Justification is generated endogenously by rational agreement (or lack of rejection in T. M. Scanlon's version). That is, the fact that everyone in a society, given their individual reasoning, would agree to a certain rule or principle is the critical justification for that rule or principle.

Social contract theory[127], clauses as old as philosophy itself, is the view that persons' moral and/or political obligations are dependent upon a contract or agreement among them to form the society in which they live. Socrates uses something quite like a social contract argument to explain to Crito[128] why he must remain in prison and accept the death penalty. However, social contract theory is rightly associated with modern moral and political theory and is given its first full exposition and defense by Thomas Hobbes[129]. After Hobbes, John Locke [130]and Jean-Jacques Rousseau[131] are the best known proponents of this enormously influential theory, which has been one of the most dominant theories within moral and political theory throughout the history of the modern West. In the twentieth century, moral and political theory regained philosophical momentum as a result of John Rawls' Kantian version of social contract theory[132], and was followed by new analyses of the subject by David Gauthier [133]and others. More recently, philosophers from different perspectives have offered new criticisms of social contract theory and in particular, feminists[134] and race-conscious philosophers[135] have argued that social contract theory is at least an incomplete picture of our moral and political lives, and may in fact camouflage some of the ways in which the contract is itself parasitical upon the subjugations of classes of persons.

In the early Platonic dialogue, *Crito*, Socrates[136] makes a compelling argument as to why he must stay in prison and accept the death penalty, rather than escape and go into exile in another Greek city. He personifies the Laws of Athens[137], and, speaking in their voice, explains that he has acquired an overwhelming obligation to obey the Laws because they have made his entire way of life, and even the fact of his very existence, possible. They made it possible for his mother and father to marry, and therefore to have legitimate children, including himself. Having been born, the city of Athens, through its laws, then required that his father care for and educate him. Socrates' life and the way in which that life has flourished in Athens are each dependent upon the Laws. Importantly, however, this relationship between citizens and the Laws of the city are not coerced. Citizens, once they have grown up, and have seen how the city conducts itself, can choose whether to leave, taking their property with them, or stay. Staying implies an agreement to abide by the Laws and accept the punishments that they mete out. And, having made an agreement that is itself just, Socrates asserts that he must keep to this agreement that he has made and obey the Laws, in this case, by staying and accepting the death penalty. Importantly, the contract described by Socrates is an implicit one: it is implied by his choice to stay in Athens, even though he is free to leave.

In Plato's most well-known dialogue, *Republic*, social contract theory is represented again, although this time less favorably. In Book II, Glaucon[138] offers a candidate for an answer to the question "what is justice?" by representing a social contract explanation for the nature of justice. What men would most want is to be able to commit injustices against others without the fear of reprisal, and what they most want to avoid is being treated unjustly by others without being able to do injustice in return. Justice then, he says, is the conventional result of the laws and covenants that men make in order to avoid these extremes.

Being unable to commit injustice with impunity (as those who wear the ring of Gyges[139] would), and fearing becoming victims themselves, men decide that it is in their interests to submit themselves to the convention of justice. Socrates rejects this view, and most of the rest of the dialogue centers on showing that justice is worth having for its own sake, and that the just man is the happy man. So, from Socrates' point of view, justice has a value that greatly exceeds the prudential value that Glaucon assigns to it.

These views, in the *Crito* and the *Republic*, might seem at first glance inconsistent: in the former dialogue Socrates uses a social contract type of argument to show why it is just for him to remain in prison, whereas in the latter he rejects social contract as the source of justice. These two views are, however, reconcilable. From Socrates' point of view, a just man is one who will, among other things, recognize his obligation to the state by obeying its laws. The state is the morally and politically most fundamental entity, and as such deserves our highest allegiance and deepest respect. Just men know this and act accordingly. Justice, however, is more than simply obeying laws in exchange for others obeying them as well. Justice is the state of a well-regulated soul, and so the just man will also necessarily be the happy man. So, justice is more than the simple reciprocal obedience to law, as Glaucon suggests, but it does nonetheless include obedience to the state and the laws that sustain it. So in the end, although Plato is perhaps the first philosopher to offer a representation of the argument at the heart of social contract theory, Socrates ultimately rejects the idea that social contract is the original source of justice.

Thomas Hobbes, 1588-1679, lived during the most crucial period of early modern England's history: the English Civil War, waged from 1642-1648. To describe this conflict in the most general of terms, it was a clash between the King and his supporters, the Monarchists, who preferred the traditional authority of a monarch, and the Parliamentarians, most notably led by Oliver Cromwell[140], who demanded more power for the quasi-democratic institution of Parliament. Hobbes represents a compromise between these two factions. On the one hand he rejects the theory of the Divine Right of Kings, which is most eloquently expressed by Robert Filmer[141] in his *Patriarcha or the Natural Power of Kings*, (although it would be left to John Locke to refute Filmer directly). Filmer's view held that a king's authority was invested in him (or, presumably, her) by God, that such authority was absolute, and therefore that the basis of political obligation lay in our obligation to obey God absolutely. According to this view, then, political obligation is subsumed under religious obligation. On the other hand, Hobbes also rejects the early democratic view, taken up by the Parliamentarians, that power ought to be shared between Parliament and the King. In rejecting both these views, Hobbes occupies the ground of one who is both radical and conservative. He argues, radically for his times, that political authority and obligation are based on the individual self-interests of members of society who are understood to be equal to one another, with no single individual invested with any essential authority to rule over the rest, while at the same time maintaining the conservative position that the monarch, which he called the Sovereign, must be ceded absolute authority if society is to survive.

Hobbes' political theory is best understood if taken in two parts: his theory of human motivation, Psychological Egoism, and his theory of the social contract, founded on the hypothetical State of Nature. Hobbes has, first and foremost, a particular theory of human nature, which gives rise to a particular view of morality and politics, as developed in his philosophical masterpiece, *Leviathan*, published in 1651[142]. The Scientific Revolution, with its important new discoveries that the universe could be both described and predicted in accordance with universal laws of nature, greatly influenced Hobbes. He sought to provide a theory of human nature that would parallel the discoveries being made in the sciences of the inanimate universe. His psychological theory is therefore informed by mechanism, the general view that everything in the universe is produced by nothing other than matter in motion. According to Hobbes, this extends to human behavior. Human macro-behavior can be aptly described as the effect of certain kinds of micro-behavior, even though some of this latter behavior is invisible to us. So, such behaviors as walking, talking, and the like are themselves produced by other actions inside of us. And these other actions are themselves caused by the interaction of our bodies with other bodies, human or otherwise, which create in us certain chains of causes and effects, and which eventually give rise to the human behavior that we can plainly observe. We, including all of our actions and choices, are then, according to this view, as explainable in terms of universal laws of nature as are the motions of heavenly bodies. The gradual disintegration of memory, for example, can be explained by inertia. As we are presented with ever more sensory information, the residue of earlier impressions 'slows down' over time. From Hobbes' point of view, we are essentially very complicated organic machines, responding to the stimuli of the world mechanistically and in accordance with universal laws of human nature.

In Hobbes' view, this mechanistic quality of human psychology implies the subjective nature of normative claims. 'Love' and 'hate', for instance, are just words we use to describe the things we are drawn to and repelled by, respectively. So, too, the terms 'good' and 'bad' have no meaning other than to describe our appetites and aversions. Moral terms do not, therefore, describe some objective state of affairs, but are rather reflections of individual tastes and preferences.

In addition to Subjectivism, Hobbes also infers from his mechanistic theory of human nature that humans are necessarily and exclusively self-interested. All men pursue only what they perceive to be in their own individually considered best interests – they respond mechanistically by being drawn to that which they desire and repelled by that to which they are averse. This is a universal claim: it is meant to cover all human actions under all circumstances – in society or out of it, with regard to strangers and friends alike, with regard to small ends and the most generalized of human desires, such as the desire for power and status. Everything we do is motivated solely by the desire to better our own situations, and satisfy as many of our own, individually considered desires as possible. We are infinitely appetitive and only genuinely concerned with our own selves. According to Hobbes, even the reason that adults care for small children can be explicated in terms of the adults' own self-interest (he claims that in saving an infant by caring for it, we become the recipient of a strong sense of obligation in one who has been helped to survive rather than allowed to die).

In addition to being exclusively self-interested, Hobbes also argues that human beings are reasonable. They have in them the rational capacity to pursue their desires as efficiently and maximally as possible. Their reason does not, given the subjective nature of value, evaluate their given ends, rather it merely acts as "Scouts, and Spies, to range abroad, and find the way to the things Desired". Rationality is purely instrumental. It can add and subtract, and compare sums one to another, and thereby endows us with the capacity to formulate the best means to whatever ends we might happen to have.

From these premises of human nature, Hobbes goes on to construct a provocative and compelling argument for why we ought to be willing to submit ourselves to political authority. He does this by imagining persons in a situation prior to the establishment of society, the State of Nature.

According to Hobbes, the justification for political obligation is this: given that men are naturally self-interested, yet they are rational, they will choose to submit to the authority of a Sovereign in order to be able to live in a civil society, which is conducive to their own interests. Hobbes argues for this by imagining men in their natural state, or in other words, the State of Nature. In the State of Nature, which is purely hypothetical according to Hobbes, men are naturally and exclusively self-interested, they are more or less equal to one another, (even the strongest man can be killed in his sleep), there are limited resources, and yet there is no power able to force men to cooperate. Given these conditions in the State of Nature, Hobbes concludes that the State of Nature would be unbearably brutal. In the State of Nature, every person is always in fear of losing his life to another. They have no capacity to ensure the long-term satisfaction of their needs or desires. No long-term or complex cooperation is possible because the State of Nature can be aptly described as a state of utter distrust. Given Hobbes' reasonable assumption that most people want first and foremost to avoid their own deaths, he concludes that the State of Nature is the worst possible situation in which men can find themselves. It is the state of perpetual and unavoidable war.

The situation is not, however, hopeless. Because men are reasonable, they can see their way out of such a state by recognizing the laws of nature, which show them the means by which to escape the State of Nature and create a civil society. The first and most important law of nature commands that each man be willing to pursue peace when others are willing to do the same, all the while retaining the right to continue to pursue war when others do not pursue peace. Being reasonable, and recognizing the rationality of this basic precept of reason, men can be expected to construct a Social Contract that will afford them a life other than that available to them in the State of Nature. This contract is constituted by two distinguishable contracts. First, they must agree to establish society by collectively and reciprocally renouncing the rights they had against one another in the State of Nature. Second, they must imbue some one person or assembly of persons with the authority and power to enforce the initial contract. In other words, to ensure their escape from the State of Nature, they must both agree to live together under common laws, and create an *enforcement mechanism* for the social contract and the laws that constitute it. Since the sovereign is invested with the authority and power to mete out punishments for breaches of the contract which are worse than not being able to act as one pleases, men have good, albeit self-interested, reason to adjust themselves to the artifice of morality in general, and justice in particular. Society becomes possible because, whereas in the State of Nature there was no power able to "overawe them all", now there is an artificially and conventionally superior and more powerful person who can force men to cooperate. While living under the authority of a Sovereign can be harsh (Hobbes argues that because men's passions can be expected to overwhelm their reason, the Sovereign must have absolute authority in order for the contract to be successful) it is at least better than living in the State of Nature. And, no matter how much we may object to how poorly a Sovereign manages the affairs of the state and regulates our own lives, we are never justified in resisting his power because it is the only thing which stands between us and what we most want to avoid, the State of Nature.

According to this argument, morality, politics, society, and everything that comes along with it, all of which Hobbes calls 'commodious living' are purely conventional. Prior to the establishment of the basic social contract, according to which men agree to live together and the contract to embody a Sovereign with absolute authority, nothing is immoral or unjust – anything goes. After these contracts are established, however, then society becomes possible, and people can be expected to keep their promises, cooperate with one another, and so on. The Social Contract is the most fundamental source of all that is good and that which we depend upon to live well. Our choice is either to abide by the terms of the contract, or return to the State of Nature, which Hobbes argues no reasonable person could possibly prefer.

Given his rather severe view of human nature, Hobbes nonetheless manages to create an argument that makes civil society, along with all its advantages, possible. Within the context of the political events of his England, he also managed to argue for a continuation of the traditional form of authority that his society had long since enjoyed, while nonetheless placing it on what he saw as a far more acceptable foundation.

For Hobbes, the necessity of an absolute authority, in the form of a Sovereign, followed from the utter brutality of the State of Nature. The State of Nature was completely intolerable, and so rational men would be willing to submit themselves even to absolute authority in order to escape it. For John Locke, 1632-1704, the State of Nature is a very different type of place, and so his argument concerning the social contract and the nature of men's relationship to authority are consequently quite different. While Locke uses Hobbes' methodological device of the State of Nature, as do virtually all social contract theorists, he uses it to a quite different end. Locke's arguments for the social contract, and for the right of citizens to revolt against their king were enormously influential on the democratic revolutions that followed, especially on Thomas Jefferson, and the founders of the United States.

Locke's most important and influential political writings are contained in his *Two Treatises on Government*. The first treatise is concerned almost exclusively with refuting the argument of Robert Filmer's *Patriarcha*, that political authority was derived from religious authority, also known by the description of the Divine Right of Kings, which was a very dominant theory in seventeenth-century England. The second treatise contains Locke's own constructive view of the aims and justification for civil government, and is titled "An Essay Concerning the True Original Extent and End of Civil Government".

According to Locke, the State of Nature, the natural condition of mankind, is a state of perfect and complete liberty to conduct one's life as one best sees fit, free from the interference of others. This does not mean, however, that it is a state of license: one is not free to do anything at all one pleases, or even anything that one judges to be in one's interest. The State of Nature, although a state wherein there is no civil authority or government to punish people for transgressions against laws, is not a state without morality. The State of Nature is pre-political, but it is not pre-moral. Persons are assumed to be equal to one another in such a state, and therefore equally capable of discovering and being bound by the Law of Nature. The Law of Nature, which is on Locke's view the basis of all morality, and given to us by God, commands that we not harm others with regards to their "life, health, liberty, or possessions" (par. 6). Because we all belong equally to God, and because we cannot take away that which is rightfully His, we are prohibited from harming one another. So, the State of Nature is a state of liberty where persons are free to pursue their own interests and plans, free from interference, and, because of the Law of Nature and the restrictions that it imposes upon persons, it is relatively peaceful.

The State of Nature therefore, is not the same as the state of war, as it is according to Hobbes. It can, however devolve into a state of war, in particular, a state of war over property disputes. Whereas the State of Nature is the state of liberty where persons recognize the Law of Nature and therefore do not harm one another, the state of war begins between two or more men once one man declares war on another, by stealing from him, or by trying to make him his slave. Since in the State of Nature there is no civil power to whom men can appeal, and since the Law of Nature allows them to defend their own lives, they may then kill those who would bring force against them. Since the State of Nature lacks civil authority, once war begins it is likely to continue. And this is one of the strongest reasons that men have to abandon the State of Nature by contracting together to form civil government.

Property plays an essential role in Locke's argument for civil government and the contract that establishes it. According to Locke, private property is created when a person mixes his labor with the raw materials of nature. So, for example, when one tills a piece of land in nature, and makes it into a piece of farmland, which produces food, then one has a claim to own that piece of land and the food produced upon it. (This led Locke to conclude that America didn't really belong to the natives who lived there, because they were, on his view, failing to utilize the basic material of nature. In other words, they didn't farm it, so they had no legitimate claim to it, and others could therefore justifiably appropriate it.) Given the implications of the Law of Nature, there are limits as to how much property one can own: one is not allowed to take more from nature than one can use, thereby leaving others without enough for themselves. Because nature is given to all of mankind by God for its common subsistence, one cannot take more than his own fair share. Property is the linchpin of Locke's argument for the social contract and civil government because it is the protection of their property, including their property in their own bodies, that men seek when they decide to abandon the State of Nature.

According to Locke, the State of Nature is not a condition of individuals, as it is for Hobbes. Rather, it is populated by mothers and fathers with their children, or families – what he calls "conjugal society" (par. 78). These societies are based on the voluntary agreements to care for children together, and they are moral but not political. Political society comes into being when individual men, representing their families, come together in the State of Nature and agree to each give up the executive power to punish those who transgress the Law of Nature, and hand over that power to the public power of a government. Having done this, they then become subject to the will of the majority. In other words, by making a compact to leave the State of Nature and form society, they make "one body politic under one government" (par. 97) and submit themselves to the will of that body. One joins such a body, either from its beginnings, or after it has already been established by others, only by explicit consent. Having created a political society and government through their consent, men then gain three things which they lacked in the State of Nature: laws, judges to adjudicate laws, and the executive power necessary to enforce these laws. Each man therefore gives over the power to protect himself and punish transgressors of the Law of Nature to the government that he has created through the compact.

Given that the end of "men's uniting into common-wealths" (par. 124) is the preservation of their wealth, and preserving their lives, liberty, and well-being in general, Locke can easily imagine the conditions under which the compact with government is destroyed, and men are justified in resisting the authority of a civil government, such as a King. When the executive power of a government devolves into tyranny, such as by dissolving the legislature and therefore denying the people the ability to make laws for their own preservation, then the resulting tyrant puts himself into a State of Nature, and specifically into a state of war with the people, and they then have the same right to self-defense as they had before making a compact to establish society in the first place. In other words, the justification of the authority of the executive component of government is the protection of the people's property and well-being, so when such protection is no longer present, or when the king becomes a tyrant and acts against the interests of the people, they have a right, if not an outright obligation, to resist his authority. The social compact can be dissolved and the process to create political society begun anew.

Because Locke did not envision the State of Nature as grimly as did Hobbes, he can imagine conditions under which one would be better off rejecting a particular civil government and returning to the State of Nature, with the aim of constructing a better civil government in its place. It is therefore both the view of human nature, and the nature of morality itself, which account for the differences between Hobbes' and Locke's views of the social contract.

Jean-Jacques Rousseau, 1712-1778, lived and wrote during what was arguably the headiest period in the intellectual history of modern France–the Enlightenment. He was one of the bright lights of that intellectual movement, contributing articles to the *Encyclopdie* of Diderot, and participating in the salons in Paris, where the great intellectual questions of his day were pursued.

Rousseau has two distinct social contract theories. The first is found in his essay, *Discourse on the Origin and Foundations of Inequality Among Men*, commonly referred to as the Second Discourse, and is an account of the moral and political evolution of human beings over time, from a State of Nature to modern society. As such it contains his *naturalized* account of the social contract, which he sees as very problematic. The second is his *normative*, or idealized theory of the social contract, and is meant to provide the means by which to alleviate the problems that modern society has created for us, as laid out in the *Social Contract*.

Rousseau wrote his *Second Discourse* in response to an essay contest sponsored by the Academy of Dijon. (Rousseau had previously won the same essay contest with an earlier essay, commonly referred to as the *First Discourse*.) In it he describes the historical process by which man began in a State of Nature and over time 'progressed' into civil society. According to Rousseau, the State of Nature was a peaceful and quixotic time. People lived solitary, uncomplicated lives. Their few needs were easily satisfied by nature. Because of the abundance of nature and the small size of the population, competition was non-existent, and persons rarely even saw one another, much less had reason for conflict or fear. Moreover, these simple, morally pure persons were naturally endowed with the capacity for pity, and therefore were not inclined to bring harm to one another.

As time passed, however, humanity faced certain changes. As the overall population increased, the means by which people could satisfy their needs had to change. People slowly began to live together in small families, and then in small communities. Divisions of labor were introduced, both within and between families, and discoveries and inventions made life easier, giving rise to leisure time. Such leisure time inevitably led people to make comparisons between themselves and others, resulting in public values, leading to shame and envy, pride and contempt. Most importantly however, according to Rousseau, was the invention of private property, which constituted the pivotal moment in humanity's evolution out of a simple, pure state into one characterized by greed, competition, vanity, inequality, and vice. For Rousseau the invention of property constitutes humanity's 'fall from grace' out of the State of Nature.

Having introduced private property, initial conditions of inequality became more pronounced. Some have property and others are forced to work for them, and the development of social classes begins. Eventually, those who have property notice that it would be in their interests to create a government that would protect private property from those who do not have it but can see that they might be able to acquire it by force. So, government gets established, through a contract, which purports to guarantee equality and protection for all, even though its true purpose is to fossilize the very inequalities that private property has produced. In other words, the contract, which claims to be in the interests of everyone equally, is really in the interests of the few who have become stronger and richer as a result of the developments of private property. This is the naturalized social contract, which Rousseau views as responsible for the conflict and competition from which modern society suffers.

The normative social contract, argued for by Rousseau in *The Social Contract* (1762), is meant to respond to this sorry state of affairs and to remedy the social and moral ills that have been produced by the development of society. The distinction between history and justification, between the factual situation of mankind and how it ought to live together, is of the utmost importance to Rousseau. While we ought not to ignore history, nor ignore the causes of the problems we face, we must resolve those problems through our capacity to choose how we ought to live. Might never makes right, despite how often it pretends that it can.

The Social Contract begins with the most oft-quoted line from Rousseau: "Man was born free, and he is everywhere in chains". This claim is the conceptual bridge between the descriptive work of the Second Discourse, and the prescriptive work that is to come. Humans are essentially free, and were free in the State of Nature, but the 'progress' of civilization has substituted subservience to others for that freedom, through dependence, economic and social inequalities, and the extent to which we judge ourselves through comparisons with others. Since a return to the State of Nature is neither feasible nor desirable, the purpose of politics is to restore freedom to us, thereby reconciling who we truly and essentially are with how we live together. So, this is the fundamental philosophical problem that *The Social Contract* seeks to address: how can we be free and live together? Or, put another way, how can we live together without succumbing to the force and coercion of others? We can do so, Rousseau maintains, by submitting our individual, particular wills to the collective or general will, created through agreement with other free and equal persons. Like Hobbes and Locke before him, and in contrast to the ancient philosophers, all men are made by nature to be equals, therefore no one has a natural right to govern others, and therefore the only justified authority is the authority that is generated out of agreements or covenants.

The most basic covenant, the social pact, is the agreement to come together and form a people, a collectivity, which by definition is more than and different from a mere aggregation of individual interests and wills. This act, where individual persons become a people is "the real foundation of society" (59). Through the collective renunciation of the individual rights and freedom that one has in the State of Nature, and the transfer of these rights to the collective body, a new 'person', as it were, is formed. The sovereign is thus formed when free and equal persons come together and agree to create themselves anew as a single body, directed to the good of all considered together. So, just as individual wills are directed towards individual interests, the general will, once formed, is directed towards the common good, understood and agreed to collectively. Included in this version of the social contract is the idea of reciprocated duties: the sovereign is committed to the good of the individuals who constitute it, and each individual is likewise committed to the good of the whole. Given this, individuals cannot be given liberty to decide whether it is in their own interests to fulfill their duties to the Sovereign, while at the same time being allowed to reap the benefits of citizenship. They must be made to conform themselves to the general will, they must be "forced to be free" (64).

For Rousseau, this implies an extremely strong and direct form of democracy. One cannot transfer one's will to another, to do with as he or she sees fit, as one does in representative democracies. Rather, the general will depends on the coming together periodically of the entire democratic body, each and every citizen, to decide collectively, and with at least near unanimity, how to live together, i.e., what laws to enact. As it is constituted only by individual wills, these private, individual wills must assemble themselves regularly if the general will is to continue. One implication of this is that the strong form of democracy which is consistent with the general will is also only possible in relatively small states. The people must be able to identify with one another, and at least know who each other are. They cannot live in a large area, too spread out to come together regularly, and they cannot live in such different geographic circumstances as to be unable to be united under common laws. (Could the present-day U.S. satisfy Rousseau's conception of democracy? It could not.) Although the conditions for true democracy are stringent, they are also the only means by which we can, according to Rousseau, save ourselves, and regain the freedom to which we are naturally entitled.

Rousseau's social contract theories together form a single, consistent view of our moral and political situation. We are endowed with freedom and equality by nature, but our nature has been corrupted by our contingent social history. We can overcome this corruption, however, by invoking our free will to reconstitute ourselves politically, along strongly democratic principles, which is good for us, both individually and collectively.

In 1972, the publication of John Rawls' extremely influential *A Theory of Justice* brought moral and political philosophy back from what had been a long hiatus of philosophical consideration. Rawls' theory relies on a Kantian understanding of persons and their capacities. For Rawls, as for Kant, persons have the capacity to reason from a universal point of view, which in turn means that they have the particular moral capacity of judging principles from an impartial standpoint. In *A Theory of Justice*, Rawls argues that the moral and political point of view is discovered via impartiality. (It is important to note that this view, delineated in *A Theory of Justice*, has undergone substantial revisions by Rawls, and that he described his later view as "political liberalism".) He invokes this point of view (the general view that Thomas Nagel describes as "the view from nowhere") by imagining persons in a hypothetical situation, the Original Position, which is characterized by the epistemological limitation of the Veil of Ignorance. Rawls' original position is his highly abstracted version of the State of Nature. It is the position from which we can discover the nature of justice and what it requires of us as individual persons and of the social institutions through which we will live together cooperatively. In the original position, behind the veil of ignorance, one is denied any particular knowledge of one's circumstances, such as one's gender, race, particular talents or disabilities, one's age, social status, one's particular conception of what makes for a good life, or the particular state of the society in which one lives. Persons are also assumed to be rational and disinterested in one another's well-being. These are the conditions under which, Rawls argues, one can choose principles for a just society which are themselves chosen from initial conditions that are inherently fair. Because no one has any of the particular knowledge he or she could use to develop principles that favor his or her own particular circumstances, in other words the knowledge that makes for and sustains prejudices, the principles chosen from such a perspective are necessarily fair. For example, if one does not know whether one is female or male in the society for which one must choose basic principles of justice, it makes no sense, from the point of view of self-interested rationality, to endorse a principle that favors one sex at the expense of another, since, once the veil of ignorance is lifted, one might find oneself on the losing end of such a principle. Hence Rawls describes his theory as "justice as fairness." Because the conditions under which the principles of justice are discovered are basically fair, justice proceeds out of fairness.

In such a position, behind such a veil, everyone is in the same situation, and everyone is presumed to be equally rational. Since everyone adopts the same method for choosing the basic principles for society, everyone will occupy the same standpoint: that of the disembodied, rational, universal human. Therefore all who consider justice from the point of view of the original position would agree upon the same principles of justice generated out of such a thought experiment. Any one person would reach the same conclusion as any other person concerning the most basic principles that must regulate a just society.

The principles that persons in the Original Position, behind the Veil of Ignorance, would choose to regulate a society at the most basic level (that is, prior even to a Constitution) are called by Rawls, aptly enough, the Two Principles of Justice. These two principles determine the distribution of both civil liberties and social and economic goods. The first principle states that each person in a society is to have as much basic liberty as possible, as long as everyone is granted the same liberties. That is, there is to be as much civil liberty as possible as long as these goods are distributed equally. (This would, for example, preclude a scenario under which there was a greater aggregate of civil liberties than under an alternative scenario, but under which such liberties were not distributed equally amongst citizens.) The second principle states that while social and economic inequalities can be just, they must be available to everyone equally (that is, no one is to be on principle denied access to greater economic advantage) and such inequalities must be to the advantage of everyone. This means that economic inequalities are only justified when the least advantaged member of society is nonetheless better off than she would be under alternative arrangements. So, only if a rising tide truly does carry all boats upward, can economic inequalities be allowed for in a just society. The method of the original position supports this second principle, referred to as the Difference Principle, because when we are behind the veil of ignorance, and therefore do not know what our situation in society will be once the veil of ignorance is lifted, we will only accept principles that will be to our advantage even if we end up in the least advantaged position in society.

These two principles are related to each other by a specific order. The first principle, distributing civil liberties as widely as possible consistent with equality, is prior to the second principle, which distributes social and economic goods. In other words, we cannot decide to forgo some of our civil liberties in favor of greater economic advantage. Rather, we must satisfy the demands of the first principle, before we move on to the second. From Rawls' point of view, this serial ordering of the principles expresses a basic rational preference for certain kinds of goods, i.e., those embodied in civil liberties, over other kinds of goods, i.e., economic advantage.

Having argued that any rational person inhabiting the original position and placing him or herself behind the veil of ignorance can discover the two principles of justice, Rawls has constructed what is perhaps the most abstract version of a social contract theory. It is highly abstract because rather than demonstrating that we would or even have signed to a contract to establish society, it instead shows us what we must be willing to accept as rational persons in order to be constrained by justice and therefore capable of living in a well ordered society. The principles of justice are more fundamental than the social contract as it has traditionally been conceived. Rather, the principles of justice constrain that contract, and set out the limits of how we can construct society in the first place. If we consider, for example, a constitution as the concrete expression of the social contract, Rawls' two principles of justice delineate what such a constitution can and cannot require of us. Rawls' theory of justice constitutes, then, the Kantian limits upon the forms of political and social organization that are permissible within a just society.

In his 1986 book, *Morals by Agreement*, David Gauthier set out to renew Hobbesian moral and political philosophy. In that book, he makes a strong argument that Hobbes was right: we can understand both politics and morality as founded upon an agreement between exclusively self-interested yet rational persons. He improves upon Hobbes' argument, however, by showing that we can establish morality without the external enforcement mechanism of the Sovereign. Hobbes argued that men's passions were so strong as to make cooperation between them always in danger of breaking down, and thus that a Sovereign was necessary to force compliance. Gauthier, however, believes that rationality alone convinces persons not only to agree to cooperate, but to stick to their agreements as well.

We should understand ourselves as individual Robinson Crusoes, each living on our own island, lucky or unlucky in terms of our talents and the natural provisions of our islands, but able to enter into negotiations and deals with one another to trade goods and services with one another. Entering into such agreements is to our own advantage, and so rationality convinces us to both make such agreements and stick to them as well.

Gauthier has an advantage over Hobbes when it comes to developing the argument that cooperation between purely self-interested agents is possible. He has access to rational choice theory and its sophisticated methodology for showing how such cooperation can arise. In particular, he appeals to the model of the Prisoner's Dilemma to show that self-interest can be consistent with acting cooperatively. (There is a reasonable argument to be made that we can find in Hobbes a primitive version of the problem of the Prisoner's Dilemma.)

According to the story of the Prisoner's Dilemma, two people have been brought in for questioning, conducted separately, about a crime they are suspected to have committed. The police have solid evidence of a lesser crime that they committed, but need confessions in order to convict them on more serious charges. Each prisoner is told that if she cooperates with the police by informing on the other prisoner, then she will be rewarded by receiving a relatively light sentence of one year in prison, whereas her cohort will go to prison for ten years. If they both remain silent, then there will be no such rewards, and they can each expect to receive moderate sentences of two years. And if they both cooperate with police by informing on each other, then the police will have enough to send each to prison for five years. The dilemma then is this: in order to serve her own interests as well as possible, each prisoner reasons that no matter what the other does she is better off cooperating with the police by confessing. Each reasons: "If she confesses, then I should confess, thereby being sentenced to five years instead of ten. And if she does not confess, then I should confess, thereby being sentenced to one year instead of two. So, no matter what she does, I should confess." The problem is that when each reason this way, they each confess, and each goes to prison for five years. However, had they each remained silent, thereby cooperating with each other rather than with the police, they would have spent only two years in prison.

According to Gauthier, the important lesson of the Prisoner's Dilemma is that when one is engaged in interaction such that others' actions can affect one's own interests, and vice versa, one does better if one acts cooperatively. By acting to further the interests of the other, one serves one's own interests as well. We should, therefore, insofar as we are rational, develop within ourselves the dispositions to constrain ourselves when interacting with others. We should become "constrained maximizers" (CMs) rather remain the "straightforward maximizers" (SMs) that we would be in a State of Nature (167).

Both SMs and CMs are exclusively self-interested and rational, but they differ with regard to whether they take into account only strategies, or both the strategies and utilities, of whose with whom they interact. To take into account the others' strategies is to act in accordance with how you expect the others will act. To take into account their utilities is to consider how they will fare as a result of your action and to allow that to affect your own actions. Both SMs and CMs take into account the strategies of the other with whom they interact. But whereas SMs do not take into account the utilities of those with whom they interact, CMs do. And, whereas CMs are afforded the benefits of cooperation with others, SMs are denied such advantage. According to Gauthier, when interacting in Prisoner's Dilemma-like situations, where the actions of others can affect one's own outcome, and vice versa, rationality shows that one's own interest is best pursued by being cooperative, and therefore agents rationally dispose themselves to the constrain the maximization of their own utility by adopting principles of morality. According to Gauthier, rationality is a force strong enough to give persons internal reasons to cooperate. They do not, therefore, need Hobbes' Sovereign with absolute authority to sustain their cooperation. The enforcement mechanism has been internalized. "Morals by agreement" are therefore created out of the rationality of exclusively self-interested agents.

Given the longstanding and widespread influence that social contract theory has had, it comes as no surprise that it is also the objects of many critiques from a variety of philosophical perspectives. Feminists and race-conscious philosophers, in particular, have made important arguments concerning the substance and viability of social contract theory.

For the most part, feminism resists any simple or universal definition. In general though, feminists take women's experiences seriously, as well as the impact that theories and practices have for women's lives. Given the pervasive influence of contract theory on social, political, and moral philosophy, then, it is not surprising that feminists should have a great deal to say about whether contract theory is adequate or appropriate from the point of view of taking women seriously. To survey all of the feminist responses to social contract theory would carry us well beyond the boundaries of the present article. I will concentrate therefore on just three of those arguments: Carole Pateman's argument about the relation between the contract and women's subordination to men, feminist arguments concerning the nature of the liberal individual, and the care argument.

Carole Pateman's 1988 book, *The Sexual Contract*, argues that lying beneath the myth of the idealized contract, as described by Hobbes, Locke, and Rousseau, is a more fundamental contract concerning men's relationship to women. Contract theory represents itself as being opposed to patriarchy and patriarchal right. (Locke's social contract, for example, is set by him in stark contrast to the work of Robert Filmer who argued in favor of patriarchal power.) Yet the "original pact" (2) that precedes the social contract entered into by equals is the agreement by men to dominate and control women. This 'original pact' is made by brothers, literally or metaphorically, who, after overthrowing the rule of the father, then agree to share their domination of the women who were previously under the exclusive control of one man, the father. The change from "classical patriarchalism" (24) to modern patriarchy is a shift, then, in who has power over women. It is not, however, a fundamental change in whether women are dominated by men. Men's relationships of power to one another change, but women's relationship to men's power does not. Modern patriarchy is characterized by a contractual relationship between men, and part of that contract involves power over women. This fact, that one form of patriarchy was not overthrown completely, but rather was replaced with a different form, in which male power was distributed amongst more men, rather than held by one man, is illustrated by Freud's story of the genesis of civilization. According to that story, a band of brothers, lorded over by a father who maintained exclusive sexual access to the women of the tribe, kill the father, and then establish a contract among themselves to be equal and to share the women. This is the story, whether we understand Freud's tale to be historically accurate or not, of modern patriarchy and its deep dependence on contract as the means by which men control and dominate women.

Patriarchal control of women is found in at least three paradigmatic contemporary contracts: the marriage contract, the prostitution contract, and the contract for surrogate motherhood. Each of these contracts is concerned with men's control of women, or a particular man's control of a particular woman generalized. According to the terms of the marriage contract, in most states in the U.S., a husband is accorded the right to sexual access, prohibiting the legal category of marital rape. Prostitution is a case in point of Pateman's claim that modern patriarchy requires equal access by men to women, in particular sexual access, access to their bodies. And surrogate motherhood can be understood as more of the same, although in terms of access to women's reproductive capacities. All these examples demonstrate that contract is the means by which women are dominated and controlled. Contract is not the path to freedom and equality. Rather, it is one means, perhaps the most fundamental means, by which patriarchy is upheld.

Following Pateman's argument, a number of feminists have also called into question the very nature of the person at the heart of contract theory. The Liberal Individual, the contractor, is represented by the Hobbesian man, Locke's proprietor, Rousseau's "Noble Savage," Rawls's person in the original position, and Gauthier's Robinson Crusoe. The liberal individual is purported to be universal: raceless, sexless, classless, disembodied, and is taken to represent an abstract, generalized model of humanity writ large. Many philosophers have argued, however, that when we look more closely at the characteristics of the liberal individual, what we find is not a representation of universal humanity, but a historically located, specific type of person. C.B. Macpherson, for example, has argued that Hobbesian man is, in particular, a bourgeois man, with the characteristics we would expect of a person during the nascent capitalism that characterized early modern Europe. Feminists have also argued that the liberal individual is a particular, historical, and embodied person. (As have race-conscious philosophers, such as Charles Mills, to be discussed below.) More specifically, they have argued that the person at the heart of liberal theory, and the social contract, is gendered. Christine Di Stefano, in her 1991 book *Configurations of Masculinity*, shows that a number of historically important modern philosophers can be understood to develop their theories from within the perspective of masculinity, as conceived of in the modern period. She argues that Hobbes's conception of the liberal individual, which laid the groundwork for the dominant modern conception of the person, is particularly masculine in that it is conceived as atomistic and solitary and as not owing any of its qualities, or even its very existence, to any other person, in particular its mother. Hobbes's human, is therefore, radically individual, in a way that is specifically owing to the character of modern masculinity. Virginia Held, in her 1993 book, *Feminist Morality*, argues that social contract theory implicitly relies on a conception of the person that can be best described as "economic man." "Economic man" is concerned first and foremost to maximize his own, individually considered interests, and he enters into contracts as a means by which to achieve this end. "Economic man", however, fails to represent all persons in all times and places. In particular, it fails to adequately represent children and those who provide them with the care they require, who have historically been women. The model of "economic man" cannot, therefore, fairly claim to be a general representation of all persons. Similarly, Annette Baier argues that Gauthier's conception of the liberal individual who enters into the social contract as a means by which to maximize his own individually considered interests is gendered in that it does not take seriously the position of either children or the women who most usually are responsible for caring for those children.

Theorizing from within the emerging tradition of care ethics, feminist philosophers such as Baier and Held argue that social contract theory fails as an adequate account of our moral or political obligations. Social contract theory, in general, only goes so far as to delineate our rights and obligations. But this may not be enough to adequately reveal the full extent of what it means to be a moral person, and how fully to respond to others with whom one interacts through relations of dependence. Baier argues that Gauthier, who conceives of affective bonds between persons as non-essential and voluntary, therefore fails to represent the fullness of human psychology and motivations. She argues that this therefore leads to a crucial flaw in social contract theory. Liberal moral theory is in fact parasitic upon the very relations between persons from which it seeks to liberate us. While Gauthier argues that we are freer the more that we can see affective relations as voluntary, we must nonetheless, in the first place, be in such relationships (e.g., the mother-child relationship) in order to develop the very capacities and qualities lauded by liberal theory. Certain kinds of relationships of dependence, in other words, are necessary in the first place if we are to become the very kinds of persons who are capable of entering into contracts and agreements. In a similar vein, Held has argued that the model of "economic man" fails to capture much of what constitutes meaningful moral relations between people. Understanding human relations in purely contractual terms constitutes, according to her argument "an impoverished view of human aspiration" (194). She therefore suggests that we consider other models of human relationships when looking for insight into morality. In particular, she offers up the paradigm of the mother-child relationship to at least supplement the model of individual self-interested agents negotiating with one another through contracts. Such a model is more likely to match up with many of the moral experiences of most people, especially women.

Feminist critiques of the contractarian approaches to our collective moral and political lives continue to reverberate through social and political philosophy. One such critique, that of Carole Pateman, has influenced philosophers writing outside of feminist traditions.

Charles Mills' 1997 book, *The Racial Contract*, is a critique not only of the history of Western political thought, institutions, and practices, but, more specifically, of the history of social contract theory. It is inspired by Carole Pateman's *The Sexual Contract*, and seeks to show that non-whites have a similar relationship to the social contract as do women. As such, it also calls into question the supposed universality of the liberal individual who is the agent of contract theory.

Mills' central argument is that there exists a 'racial contract' that is even more fundamental to Western society than the social contract. This racial contract determines in the first place who counts as full moral and political persons, and therefore sets the parameters of who can 'contract in' to the freedom and equality that the social contract promises. Some persons, in particular white men, are full persons according to the racial contract. As such they are accorded the right to enter into the social contract, and into particular legal contracts. They are seen as fully human and therefore as deserving of equality and freedom. Their status as full persons accords them greater social power. In particular, it accords them the power to make contracts, to be the subjects of the contract, whereas other persons are denied such privilege and are relegated to the status of objects of contracts.

This racial contract is to some extent a meta-contract, which determines the bounds of personhood and parameters of inclusion and exclusion in all the other contracts that come after it. It manifests itself both formally and informally. It is an agreement, originally among European men in the beginning of the modern period, to identify themselves as 'white' and therefore as fully human, and to identify all others, in particular the natives with whom they were beginning to come into contact, as 'other': non-white and therefore not fully human. So, race is not just a social construct, as others have argued, it is more especially a political construct, created to serve a particular political end, and the political purposes of a specific group. The contract allows some persons to treat other persons, as well as the lands they inhabit, as resources to be exploited. The enslavement of millions of Africans and the appropriation of the Americas from those who inhabited them, are examples of this racial contract at work in history (such as Locke's claim that Native Americans did not own the land they lived on because they did not farm it and therefore did not own it). This contract is not hypothetical, as Hobbes describes the one argued for in his *Leviathan*. This is an actual contract, or series of contracts, made by real men of history. It is found in such documents as Papal Bulls and Locke's writings on Native Americans, and acted upon in such historical events as the voyages of discovery made by Europeans and the colonization of Africa, Asia, and the Americas. The racial contract makes possible and justifies some people, in virtue of their alleged superiority, exploiting the peoples, lands, and resources of other races.

From Mills' perspective then, racism is not just an unhappy accident of Western democratic and political ideals. It is not the case that we have a political system that was perfectly conceived and unfortunately imperfectly applied. One of the reasons that we continue to think that the problem of race in the West is relatively superficial, that it does not go all the way down, is the hold that the idealized social contract has on our imagination. We continue to believe, according to Mills, in the myths that social contract theory tells us – that everyone is equal, that all will be treated the same before the law, that the Founding Fathers were committed to equality and freedom for all persons, etc. One of the very purposes of social contract theory, then, is to keep hidden from view the true political reality – some persons will be accorded the rights and freedoms of full persons, and the rest will be treated as sub-persons. The racial contract informs the very structure of our political systems, and lays the basis for the continuing racial oppression of non-whites. We cannot respond to it, therefore, by simply adding more non-whites into the mix of our political institutions, representation, and so on. Rather, we must reexamine our politics in general, from the point of view of the racial contract, and start from where we are, with full knowledge of how our society has been informed by the systematic exclusion of some persons from the realm of politics and contract. This "naturalized" feature of the racial contract, meaning that it tells a story about who we actually are and what is included in our history, is better, according to Mills, because it holds the promise of making it possible for us to someday actually live up to the norms and values that are at the heart of the Western political traditions.

Virginia Held has argued that "Contemporary Western society is in the grip of contractual thinking" (193). Contractual models have come to inform a vast variety of relations and interaction between persons, from students and their teachers, to authors and their readers. Given this, it would be difficult to overestimate the effect that social contract theory has had, both within philosophy, and on the wider culture. Social contract theory is undoubtedly with us for the foreseeable future. But so too are the critiques of such theory, which will continue to compel us to think and rethink the nature of both ourselves and our relations with one another.

John Rawl and Theory of Justice

John Rawls was born and raised in Baltimore, Maryland. His father was a prominent lawyer, his mother was a chapter president of the League of Women Voters. Rawls studied at Princeton and Cornell, where he was influenced by Wittgenstein[143]'s student Norman Malcolm[144]; and at Oxford, where he worked with H. L. A. Hart[145], Isaiah Berlin[146], and Stuart Hampshire[147]. His first professorial appointments were at Cornell and MIT. In 1962 Rawls joined the faculty at Harvard, where he taught for more than thirty years.

Rawls's adult life was a scholarly one: its major events occurred within his writings. The exceptions were two wars. As a college student, Rawls wrote an intensely religious senior thesis (*BI*) and had considered studying for the priesthood. Yet Rawls lost his Christian faith as an infantryman in World War II on seeing the capriciousness of death in combat and learning of the horrors of the Holocaust. Then in the 1960s, Rawls spoke out against the draft for the Vietnam war because it discriminated against black and poor Americans. The Vietnam conflict impelled Rawls to analyze the defects in the American political system that led it to prosecute so ruthlessly what he saw as an unjust war, and to consider how citizens could conscientiously resist their government's aggressive policies.

Rawls's most discussed work is his theory of a just liberal society, called *justice as fairness*. Rawls first set out justice as fairness in systematic detail in his 1971 book, *A Theory of Justice*. Rawls continued to rework justice as fairness throughout his life, restating the theory in *Political Liberalism* (1993)[148], *The Law of Peoples* (1999)[149], and *Justice as Fairness* (2001)[150].

This entry reflects Rawls's final statement of his views on justice as fairness, as well as on political liberalism and on the law of peoples.

Rawls sees political philosophy as fulfilling at least four roles in a society's public culture. The first role is practical: philosophy can propose grounds for reasoned agreement when sharp political divisions threaten to lead to violent conflict. Rawls cites Hobbes's *Leviathan* as an attempt to solve the problem of order during the English civil war, Locke's *Letter on Toleration* as responding to the Wars of Religion, as well as the philosophy that emerged from the debates over the US Constitution, and from debates over the extension of slavery before the American civil war.

A second role of political philosophy is to help citizens to orient themselves within their own social world. Philosophy can meditate on what it is to be a member of a certain society—in a democracy, an equal citizen—and offer a unifying framework for answering divisive questions about how people with that political status should relate to each other.

A third role is to probe the limits of political possibility. Political philosophy must describe workable political arrangements that can gain support from real people. Yet within these limits, philosophy can be utopian: it can depict a social order that is the best that we can hope for. Given humans as they are, philosophy imagines laws as they might be.

A fourth role of political philosophy is reconciliation: "to calm our frustration and rage against our society and its history by showing us the way in which its institutions…are rational, and developed over time as they did to attain their present, rational form". Philosophy can show that human life is not simply domination and cruelty, prejudice, folly and corruption; but that, at least in some ways, it is better that it has become as it is.

Rawls views his own work as a practical contribution to resolving the long-standing tension in democratic thought between liberty and equality, and to limning the limits of civic and of international toleration. He offers the members of democratic countries a way of understanding themselves as free and equal citizens of a society that is fair to all, and he describes a hopeful vision of a stably just constitutional democracy doing its part within a peaceful international community. To individuals who are frustrated that their fellow citizens and fellow humans do not see the whole truth as they do, Rawls offers the reconciling thought that this diversity of worldviews results from, and can support, a social order with greater freedom for all.

In contrast to the utilitarian, for Rawls political philosophy is not simply applied moral philosophy. The utilitarian holds to one universal moral principle ("maximize utility"), which she applies to individual actions, political constitutions, international relations, and all other subjects as required. Rawls has no universal principle: "The correct regulative principle for anything," he says, "depends on the nature of that thing". Rawls confines his theorizing to the political domain, and within this domain he holds that the correct principles for each sub-domain depend on its particular agents and constraints.

Rawls covers the domain of the political by addressing its sub-domains in sequence. The first sub-domain that he addresses is a self-contained democratic society reproducing itself across generations. Once principles are in place for such a society, Rawls moves to a second sub-domain: a society of nations, of which this democratic society is a member. Rawls suggests (though he does not show) that his sequence of theories could extend to cover further sub-domains, such as human interactions with animals. Universal coverage will have been achieved once this sequence is complete, each sub-domain having received the principles appropriate to it.

Within each sub-domain of the political Rawls also follows a sequence: ideal theory before non-ideal theory. *Ideal theory* makes two types of idealizing assumptions about its subject matter. First, ideal theory assumes that all actors (citizens or societies) are generally willing to comply with whatever principles are chosen. Ideal theory thus idealizes away the possibility of law-breaking, either by individuals (crime) or societies (aggressive war). Second, ideal theory assumes reasonably favorable social conditions, wherein citizens and societies are able to abide by principles of political cooperation. Citizens are not so driven by hunger, for example, that their capacity for moral reasoning is overwhelmed; nor are nations struggling to overcome famine or the failure of their states.

Completing ideal theory first, Rawls says, yields a systematic understanding of how to reform our non-ideal world, and fixes a vision (mentioned above) of what is the best that can be hoped for. Once ideal theory is completed for a political sub-domain, *non-ideal theory* can be set out by reference to the ideal. For instance, once we find ideal principles for citizens who can be productive members of society over a complete life, we will be better able to frame non-ideal principles for providing health care to citizens with serious illnesses or disabilities. Similarly, once we understand the ideal principles of international relations, we will better see how the international community should act toward failed states, as well as toward aggressive states that threaten the peace.

The aim of political philosophy is to reach justified conclusions about how political life should proceed. For Rawls, how justified one is in one's political convictions depends on how close one is to achieving *reflective equilibrium*. In reflective equilibrium all of one's beliefs, on all levels of generality, cohere perfectly with one another.

Thus, in reflective equilibrium one's specific political judgments (e.g., "religious intolerance is unjust," "racial discrimination is unjust") support one's more general political convictions (e.g., "all citizens have certain basic rights") which support one's very abstract beliefs about the political world (e.g., "all citizens are free and equal"). Viewed from the opposite direction, in reflective equilibrium one's abstract beliefs explain one's more general convictions, which in turn explain one's specific judgments. Were one to attain reflective equilibrium, the justification of each belief would follow from all beliefs relating in these networks of mutual support and explanation.

Though perfect reflective equilibrium is unattainable, one can use the *method of reflective equilibrium* to get closer to it and so increase the justifiability of one's beliefs. In carrying through this method, one begins with one's considered moral judgments: those made consistently and without hesitation when one is under good conditions for thinking (e.g., "slavery is wrong," "all citizens are political equals"). One treats these considered judgments as provisional fixed points, and then starts the process of bringing one's beliefs into relations of mutual support and explanation as described above. Doing this inevitably brings out conflicts where, for example, a specific judgment clashes with a more general conviction, or where an abstract principle cannot accommodate a particular kind of case. One proceeds by revising these beliefs as necessary, striving always to increase the coherence of the whole.

Carrying through this process of mutual adjustment brings one closer to *narrow reflective equilibrium*: coherence among one's initial beliefs. One then adds to this narrow equilibrium one's responses to the major theories in the history of political philosophy, as well as one's responses to theories critical of political philosophizing as such. One continues to adjust one's scheme of beliefs as one reflects on these alternatives, aiming for the end-point of *wide reflective equilibrium*, in which coherence is maintained after many alternatives have been considered.

Because of its emphasis on coherence, reflective equilibrium is often contrasted with foundationalism as an account of justified belief. Within foundationalist approaches, some subset of beliefs is considered to be unrevisable, thereby serving as a foundation on which all other beliefs are to be based. Reflective equilibrium privileges no such subset of beliefs: any belief at any level of generality is subject to revision, if revision will help to bring one's considered convictions into greater coherence overall.

In working toward greater reflective equilibrium, any type of belief can in principle be relevant to one's conclusions about how political institutions should be arranged. Metaphysical beliefs about free will or personal identity might be relevant, as could epistemological beliefs about how we come to know what moral facts there are. However, while this is correct in principle, Rawls holds that in practice productive moral and political theorizing will proceed to a large extent independent of metaphysics and epistemology. Indeed, as a methodological presumption Rawls reverses the traditional order of priority. Progress in metaethics will derive from progress in substantive moral and political theorizing, instead of (as often assumed) vice versa.

Rawls's own metaethical theory of the objectivity and validity of political judgments, political constructivism, will be described below, after the substantive political theory from which it emerges.

In a free society, citizens will have disparate worldviews. They will believe in different religions or none at all; they will have differing conceptions of right and wrong; they will disagree on how to live and on what relationships to value. Citizens will have contrary commitments, yet within any country there can only be one law. The law must either establish a national church, or not; women must either have equal rights, or not; abortion and gay marriage must either be permissible, or not; the economy must be set up in one way or another.

Rawls holds that the need to impose a unified law on a diverse citizenry raises two fundamental challenges. The first is the challenge of *legitimacy*: the legitimate use of coercive political power. How can it be legitimate to coerce all citizens to follow just one law, given that citizens will inevitably hold divergent worldviews?

The second challenge is the challenge of *stability*, which looks at political power from the receiving end. Why would a citizen willingly obey a law that is imposed on her by a collective body whose members have beliefs and values so different to her own? Yet unless most citizens willingly obey the law, no social order can be stable for long.

Rawls answers these challenges of legitimacy and stability with his theory of *political liberalism*. Political liberalism is not yet Rawls's theory of justice (justice as fairness). Political liberalism answers the conceptually prior questions of legitimacy and stability, so fixing the context and starting points for justice as fairness.

In a democracy, political power is always the power of the people as a collective body. In light of the diversity within a democracy, what would it mean for citizens legitimately to exercise coercive political power over one another? Rawls's test for the acceptable use of political power in a democracy is his *liberal principle of legitimacy*:

Our exercise of political power is fully proper only when it is exercised in accordance with a constitution the essentials of which all citizens as free and equal may reasonably be expected to endorse in the light of principles and ideals acceptable to their common human reason.

According to this principle, political power may only be used in ways that all citizens can reasonably be expected to endorse. The use of political power must fulfill a *criterion of reciprocity*: citizens must reasonably believe that all citizens can reasonably accept the enforcement of a particular set of basic laws. Those coerced by law must be able to endorse the society's fundamental political arrangements freely, not because they are dominated or manipulated or kept uninformed.

The liberal principle of legitimacy intensifies the challenge of legitimacy: how can any particular set of basic laws legitimately be imposed upon a pluralistic citizenry? What constitution could all citizens reasonably be expected to endorse? Rawls's answer to this challenge begins by explaining what it means for citizens to be *reasonable.*

Reasonable citizens want to live in a society in which they can cooperate with their fellow citizens on terms that are acceptable to all. They are willing to propose and abide by mutually acceptable rules, given the assurance that others will also do so. They will also honor these rules, even when this means sacrificing their own particular interests. Reasonable citizens want, in short, to belong to a society where political power is legitimately used.

Each reasonable citizen has her own view about God and life, right and wrong, good and bad. Each has, that is, what Rawls calls her own *comprehensive doctrine.* Yet because reasonable citizens are reasonable, they are unwilling to impose their own comprehensive doctrines on others who are also willing to search for mutually agreeable rules. Though each citizen may believe that she knows the truth about the best way to live, none is willing to force other reasonable citizens to live according to her beliefs, even if she belongs to a majority that has the power to enforce those beliefs on everyone. After all, Rawls says mentioning the Inquisition, oppressive use of state power will be necessary to unite a society around any comprehensive doctrine, including the comprehensive liberalism of Kant or Mill.

One reason that reasonable citizens are so tolerant, Rawls says, is that they accept a certain explanation for the diversity of worldviews in their society. Reasonable citizens accept the *burdens of judgment.* The deepest questions of religion, philosophy, and morality are very difficult to think through. Even conscientious people will answer these questions in different ways, because of their particular life experiences (their upbringing, class, occupation, and so on). Reasonable citizens understand that these deep issues are ones on which people of good will can disagree, and so will be unwilling to impose their own worldviews on those who have reached conclusions different than their own.

Rawls's account of the reasonable citizen highlights his view of human nature. Humans are not irredeemably self-centered, dogmatic, or driven by what Hobbes called, "a perpetual and restless desire of power after power" (1651, 58). Humans have at least the capacity for genuine toleration and mutual respect.

This human capacity raises the hope that the diversity of worldviews in a democratic society may represent not merely pluralism, but *reasonable pluralism.* Rawls hopes, that is, that the religious, moral, and philosophical doctrines that citizens accept will themselves endorse toleration and accept the essentials of a democratic regime. In the religious sphere, for example, a reasonable pluralism might contain a reasonable Catholicism, a reasonable interpretation of Islam, a reasonable atheism, and so on. Being reasonable, none of these doctrines will advocate the use of coercive political power to impose religious conformity on citizens with different beliefs.

The possibility of reasonable pluralism softens but does not solve the challenge of legitimacy: how one law can legitimately be imposed on diverse citizens. For even in a society of reasonable pluralism, it would be unreasonable to expect everyone to endorse, say, a reasonable Catholicism as the basis for a constitutional settlement. Reasonable Muslims or atheists cannot be expected to endorse Catholicism as setting the basic terms for social life. Nor, of course, can Catholics be expected to accept Islam or atheism as the fundamental basis of law. *No comprehensive doctrine can be accepted by all reasonable citizens, and so no comprehensive doctrine can serve as the basis for the legitimate use of coercive political power.*

Yet where else then to turn to find the ideas that will define society's most basic laws, which all citizens will be required to obey? For Rawls, there is only one source of fundamental ideas that can serve as a focal point for all reasonable citizens of a liberal society. This is the society's *public political culture.*

Since justification is addressed to others, it proceeds from what is, or can be, held in common; and so we begin from shared fundamental ideas implicit in the public political culture in the hope of developing from them a political conception that can gain free and reasoned agreement in judgment.

The public political culture of a democratic society, Rawls says, "comprises the political institutions of a constitutional regime and the public traditions of their interpretation (including those of the judiciary), as well as historic texts and documents that are common knowledge". Rawls looks to fundamental ideas implicit, for example, in the constitution's list of individual rights, in the design of the society's government, and in the historic decisions of important courts. These fundamental ideas from the public political culture can be crafted into a shared political conception of justice.

Rawls's solution to the challenge of legitimacy in a liberal society is for political power to be exercised in accordance with a *political conception of justice.* A political conception of justice is an interpretation of the fundamental ideas implicit in that society's public political culture.

A political conception is not derived from any particular comprehensive doctrine, nor is it a compromise among the worldviews that happen to exist in society at the moment. Rather, a political conception is freestanding: its content is set out independently of the comprehensive doctrines that citizens affirm. Reasonable citizens, who want to cooperate with one another on mutually acceptable terms, will see that a freestanding political conception generated from ideas in the public political culture is the only basis for cooperation that all citizens can reasonably be expected to endorse. The use of coercive political power guided by the principles of a political conception of justice will therefore be legitimate.

The three most fundamental ideas that Rawls finds in the public political culture of a democratic society are that citizens are *free* and *equal*, and that society should be a *fair* system of cooperation. All liberal political conceptions of justice will therefore be centered on interpretations of these three fundamental ideas.

Because there are many reasonable interpretations of "free," "equal" and "fair," there will be many liberal political conceptions of justice. Since all the members of this family interpret the same three fundamental ideas, however, all liberal political conceptions of justice will share certain basic features:

1. A liberal political conception of justice will ascribe to all citizens familiar individual rights and liberties, such as rights of free expression, liberty of conscience, and free choice of occupation;
2. A political conception will give special priority to these rights and liberties, especially over demands to further the general good (e.g., to increase national wealth) or perfectionist values (e.g., to promote a particular view of human flourishing);
3. A political conception will assure for all citizens sufficient all-purpose means to make effective use of their freedoms.

These abstract features must, Rawls says, be realized in certain kinds of institutions. He mentions several demands that all liberal conceptions of justice will make on institutions: a decent distribution of income and wealth; fair opportunities for all citizens, especially in education and training; government as the employer of last resort; basic health care for all citizens; and public financing of elections.

The use of political power in a liberal society will be legitimate if it is employed in accordance with the principles of any liberal conception of justice. By Rawls's criteria, a libertarian conception of justice (such as Nozick's in *Anarchy, State, and Utopia*) is not a liberal political conception of justice. Libertarianism does not assure all citizens sufficient means to make use of their basic liberties, and it permits excessive inequalities of wealth and power. By contrast, Rawls's own conception of justice (justice as fairness) does qualify as a member of the family of liberal political conceptions of justice.

Political power is used legitimately in a liberal society when it is used in accordance with a political conception of justice. Yet the challenge of stability remains. Legitimacy means that the law may be enforced, but Rawls still needs to explain why citizens are willing to abide by it. If citizens do not believe that they have reasons to abide by the law from within their own perspectives, social order may disintegrate.

Rawls places his hopes for social stability on an *overlapping consensus*. In an overlapping consensus, citizens all endorse a core set of laws for different reasons. In Rawlsian terms, each citizen supports a political conception of justice for reasons internal to her own comprehensive doctrine.

Recall that the content of a political conception is freestanding: it is specified without reference to any comprehensive doctrine. This allows a political conception to be a "module" that can fit into any number of worldviews that citizens might have. In an overlapping consensus, each reasonable citizen affirms this common "module" from within her point of view.

Here is an example. The quotation below from the second Vatican Council of the Catholic Church shows how a particular comprehensive doctrine (Catholicism) affirms one component of a liberal political conception (a familiar individual liberty) for its own reasons:

This Vatican Council declares that the human person has a right to religious freedom. This freedom means that all men are to be immune from coercion on the part of individuals or of social groups and of any human power, in such wise that in matters religious no one is forced to act in a manner contrary to his own beliefs. Nor is anyone to be restrained from acting in accordance with his own beliefs, whether privately or publicly, whether alone or in association with others, within due limits. The council further declares that the right to religious freedom has its foundation in the very dignity of the human person, as this dignity is known through the revealed Word of God and by reason itself. This right of the human person to religious freedom is to be recognized in the constitutional law whereby society is governed and thus it is to become a civil right.

Catholic doctrine here supports the liberal right to religious freedom for reasons internal to Catholicism. A reasonable Islamic doctrine, and a reasonable atheistic doctrine, might also affirm this same right to religious freedom—not, of course, for the same reasons as Catholic doctrine, but each for its own reasons. In an overlapping consensus, all reasonable comprehensive doctrines will support the right to religious freedom, each for its own reasons. Indeed, in an overlapping consensus, all reasonable comprehensive doctrines will endorse all of a political conception of justice, each from within its own point of view.

Citizens within an overlapping consensus work out for themselves how the liberal "module" fits with their own worldviews. Some citizens may see liberalism as derived directly from their deepest beliefs, as in the quotation from Vatican II above. Others may accept a liberal conception as attractive in itself, but mostly separate from their other concerns. What is crucial is that all citizens view the values of a political conception of justice as very great values, which normally outweigh their other values should these conflict on some particular issue. All citizens, for their own reasons, give the political conception priority in their reasoning about how their society's basic laws should be ordered.

Rawls sees an overlapping consensus as the most desirable form of stability in a free society. Stability in an overlapping consensus is better than a mere balance of power (a *modus vivendi*) among citizens who hold contending worldviews. After all, power often shifts, and when it does the stability of a *modus vivendi* may be lost.

In an overlapping consensus, citizens affirm a political conception wholeheartedly from within their own perspectives, and so will continue to do so even if their group gains or loses political power. Rawls says that an overlapping consensus is *stable for the right reasons*: each citizen affirms a moral doctrine (a liberal conception of justice) for moral reasons (as given by their comprehensive doctrine). Abiding by liberal basic laws is not a citizen's second-best option in the face of the power of others; it is each citizen's first-best option given her own beliefs.

Rawls does not assert that an overlapping consensus is achievable in every liberal society. Nor does he say that, once established, an overlapping consensus must forever endure. Citizens in some societies may have too little in common to converge on a liberal political conception of justice. In other societies, unreasonable doctrines may spread until they overwhelm liberal institutions.

Rawls does hold that history shows both convergence in beliefs and deepening trust among citizens in many liberal societies. This gives hope that an overlapping consensus is at least possible. Where an overlapping consensus is possible, Rawls believes, it is the best support for social stability that a free society can achieve.

Having seen how Rawls answers the challenges of legitimacy and stability, we can return to legitimacy and its criterion of reciprocity: citizens must reasonably believe that all citizens can reasonably accept the enforcement of a particular set of basic laws. It is unreasonable for citizens to attempt to impose what they see as the whole truth on others— political power must be used in ways that all citizens may reasonably be expected to endorse. With his doctrine of *public reason*, Rawls extends this requirement of reciprocity to apply directly to how citizens explain their political decisions to one another. In essence, public reason requires citizens to be able to justify their political decisions to one another using publicly available values and standards.

To take a straightforward example: a Supreme Court justice deciding on a gay marriage law would violate public reason were she to base her opinion on God's forbidding gay sex in the book of Leviticus, or on a personal spiritual revelation that upholding such a law would hasten the end of days. This is because not all members of society can reasonably be expected to accept Leviticus as stating an authoritative set of political values, nor can a religious premonition be a common standard for evaluating public policy. These values and standards are not public.

Rawls's doctrine of public reason can be summarized as follows:

Citizens engaged in certain political activities have a duty of civility to be able to justify their decisions on fundamental political issues by reference only to public values and public standards.

Each of the highlighted terms in this doctrine can be further elucidated as follows:

- The public values that citizens must be able to appeal to are the values of a political conception of justice: those related to the freedom and equality of citizens, and society as a fair system of cooperation over time. Among such public values are the freedom of religious practice, the political equality of women and of racial minorities, the efficiency of the economy, the preservation of a healthy environment, and the stability of the family (which helps the orderly reproduction of society from one generation to the next). Nonpublic values include values internal to associations like churches (e.g., that women may not hold the highest offices) or private clubs (e.g., that racial minorities can be excluded) which cannot be squared with public values such as these.
- Similarly, citizens should be able to justify their political decisions by public standards of inquiry. Public standards are principles of reasoning and rules of evidence that all citizens can reasonably endorse. So citizens should not justify their political decisions by appeal to divination, or to complex and disputed economic or psychological theories. Rather, publicly acceptable standards are those that rely on common sense, on facts generally known, and on the conclusions of science that are well established and not controversial.
- The duty to abide by public reason applies when the most fundamental political issues are at stake: issues such as who has the right to vote, which religions are to be tolerated,

who will be eligible to own property, and what are suspect classifications for discrimination in hiring decisions. These are what Rawls calls *constitutional essentials and matters of basic justice*. Public reason applies more weakly, if at all, to less momentous political questions, for example to most laws that set rates of taxation, or that put aside public money to maintain national parks.

- Citizens have a duty to constrain their decisions by public reason only when they engage in certain political activities, usually when exercising powers of public office. So judges are bound by public reason when they issue their rulings, legislators should abide by public reason when speaking and voting in the legislature, and the executive and candidates for high office should respect public reason in their public pronouncements. Significantly, Rawls says that voters should also heed public reason when they vote. All of these activities are or support exercises of political power, so (by the liberal principle of legitimacy) all must be justifiable in terms that all citizens might reasonably endorse. However, citizens are not bound by any duties of public reason when they engage in other activities, for example when they worship in church, perform on stage, pursue scientific research, send letters to the editor, or talk politics around the dinner table.

- The duty to be able to justify one's political decisions with public reasons is a moral duty, not a legal duty: it is a duty of civility. All citizens always have their full legal rights to free expression, and overstepping the bounds of public reason is never in itself a crime. Rather, citizens have a moral duty of mutual respect and civic friendship not to justify their political decisions on fundamental issues by appeal to partisan values or controversial standards of reasoning that cannot be publicly redeemed.

In an important proviso, Rawls adds that citizens may speak the language of their controversial comprehensive doctrines—even as public officials, and even on the most fundamental issues—so long as it can be shown that these assertions appeal to public values. So President Lincoln, for instance, could legitimately use Biblical imagery to condemn the evil of slavery, since his condemnations appealed to the public values of freedom and equality. Thus even within its limited range of application, Rawls's doctrine of public reason is rather permissive concerning what citizens may say and do within the bounds of civility.

Justice as fairness is Rawls's theory of justice for a liberal society. As a member of the family of liberal political conceptions of justice it provides a framework for the legitimate use of political power. Yet legitimacy is only the minimal standard of moral acceptability; a political order can be legitimate without being just. Justice sets the maximal standard: the arrangement of social institutions that is morally best.

Rawls constructs justice as fairness around specific interpretations of the ideas that citizens are free and equal, and that society should be fair. He sees it as resolving the tensions between the ideas of freedom and equality, which have been highlighted both by the socialist critique of liberal democracy and by the conservative critique of the modern welfare state. Rawls also argues that justice as fairness is superior to the dominant tradition in modern political thought: utilitarianism.

In Rawls's egalitarian liberalism, citizens relate to each other as equals within a social order defined by reciprocity, instead of within the unjust status hierarchies familiar from today.

Significant political and economic inequalities are often associated with inequalities of social status that encourage those of lower status to be viewed both by themselves and by others as inferior. This may arouse widespread attitudes of deference and servility, on one side, and a will to dominate and arrogance on the other. These effects of social and economic inequalities can be serious evils and the attitudes they engender great vices…Fixed status ascribed by birth, or by gender or race, is particularly odious (*JF*, 131).

Justice as fairness aims to describe a just arrangement of the major political and social institutions of a liberal society: the political constitution, the legal system, the economy, the family, and so on. Rawls calls the arrangement of these institutions a society's *basic structure*. The basic structure is the location of justice because these institutions distribute the main benefits and burdens of social life: who will receive social recognition, who will have which basic rights, who will have opportunities to get what kind of work, what the distribution of income and wealth will be, and so on.

The form of a society's basic structure will have profound effects on the lives of citizens. The basic structure will influence not only citizens' life prospects, but more deeply their goals, their attitudes, their relationships, and their characters. Institutions that will have such pervasive influence on people's lives require justification. Since leaving one's society is not a realistic option for most people, the justification cannot be that citizens have consented to a basic structure by staying in the country. And since the rules of any basic structure will be coercively enforced, often with serious penalties, the demand to justify the imposition of any particular set of rules intensifies further.

In setting out justice as fairness, Rawls assumes that the liberal society in question is marked by reasonable pluralism as described above, and also that it is under reasonably favorable conditions: that there are enough resources for it to be possible for everyone's basic needs to be met. Rawls makes the simplifying assumption that the society is self-sufficient and closed, so that citizens enter it only by birth and leave it only at death. He also confines his attention mainly to ideal theory, putting aside non-ideal theory such as on criminal justice.

Social cooperation in some form is necessary for citizens to be able to lead decent lives. Yet citizens are not indifferent to how the benefits and burdens of cooperation will be divided amongst them. Rawls's principles of justice as fairness articulate the central liberal ideas that cooperation should be fair to all citizens regarded as free and as equals. The distinctive interpretation that Rawls gives to these concepts can be seen as combining a negative and a positive thesis.

Rawls's negative thesis starts with the idea that citizens do not deserve to be born into a rich or a poor family, to be born naturally more or less gifted than others, to be born female or male, to be born a member of a particular racial group, and so on. Since these features of persons are morally arbitrary in this sense, citizens are not entitled to more of the benefits of social cooperation simply because of them. For example, the fact that a citizen was born rich, white, and male provides no reason in itself for this citizen to be favored by social institutions.

This negative thesis does not say how social goods should be distributed; it merely clears the decks. Rawls's positive distributive thesis is equality-based reciprocity. All social goods are to be distributed equally, unless an unequal distribution would be to everyone's advantage. The guiding idea is that since citizens are fundamentally equal, reasoning about justice should begin from a presumption that cooperatively-produced goods should be equally divided. Justice then requires that any inequalities must benefit all citizens, and particularly must benefit those who will have the least. Equality sets the baseline; from there any inequalities must improve everyone's situation, and especially the situation of the worst-off. These strong requirements of equality and reciprocal advantage are hallmarks of Rawls's theory of justice.

These guiding ideas of justice as fairness are given institutional form by its two principles of justice:

First Principle: Each person has the same indefeasible claim to a fully adequate scheme of equal basic liberties, which scheme is compatible with the same scheme of liberties for all;

Second Principle: Social and economic inequalities are to satisfy two conditions:

a. They are to be attached to offices and positions open to all under conditions of *fair equality of opportunity*;
b. They are to be to the greatest benefit of the least-advantaged members of society (the *difference principle*) (*JF*, 42–43).

The first principle of equal basic liberties is to be embodied in the political constitution, while the second principle applies primarily to laws governing economic institutions. Fulfillment of the first principle takes priority over fulfillment of the second principle, and within the second principle fair equality of opportunity takes priority over the difference principle.

The first principle affirms that all citizens should have the familiar basic rights and liberties: liberty of conscience and freedom of association, freedom of speech and liberty of the person, the rights to vote, to hold public office, to be treated in accordance with the rule of law, and so on. The first principle accords these rights and liberties to all citizens equally. Unequal rights would not benefit those who would get a lesser share of the rights, so justice requires equal rights for all, in all normal circumstances.

Rawls's first principle confirms widespread convictions about the importance of equal basic rights and liberties. Two further features make this principle distinctive. First is its priority: the basic rights and liberties must not be traded off against other social goods. The first principle disallows, for instance, a policy that would give draft exemptions to college students on the grounds that educated civilians will increase economic productivity. The draft is a drastic infringement on basic liberties, and if a draft is implemented then all who are able to serve must be equally subject to it, even if this means slower growth. Citizens' equal liberty must have priority over economic policy.

The second distinctive feature of Rawls's first principle is that it requires *fair value of the political liberties*. The political liberties are a subset of the basic liberties, concerned with the right to hold public office, the right to affect the outcome of national elections and so on. For these liberties, Rawls requires that citizens should be not only formally but also substantively equal. That is, citizens who are similarly endowed and motivated should have similar opportunities to hold office, to influence elections, and so on regardless of how rich or poor they are. This requirement of the fair value of the political liberties has major implications for how elections should be funded and run, as will be discussed below.

Rawls's second principle of justice has two parts. The first part, fair equality of opportunity, requires that citizens with the same talents and willingness to use them have the same educational and economic opportunities regardless of whether they were born rich or poor. "In all parts of society there are to be roughly the same prospects of culture and achievement for those similarly motivated and endowed".

So, for example, if we assume that natural endowments and the willingness to use them are evenly distributed across children born into different social classes, then within any type of occupation (generally specified) we should find that roughly one quarter of people in that occupation were born into the top 25% of the income distribution, one quarter were born into the second-highest 25% of the income distribution, one quarter were born into the second-lowest 25%, and one-quarter were born into the lowest 25%. Since class of origin is a morally arbitrary fact about citizens, justice does not allow class of origin to turn into unequal opportunities for education or meaningful work.

The second part of the second principle is the difference principle, which regulates the distribution of wealth and income. Allowing inequalities of wealth and income can lead to a larger social product: higher wages can cover the costs of training and education, for example, and can provide incentives to fill jobs that are more in demand. The difference principle allows inequalities of wealth and income, so long as these will be to everyone's advantage, and specifically to the advantage of those who will be worst off. The difference principle requires, that is, that any economic inequalities be to the greatest advantage of those who are advantaged least.

The difference principle is partly based on the negative thesis that the distribution of natural assets is undeserved. A citizen does not merit more of the social product simply because she was lucky enough to be born with the potential to develop skills that are currently in high demand. Yet this does not mean that everyone must get the same shares. The fact that citizens have different talents and abilities can be used to make everyone better off. In a society governed by the difference principle, citizens regard the distribution of natural endowments as a common asset that can benefit all. Those better endowed are welcome to use their gifts to make themselves better off, so long as their doing so also contributes to the good of those less well endowed.

The difference principle thus expresses a positive ideal, an ideal of social unity. In a society that satisfies the difference principle, citizens know that their economy works to everyone's benefit, and that those who were lucky enough to be born with greater natural potential are not getting richer at the expense of those who were less fortunate. One might contrast Rawls's positive ideal to Nozick's ideal of libertarian freedom, or to meritocratic ideas about economic justice that are dominant within many democracies. "In justice as fairness," Rawls says, "men agree to share one another's fate".

Having surveyed Rawls's two principles of justice as fairness, we can return to Rawls's interpretations of the liberal ideas that citizens are free and equal, and that society should be fair. Rawls uses these conceptions of citizens and society to construct the official justification for the two principles: the argument from the original position.

Rawls's interpretation of the idea that citizens are free is as follows. Citizens are free in that each sees herself as being entitled to make claims on social institutions in her own right—citizens are not slaves or serfs, dependent for their social status on others. Citizens are also free in that they see their public identities as independent of any particular comprehensive doctrine: a citizen who converts to Islam, or who recants her faith, will expect, for example, to retain all her political rights and liberties throughout the transition. Finally, citizens are free in being able to take responsibility for planning their own lives, given the opportunities and resources that they can reasonably expect.

Citizens are equal, Rawls says, in virtue of having the capacities to participate in social cooperation over a complete life. Citizens may have greater or lesser skills, talents, and powers "above the line" that cooperation requires, but differences above this line have no bearing on citizens' equal political status.

Rawlsian citizens are not only free and equal, they are also reasonable and rational. The idea that citizens are reasonable is familiar from political liberalism. Reasonable citizens have the capacity to abide by fair terms of cooperation, even at the expense of their own interests, provided that others are also willing to do so. In justice as fairness, Rawls calls this reasonableness the capacity for a *sense of justice*. Citizens are also rational: they have the capacity to pursue and revise their own view of what is valuable in human life. Rawls calls this the capacity for *a conception of the good*. Together these capacities are called the *two moral powers*.

Like every theory of justice (for example those of Locke, Rousseau, and Mill), justice as fairness requires an account of citizens' fundamental interests: what citizens need *qua* citizens. Rawls derives his account of *primary goods* from the conception of the citizen as free and equal, reasonable and rational. Primary goods are essential for developing and exercising the two moral powers, and are useful for pursuing a wide range of specific conceptions of the good life. Primary goods are these:

- The basic rights and liberties;
- Freedom of movement, and free choice among a wide range of occupations;
- The powers of offices and positions of responsibility;
- Income and wealth;
- The social bases of self-respect: the recognition by social institutions that gives citizens a sense of self-worth and the confidence to carry out their plans (*JF*, 58–59).

All citizens are assumed to have fundamental interests in getting more of these primary goods, and political institutions are to evaluate how well citizens are doing according to what primary goods they have. It is equalities and inequalities of these primary goods that, Rawls claims, are of the greatest political significance.

Rawls's conception of society is defined by fairness: social institutions are to be fair to all cooperating members of society, regardless of their race, gender, religion, class of origin, natural talents, reasonable conception of the good life, and so on.

Rawls also emphasizes *publicity* as an aspect of fairness. In what he calls a *well-ordered society* all citizens accept the principles of justice and know that their fellow citizens also do so, and all citizens recognize that the basic structure is just. The full philosophical justifications for the principles of justice are also knowable by and acceptable to all reasonable citizens.

The idea behind publicity is that since the principles for the basic structure will be coercively enforced on free citizens, they should stand up to public scrutiny. The publicity condition requires that a society's operative principles of justice not be too esoteric, and not be screens for deeper power relations. Fairness requires that, in "public political life, nothing need be hidden…there is no need for the illusions and delusions of ideology for society to work properly and for citizens to accept it willingly".

Rawls's conceptions of citizens and society are still quite abstract, and some might think innocuous. The *original position* aims to move from these abstract conceptions to determinate principles of social justice. It does so by translating the question: "What are fair terms of social cooperation for free and equal citizens?" into the question "What terms of cooperation would free and equal citizens agree to under fair conditions?" The move to agreement among citizens is what places Rawls's justice as fairness within the social contract tradition of Locke, Rousseau, and Kant.

The strategy of the original position is to construct a method of reasoning that models abstract ideas about justice so as to focus their power together onto the choice of principles. So Rawls's conceptions of citizens and of society are built into the design of the original position itself. Rawls's intent is that readers will see the outcome of the original position as justified because they will see how it embodies plausible understandings of citizens and society, and also because this outcome confirms many of their considered convictions about justice on specific issues.

The original position is a thought experiment: an imaginary situation in which each real citizen has a representative, and all of these representatives come to an agreement on which principles of justice should order the political institutions of the real citizens. This thought experiment is better than trying to get all real citizens actually to assemble in person to try to agree to principles of justice for their society. Even if that were possible, the bargaining among real citizens would be influenced by all sorts of factors irrelevant to justice, such as who could threaten the others most, or who could hold out for longest.

The original position abstracts from all such irrelevant factors. The original position is a fair situation in which each citizen is represented as only a free and equal citizen: each representative wants only what free and equal citizens want, and each tries to agree to principles for the basic structure while situated fairly with respect to the other representatives. The design of the original position thus models the ideas of freedom, equality, and fairness. For example, fairness and equality are modeled in the original position by the symmetrical situation of the parties: no citizen's representative is able to threaten any other citizen's representative, or to hold out longer for a better deal.

The most striking feature of the original position is the *veil of ignorance*, which prevents arbitrary facts about citizens from influencing the agreement among their representatives. As we have seen, Rawls holds that the fact that a citizen is of a certain race, class, and gender is no reason for social institutions to favor or disfavor her. Each representative in the original position is therefore deprived of knowledge of the race, class, and gender of the real citizen that they represent. In fact, the veil of ignorance deprives the parties of all facts about citizens that are irrelevant to the choice of principles of justice: not only facts about their race, class, and gender but also facts about their age, natural endowments, and more. Moreover the veil of ignorance also screens out specific information about what society is like right now, so as to get a clearer view of the permanent features of a just social system.

Behind the veil of ignorance, the informational situation of the parties that represent real citizens is as follows:

- Parties do not know
  - The race, ethnicity, gender, age, income, wealth, natural endowments, comprehensive doctrine, etc. of any of the citizens in society, or to which generation in the history of the society these citizens belong;

- The political system of the society, its class structure, economic system, or level of economic development.
- Parties do know
  - That citizens in the society have different comprehensive doctrines and plans of life; that all citizens have interests in more primary goods;
  - That the society is under conditions of moderate scarcity: there is enough to go around, but not enough for everyone to get what they want;
  - General facts and common sense about human social life; general conclusions of science (including economics and psychology) that are uncontroversial.

The veil of ignorance situates the representatives of free and equal citizens fairly with respect to one another. No party can press for agreement on principles that will arbitrarily favor the particular citizen they represent, because no party knows the specific attributes of the citizen they represent. The situation of the parties thus embodies reasonable conditions, within which the parties can make a rational agreement. Each party tries to agree to principles that will be best for the citizen they represent (i.e., that will maximize that citizen's share of primary goods). Since the parties are fairly situated, the agreement they reach will be fair to all actual citizens.

The design of the original position also models other aspects of Rawls's conceptions of citizens and society. For example, the publicity of a well-ordered society is modeled by the fact that the parties must choose among principles that can be publicly endorsed by all citizens. There are also some assumptions that make the hypothetical agreement determinate and decisive: the parties are not motivated by envy (i.e., by how much citizens besides their own end up with); the parties are neither risk-seeking nor risk-averse; and the parties must make a final agreement on principles for the basic structure: there are no "do-overs" after the veil of ignorance is lifted and the parties learn which real citizen they represent.

The argument from the original position has two parts. In the first part, the parties agree to principles of justice. In the second part, the parties check that a society ordered by these principles could be stable over time. Rawls only attempts to show that his two principles of justice as fairness would be favored over utilitarian principles, since he sees utilitarianism as the main competing tradition of reasoning about justice. The parties are thus presented with a choice between Rawls's two principles and utilitarian principles, and asked which principles they would prefer to agree to.

The first part of the original position contains two fundamental comparisons between Rawls's principles and utilitarian principles. In the first comparison, the parties compare Rawls's principles to *the principle of average utility*: the principle that the basic structure should be arranged so as to produce the highest level of utility averaged among all citizens. Rawls argues that the parties would favor his principles in this comparison, because the first principle of justice as fairness secures equal liberties for all citizens.

In this first comparison, Rawls argues that it is rational for the parties to use *maximin* reasoning: to maximize the minimum level of primary goods that the citizens they represent might find themselves with. And maximin reasoning, he says, favors justice as fairness.

Under average utilitarianism, Rawls argues, the basic liberties of some citizens might be restricted for the sake of greater benefits to other citizens. For example, restricting the political and religious liberties of a weak minority might work to the benefit of the majority, and so produce a higher average level of utility in the society. A party in the original position will find the possibility that their citizen might be denied political and religious liberties intolerable, given that the party could instead secure equal liberties for their citizen by choosing justice as fairness. A party will not be willing to gamble with the political standing and deepest commitments of the citizen they represent, Rawls says, when they could safeguard the standing and commitments of their citizen even if their citizen turns out to be in a weak minority.

Moreover, Rawls says, a society ordered by the principles of justice as fairness has other advantages over a utilitarian society. Securing equal basic liberties for all encourages a spirit of cooperation among citizens on a basis of mutual respect, and takes divisive conflicts about whether to deny liberties to some citizens off of the political agenda. By contrast, a utilitarian society would be riven by mutual suspicions, as different groups put forward highly speculative arguments that average utility could be increased by implementing their partisan policies. Rawls's first principle, by securing permanent equal liberties for all citizens, increases social harmony by making it easier for justice to be seen to be done. The balance of considerations in favor of justice as fairness over average utility here is, Rawls claims, decisive.

In the second fundamental comparison, the parties are offered a choice between justice as fairness and *the principle of restricted utility*. The principle of restricted utility is identical to Rawls's two principles, except that the difference principle is replaced with a principle which says that the distribution of wealth and income should maximize average utility, constrained by a guaranteed minimum level of income for all. While the first comparison turned on the importance of the basic liberties, the second comparison contains Rawls's formal argument for the difference principle.

Maximin reasoning plays no role in the argument for the difference principle. Nor does aversion to uncertainty (*JF*, xvii, 43, 95, 96).

In this second comparison, Rawls argues that the parties will favor justice as fairness because its principles provide a better basis for enduring cooperation among all citizens. The difference principle, he says, asks less of the better-off than restricted utility asks of the worst-off. Under the difference principle, he says, those who are better endowed are permitted to gain more wealth and income, on the condition that their doing so also benefits their fellow citizens. Under restricted utility, by contrast, those living at the minimum will suspect that their interests have been sacrificed to make the better-off better off still. These citizens at the minimum may become cynical about their society, and withdraw from active participation in public life.

Moreover, it is again difficult to maintain a public agreement as to which economic policies actually will maximize average utility, and debates over where to set the guaranteed minimum may lead to mistrust among social classes. The difference principle instead encourages mutual trust and the cooperative virtues by instantiating an ideal of economic reciprocity. Each party will see the advantages for the citizen they represent of securing the more harmonious social world of justice as fairness.

Having selected the two principles of justice as fairness, the parties turn to the second part of the original position: the check that these principles can order a society stably over time. The parties check, that is, whether those who grow up under institutions arranged by these principles will develop sufficient willingness to abide by them that the principles can serve as the focus of an enduring overlapping consensus.

Rawls argues that the parties will see that his two principles are congruent with each citizen's good. Under the two principles, the society's basic institutions affirm the freedom and equality of each citizen, giving a public basis for each citizen's self-respect. This public basis of self-respect is vital for citizens to be able to pursue their life plans with energy and confidence. Citizens will also see that the basic liberties allow sufficient social space for them to pursue their reasonable conceptions of the good. Whether poor or rich, citizens will tend not to be envious or imperious, as they will see how the economy works toward the reciprocal advantage of all. And citizens may be satisfied by reflecting on the collective good that they can achieve with each other, by working together to maintain just institutions over time.

Given that the two principles are congruent with citizens' good, Rawls argues that it is reasonable to suppose that citizens will develop a desire to act in accordance with them. People become attached to people and institutions that they see benefiting them, and the two principles create a social world in which each citizen can pursue her own ends on a basis of mutual respect with other citizens. Since this is experienced as a good, the principles will gain citizens' willing and stable allegiance. "The most stable conception of justice," Rawls says, "is one that is perspicuous to our reason, congruent with our good, and rooted not in abnegation but in affirmation of the self" (*TJ*, 261).

The two parts of the argument for justice as fairness above occur at the first stage of the original position. At this first stage, the parties also agree to a *principle of just savings* to regulate how much each generation must save for future generations. Since the parties do not know which era the citizens they represent live in, it is rational for them to choose a savings principle that is fair to all generations. Rawls says that the parties need not choose a savings principle that requires endless economic growth. Rather, the parties may prefer a Millian "steady state" of zero real growth, once a generation has been reached in which the two principles are satisfied.

After agreeing on the two principles and a principle of just savings, the parties then proceed further through the *four-stage sequence*, tailoring these general principles to the particular conditions of the society of the citizens they represent. Through this four-stage sequence, the veil of ignorance that screens out information about society's general features gradually becomes thinner, and the parties use the new information to decide on progressively more determinate applications of the principles already agreed upon. The parties, that is, progressively fill in the institutional details of what justice requires in the real world.

At the second stage of the original position, the parties are given more information about society's political culture and economic development, and take on the task of crafting a *constitution* that realizes the two principles of justice. At the third stage, the parties learn still more about the details of society, and agree to specific *legislation* that realize the two principles within the constitutional framework decided at the second stage. At the fourth stage, the parties have full information about society, and reason as *judges and administrators* to apply the previously-agreed legislation to particular cases. When the four stages are complete, the principles of justice as fairness are fully articulated for society's political life.

To illustrate: at the constitutional (second) and legislative (third) stages, the parties specify basic liberties such as "freedom of thought" into more particular rights, like the right to free political speech. The right to political speech is itself then further specified as the right to criticize the government, the rights protecting the press from political interference, and so on. Through the four-stage sequence, the parties also adjust the basic liberties to fit with one another and with other values, always aiming for an overall scheme of liberties that will best enable citizens to develop and exercise their two moral powers and pursue their determinate conceptions of the good (*PL*, 289–371).

At the later stages, the parties also work out the institutions that will be necessary to realize the fair value of the equal political liberties. On this topic, Rawls is adamant: unless there are public funds for elections, restrictions on campaign contributions, and substantially equal access to the media, politics will be captured by concentrations of private economic power. This will make it impossible for equally-able citizens to have equal opportunities to influence politics regardless of their wealth, as fair value demands. As he says in a discussion of public reason, public deliberation must be "set free from the curse of money".

The parties attempt to realize the second principle of justice at the legislative stage, by shaping the laws that regulate property, contract, taxation, inheritance, hiring, minimum wages, and so on. Their task is not to allocate some fixed set of goods that appear from nowhere, but rather to devise a set of institutions for education, production, and distribution whose operation will realize fair equality of opportunity and the difference principle over time.

For fair equality of opportunity, Rawls emphasizes that laws and policies must go beyond merely preventing discrimination in education and hiring. To ensure fair opportunity regardless of social class of origin, the state must also fund high-quality education for the less well-off. Moreover, the state must also guarantee both a basic minimum income and health care for all.

On realizing the difference principle, Rawls says that the goal is an economic order that maximizes the position of the worst-off group (e.g., unskilled laborers, or those with less than half of the median wealth and income over their lifetimes). Given that institutions realizing the prior principles are already in place, this should be approximately achievable by, for example, varying marginal rates of tax and tax exemptions.

Rawls explicitly rejects the welfare state. Welfare-state capitalism leaves control of the economy in the hands of a group of rich private actors. It therefore fails to ensure for all citizens enough resources to have roughly equal chances of influencing politics, or to have sufficiently equal opportunities in education and employment. The welfare state therefore tends to generate a demoralized under-class.

Laissez-faire capitalism is even worse for equality than the welfare state along these dimensions. And a socialist command economy would put too much power in the hands of the state, again endangering political equality and also threatening basic liberties such as free choice of employment.

Justice as fairness, Rawls says, favors either a *property-owning democracy* or liberal (democratic) socialism. The government of a property-owning democracy takes steps to encourage widespread ownership of productive assets and broad access to education and training. Liberal socialism is similar, but features worker-managed firms. The aim of both systems of political economy is to enable all citizens, even the least advantaged, to manage their own affairs within a context of significant social and economic equality. "The least advantaged are not, if all goes well, the unfortunate and unlucky—objects of our charity and compassion, much less our pity—but those to whom reciprocity is owed as a matter of basic justice".

Rawls describes the original position as a useful device for reaching greater reflective equilibrium. He holds that the value of the original position as a method of reasoning is affirmed when it selects the first principle of justice, since the first principle accords with many people's settled convictions about the importance of assuring the basic rights and liberties for all. Having gained credibility by confirming these settled moral judgments, the original position then goes on to select principles for issues on which people's judgments may be less certain, such as how society should structure employment opportunities, and what a just distribution of wealth and income might be.

In this way, the original position first confirms and then extends common judgments about justice. For Rawls it is important that the same method of reasoning that explains the equal basic liberties also justifies more political and economic equality than many people might have initially expected. The momentum of the argument for the first principle carries through to the argument for the second principle. Those who believe in equal basic liberties, but who reject the other egalitarian features of justice as fairness, must try to find some other route to justifying those basic liberties.

The original position is also the crux of Rawls's metaethical theory, *political constructivism*. Political constructivism is Rawls's account of the objectivity and validity of political judgments.

The original position embodies, Rawls says, all of the relevant conceptions of person and society, and principles of practical reasoning, for making judgments about justice. When there is an overlapping consensus focused on justice as fairness, the original position specifies a shared public perspective from which all citizens can reason about the principles of justice and their application to their society's institutions. Judgments made from this perspective are then objectively correct, in the sense of giving reasons to citizens to act regardless of their actual motivations, or the reasons they think they have within their particular points of view.

Political constructivism does not maintain that the original position shows that the principles of justice as fairness are true. Questions of truth are ones about which reasonable citizens may disagree, and are to be addressed by each citizen from within her own comprehensive doctrine. Judgments made from the original position are, however, valid, or as Rawls says, reasonable.

With the theories of legitimacy and justice for a self-contained liberal society completed, Rawls then extends his approach to international relations with the next in his sequence of theories: the law of peoples.

Rawls assumes that no tolerable world state could be stable. He cites Kant in asserting that a world government would either be a global despotism or beleaguered by groups fighting to gain their political independence. So the law of peoples will be international, not cosmopolitan: it will be a foreign policy that guides a liberal society in its interactions with other societies, both liberal and non-liberal.

Rawls describes the main ideas motivating his law of peoples as follows:

Two main ideas motivate the Law of Peoples. One is that the great evils of human history—unjust war and oppression, religious persecution and the denial of liberty of conscience, starvation and poverty, not to mention genocide and mass murder—follow from political injustice, with its own cruelties and callousness…The other main idea, obviously connected with the first, is that, once the gravest forms of political injustice are eliminated by following just (or at least decent) social policies and establishing just (or at least decent) basic institutions, these great evils will eventually disappear.

The most important feature of the "realistic utopia" that Rawls envisages in *The Law of Peoples* is that the great evils of human history no longer occur. The most important condition for this realistic utopia to come about is that all societies are internally well-ordered: that all have just, or at least decent, domestic political institutions.

Much of Rawls's presentation of the law of peoples parallels the presentations of political liberalism and justice as fairness. As a liberal society has a basic structure of institutions so, Rawls says, there is an international basic structure. While Rawls does not say that the international basic structure has a pervasive impact on the life chances of individuals, the rules of this basic structure are coercively enforced (for example, Iraq's invasion of Kuwait in 1990 was coercively reversed by a coalition of other countries). The principles that should regulate this international basic structure thus require justification. The justification of these principles must accommodate the fact that there is even more pluralism in worldviews among contemporary societies than there is within a single liberal society.

Rawls puts forward eight principles for ordering the international basic structure:

1. Peoples are free and independent, and their freedom and independence are to be respected by other peoples.

2. Peoples are to observe treaties and undertakings.
3. Peoples are equal and are parties to the agreements that bind them.
4. Peoples are to observe the duty of nonintervention (except to address grave violations of human rights).
5. Peoples have a right of self-defense, but no right to instigate war for reasons other than self-defense.
6. Peoples are to honor human rights.
7. Peoples are to observe certain specified restrictions in the conduct of war.
8. Peoples have a duty to assist other peoples living under unfavorable conditions that prevent their having a just or decent political and social regime.

All of these principles, with the exception of the last one, are familiar from contemporary international law (though Rawls's list of human rights for principles 4 and 6 is shorter than the list in international law). Rawls also leaves room for his law of peoples to accommodate various organizations that may help societies to increase their political and economic coordination, such as idealized versions of a United Nations, a World Trade Organization, and a World Bank.

The actors in Rawls's international theory are not individuals (citizens) but societies (*peoples*). A people is a group of individuals ruled by a common government, bound together by common sympathies, and firmly attached to a common conception of right and justice. "People" is a moralized concept, and not all states currently on the world map qualify as such.

Rawls's conception of peoples within the law of peoples parallels his conception of citizens within justice as fairness. Peoples see themselves as free in the sense of being rightfully politically independent; and as equal in regarding themselves as equally deserving of recognition and respect. Peoples are reasonable in that they will honor fair terms of cooperation with other peoples, even at cost to their own interests, given that other peoples will also honor those terms. Reasonable peoples are thus unwilling to try to impose their political or social ideals on other reasonable peoples. They satisfy the criterion of reciprocity with respect to one another.

Rawls describes the fundamental interests of a people as follows:

- Protecting its political independence, its territory, and the security of its citizens;
- Maintaining its political and social institutions and its civic culture;
- Securing its proper self-respect as a people, which rests on its citizens' awareness of its history and cultural accomplishments.

Rawls contrasts peoples with *states*. A state, Rawls says, is moved by the desires to enlarge its territory, or to convert other societies to its religion, or to enjoy the power of ruling over others, or to increase its relative economic strength. Peoples are not states, and as we will see peoples may treat societies that act like states as international outlaws.

Peoples are of two types, depending on the nature of their domestic political institutions. *Liberal peoples* satisfy the requirements of political liberalism: they have legitimate liberal constitutions, and they have governments that are under popular control and not driven by large concentration of private economic power.

Decent peoples are not internally just from a liberal perspective. Their basic institutions do not recognize reasonable pluralism or embody any interpretation of the liberal ideas of free and equal citizens cooperating fairly. The institutions of a decent society may be organized around a single comprehensive doctrine, such as a dominant religion. The political system may not be democratic, and women or members of minority religions may be excluded from public office. Nevertheless, decent peoples are well-ordered enough, Rawls says, to merit equal membership in international society.

Like all peoples, decent peoples do not have aggressive foreign policies. Beyond this, Rawls describes one type of decent society—a *decent hierarchical society*—to illustrate what decency requires.

A decent hierarchical society's basic structure specifies a decent system of social cooperation. First, it secures a core list of *human rights*. Second, its political system takes the fundamental interests of all persons into account through a *decent consultation hierarchy*. This means that the government genuinely consults with the representatives of all social groups, which together represent all persons in the society, and that the government justifies its laws and policies to these groups. The government does not close down protests, and responds to any protests with conscientious replies. The government also supports the right of citizens to emigrate.

Rawls imagines a decent hierarchical society that he calls "Kazanistan." In Kazanistan, Islam is the favored religion, and only Muslims can hold the high office. However non-Muslim religions may be practiced without fear, and believers in them are encouraged to take part in the civic culture of the wider society. Minorities are not subject to arbitrary discrimination by law, or treated as inferior by Muslims. Kazanistan would qualify, Rawls says, as a decent, well-ordered member of the society of peoples, entitled to respectful toleration and equal treatment by other peoples.

Liberal peoples tolerate decent peoples, and indeed treat them as equals. Not to do so, Rawls says, would be to fail to express sufficient respect for acceptable ways of ordering a society. Liberal peoples should recognize the good of national self-determination, and let decent societies decide their futures for themselves. The government of a liberal people should not criticize decent peoples for failing to be liberal, or set up incentives for them to become more so. Criticism and inducements may cause bitterness and resentment within decent peoples, and so be counter-productive.

Indeed public reason imposes duties of civility upon the members of international society, just as it does upon members of a liberal society. Government officials and candidates for high office should explain their foreign policy positions to other peoples in terms of the principles and values of the law of peoples, and should avoid reliance on contentious parochial reasons that all peoples cannot reasonably share.

One major reason that liberal peoples tolerate decent peoples, Rawls says, is that decent peoples secure for all persons within their territory a core list of human rights. These core human rights include rights to subsistence, security, personal property, and formal equality before the law, as well as freedoms from slavery, protections of ethnic groups against genocide, and some measure of liberty of conscience (but not, as we have seen, a right to democratic participation). These core human rights are the minimal conditions required for persons to be able to engage in social cooperation in any real sense, so any well-ordered society must protect them.

The role of human rights in the law of peoples is thus to set limits on international toleration. Any society that guarantees Rawls's list of human rights is to be immune from coercive intervention from other peoples. Societies that violate human rights overstep the limits of toleration, and may rightly be subject to economic sanctions or even military intervention.

The international original position parallels the domestic original position of justice as fairness. This original position answers the question: "What terms of cooperation would free and equal peoples (liberal and decent) agree to under fair conditions?" The strategy is to build the conception of peoples into the design of this original position, along with restrictions on reasons for favoring basic principles of international law. The strategy, that is, is to describe reasonable conditions under which a rational agreement on principles can be made.

In the international original position, representatives of each people agree on principles for the international basic structure. Each party is behind a veil of ignorance, deprived of information about the people they represent, such as the size of its territory and population, and its relative political and economic strength. Each party tries to do the best they can for the people they represent, in terms of the fundamental interests that all peoples have.

Rawls claims that the parties in the international original position would favor the eight principles listed above. Starting from a baseline of equality and independence, the parties would see no reason to introduce inequalities into the relationships among peoples (beyond certain functional inequalities in the design of cooperative organizations, such as richer countries contributing more to an idealized United Nations). The parties would reject international utilitarian principles, as no people is prepared to accept that it should sacrifice its fundamental interests for the sake of greater total global utility.

After selecting the eight principles of the law of peoples, the parties next check that these principles can stably order international relations over time. Analogously to the domestic case, the parties will see that the principles of the law of peoples affirm the good of peoples, and that peoples will develop trust and confidence in one another as all willingly continue to abide by these principles. The stability of the international political order will thus be stability for the right reasons (and not a mere *modus vivendi*), since each people will affirm the principles as its first-best option whatever the international balance of power might become.

Rawls also attempts to draw empirical support for his stability argument from the literature on the democratic peace. Social scientists have found that historically democracies have tended not to go to war with one another. Rawls explains this by saying that liberal societies are, because of their internal political structures, *satisfied*. Liberal peoples have no desires for imperial glory, territorial expansion, or to convert others to their religion, and whatever goods and services they need from other countries they can obtain through trade. Liberal peoples, Rawls says, have no reasons to fight aggressive wars, so a genuine peace can endure among them. And since decent peoples are defined as non-aggressive, any decent people can join this liberal peace as well.

Once the parties have agreed to the eight principles of the law of peoples, they then continue to specify these principles more precisely in a process analogous to the domestic four-stage sequence.

The principles selected in the international original position contain provisions for non-ideal situations: situations in which nations are unwilling to comply with the ideal principles, or are unable to cooperate on their terms. These provisions are embedded in principles 4 through 8 of the law of peoples.

Outlaw states are non-compliant: they threaten the peace by attempting to expand their power and influence, or by violating the human rights of those within their territory. The principles of the law of peoples allow peoples to fight these outlaw states in self-defense, and to take coercive actions against them to stop their violations of human rights. In any military confrontations with outlaw states, peoples must obey the principles of the just prosecution of war, such as avoiding direct attacks on enemy civilians in all but the most desperate circumstances. The aim of war, Rawls says, must be to bring all societies to honor the law of peoples, and eventually to become fully participating members of international society.

Burdened societies struggle with social and economic conditions that make it difficult for them to maintain either liberal or decent institutions. A burdened society may lack sufficient material or social resources to support a scheme of social cooperation, perhaps because its population has grown beyond its territory's means to support it. It is the basic structure and political culture of a society that are most crucial for its self-sufficiency; the international community must help a burdened society to rise above this threshold. The law of peoples (eighth principle) requires that burdened peoples be assisted until they can handle their own affairs (i.e., become well-ordered).

This duty of assistance is Rawls's greatest divergence from the rules of today's international law. Accepting this duty would require significant changes in how nations respond to global poverty and failed states.

Rawls's vision is of a perpetually peaceful and cooperative international order, where liberal and decent peoples stand ready to pacify aggressive states, to secure core human rights, and to help struggling countries until they become self-sufficient.

Compared to other theories, Rawls's international theory has limited ambitions. Officials of democratic societies can do little more than hope that decent societies will become internally more tolerant and democratic. Once the duty to assist burdened peoples is satisfied, there are no further requirements on international economic distributions: for Rawls, international economic inequalities are of no political concern as such. Moreover, individuals around the world may suffer greatly from bad luck, and they may be haunted by spiritual emptiness. These are not concerns reached by a Rawlsian foreign policy.

The limited practical goal of Rawls's law of peoples is the elimination of the great evils of human history: unjust war and oppression, religious persecution and the denial of liberty of conscience, starvation and poverty, genocide and mass murder. The limits of this ambition mean that there will be much in the world to which Rawls's political philosophy offers no reconciliation.

Nevertheless, while Rawls's vision is limited, it is also utopian. To believe that Rawls's vision is possible is to believe that individuals are not inevitably selfish or amoral, and that international relations can be more than merely a contest for domination, wealth, and glory. Human life, and human history, need not be merely a Hobbesian "perpetual and restless desire of power after power" (1651, 58). Affirming the possibility of a just and peaceful future can inoculate us against a cynicism that undermines the decency, reciprocity, and reasonableness that exist now and that may grow from now on.

"By showing how the social world may realize the features of a realistic utopia," Rawls says, "political philosophy provides a long-term goal of political endeavor, and in working toward it gives meaning to what we can do today".

Although contract theorists differ in their account of the reasons of individuals, with some being attracted to more objectivist accounts (Scanlon 2013), most follow Hobbes in modeling individual reasons as subjective, motivationally internal, or at least agent-relative. This may be because of skepticism about moral reasons generally (Harman 1975, Gauthier 1986, Binmore 1998), a conviction about the overwhelming importance of self-interest to the social order (Hobbes 1651, Buchanan 2000 [1975], Brennan and Buchanan 1985), a concern to take seriously the disagreement of individual view in modern society (Gaus 2011a, 2016; Muldoon 2017; Moehler 2014, 2015, 2018) or because this approach is consistent with the most well-developed theories of rational choice in the social sciences (Binmore 2005, Buchanan 2000 [1975]). In any case, the reasons individuals have for agreeing to some rules or principles are importantly their own reasons, not "good reasons" from the impartial perspective. Of course, those same individuals may care about what they perceive to be the impartial good or some other non-individualistic notion—they need not be egoists—but what they care about, and so their reasons will differ from one another. This point, as Rawls highlights in his later work, is crucial to understanding political justification in a diverse society where members of a society cannot reasonably be expected to have similar conceptions of the good (Rawls 1996). Recent contractarian accounts put even greater weight on heterogeneity (Southwood 2010, Gaus 2016, Muldoon 2017, Moehler 2018, Sugden 2018).

How contract theorists model the representative choosers (N) is determined by *our* (actual) justificatory problem and what is relevant to solving it. A major divide among contemporary social contract theories thus involves defining the justificatory problem. A distinction is often drawn between the Hobbesian/Lockean ("contractarian") and Rousseavian/Kantian ("contractualist") interpretations of the justificatory problem. These categories are imprecise, and there is often as much difference within these two approaches as between them, yet, nevertheless, the distinction can be useful for isolating some key disputes in contemporary social contract theory.

Among those "contractarians" who—*very* roughly—can be called followers of Hobbes and/or Locke, the crucial justificatory task is, as Gauthier (1991, 16) puts it, to resolve the "foundational crisis" of morality:

From the standpoint of the agent, moral considerations present themselves as constraining his choices and action, in ways independent of his desires, aims, and interests…And so we ask, what reason can a person have for recognizing and accepting a constraint that is independent of his desires and interests?…[W]hat justifies paying attention to morality, rather than dismissing it as an appendage of outworn beliefs?

If our justificatory problem is not simply to understand what morality requires, but whether morality ought to be paid attention to, or instead dismissed as a superstition based on outmoded metaphysical theories, then obviously the parties to the agreement must not employ moral judgments in their reasoning. Another version of this concern is Gregory Kavka's (1984) description of the project to reconcile morality with prudence. On both these accounts, the aim of the contract is to show that commitment to morality is an effective way to further one's non-moral aims and interests, answering the question "why be moral?" The political version of this project, is similar, though the target of justification is a set of political rules or constitution rather than morality generally (Buchanan 2000 [1975], Coleman 1985, Kavka 1986, Sudden 2018). This "contractarian" project is reductionist in a pretty straightforward sense: it derives moral or political reasons from non-moral ones. Or, to use Rawls's terminology, it attempts to generate the reasonable out of the rational (1996, 53).

The reductionist approach is appealing for several reasons. First, insofar as we doubt the normative basis of moral reasons, such a reductionist strategy promises to ground morality—or at least a very basic version of it—on the prosaic normativity of the basic requirements of instrumentalist practical rationality (Moehler 2018). The justificatory question "why be moral?" is transformed into the less troubling question "why be rational?" Second, even if we recognize that moral reasons are, in some sense, genuine, contractarians like Kavka also want to show that prudent individuals, not independently motivated by morality would have reason to reflectively endorse morality. Furthermore, if we have reason to suspect that some segment of the population is, in fact, knavish then we have good defensive reasons based on stability to build our social institutions and morality so as to restrain those who are only motivated by prudence, even if we suspect that most persons are not so motivated. Geoffrey Brennan and James Buchanan argue that a version of Gresham's law holds in political and social institutions that "bad behavior drives out good and that all persons will be led themselves by even the presence of a few self-seekers to adopt self-interested behavior" (2008 [1985], 68). We need not think people are mostly self-seeking to think that social institutions and morality should be justified to and restrain those who are.

On the other hand, "contractualists," such as Rawls, John Harsanyi (1977), Thomas Scanlon (1998), Stephen Darwall (2006), Nicholas Southwood (2010) and Gerald Gaus (2011) attribute ethical or political values to the deliberative parties, as well as a much more substantive, non-instrumentalist form of practical reasoning. The kinds of surrogates that model the justificatory problem are already so situated that their deliberations will be framed by ethico-political considerations. The agents' deliberations are not, as with the Hobbesian theorists, carried out in purely prudential or instrumentalist terms, but they are subject to the 'veil of ignorance' or other substantive conditions. Here the core justificatory problem is not whether the very idea of moral and political constraints makes sense, but what sorts of moral or political principles meet certain basic moral demands, such as treating all as free and equal moral persons, or not subjecting any person to the will or judgment of another (Reiman 1990, chap. 1). This approach, then, is non-reductionist in the sense that justification is not derived from the non-moral.

A benefit of the non-reductive approach is that the choosers in the contractual procedure (N) share many of the normative concerns of their actual counterparts (N^*). This should ensure a closer normative link between the two parties and allow for the contract to generate a thicker, more substantive morality, presumably closer to that already held by N^*. Whether this is so, however, depends on how closely the non-reductionist model of rationality is to the reasoning of actual individuals.

At this point, the debate seems to be centered on two positions, which we might call the *robustness* and *sensitivity* positions. According to the proponents of robustness, whatever else moral agents may disagree about, we can safely assume that they would all be committed to basic standards of rationality (Moehler 2013, 2017, 2018). We should thus suppose this same basic, shared conception of rationality and agency: when people fall short of more moralistic ideals and virtue, the contract will still function. It will be robust. According to this view, we are better off following Hume (1741) in assuming every person to be a knave, even though that maxim is false in fact.

The sensitivity position rejects this, holding that, if, in fact, individuals in N^* are not resolutely self-interested, the problems of N, resolutely self-interested individuals, and their contractual solutions, will be inappropriate to N^*. Perhaps whereas N^* can count on social trust, the self-interested contractors will find it elusive and arrive at second-best alternatives that trusting folks would find silly and inefficient. Indeed, the sensitivity theorist may insist that even if the self-interested agents can talk themselves into acting as moral agents they do so for the wrong sort of reasons (Gaus 2011, 185ff).

Idealization and Identification

The core idea of social contract theories, we have been stressing, is that the deliberation of the parties is supposed to model the justificatory problem of ordinary moral agents and citizens. Now this pulls social contract theories in two opposing directions. On the one hand, if the deliberations of the hypothetical parties are to model *our* problem and their conclusions are to be of relevance to us, the parties must be similar to us. The closer the parties are to "you and me" the better their deliberations will model you and me, and be of relevance to us. On the other hand, the point of contract theories is to make headway on our justificatory problem by constructing parties that are models of you and me, suggesting that some idealization is necessary and salutary in constructing a model of justification. To recognize that some forms of idealization are problematic does not imply that we should embrace what Gaus has called "justificatory populism" that every person in society must actually assent to the social and moral institutions in question (Gaus 1996, 130–131). Such a standard would take us back to the older social contract tradition based on direct consent and as we argue in §3, modern contract theories are concerned with appeals to our reason, not our self-binding power of consent.

Despite possible problems, there are two important motivations behind idealization in the modeling of the deliberative parties. First, you and I, as we now are, may be confused about what considerations are relevant to our justificatory problem. We have biases and false beliefs; to make progress on solving our problem of justification we wish, as far as possible, to see what the result would be if we only reasoned correctly from sound and relevant premises. So in constructing the hypothetical parties we wish to idealize them in this way. Ideal deliberation theorists like Jürgen Habermas (1985) and Southwood (2010), in their different ways, are deeply concerned with this reason for idealization. On the face of it, such idealization does not seem especially troublesome, since our ultimate concern is with what is justified, and so we want the deliberations of the parties to track good reasons. But if we idealize too far from individuals and citizens as they presently are (e.g., suppose we posit that they are fully rational in the sense that they know all the implications of all their beliefs and have perfect information) their deliberations may not help much in solving our justificatory problems. We will not be able to identify with their solutions (Suikkanen 2014, Southwood 2019). For example, suppose that hyper-rational and perfectly informed parties would have no religious beliefs, so they would not be concerned with freedom of religion or the role of religion of political decision making. But our problem is that among tolerably reasonable but far from perfectly rational citizens, pluralism of religious belief is inescapable. Consequently, to gain insight into the justificatory problem among citizens of limited rationality, the parties must model our imperfect rationality.

Homogeneity vs. Heterogeneity

Social contract theories model representative choosers (N) so as to render the choice situation determinate. This goal of determinacy, however, can have the effect of eliminating the pluralism of the parties that was the original impetus for contracting in the first place. In his *Lectures on the History of Political Philosophy* Rawls tells us that "a normalization of interests attributed to the parties" is "common to social contract doctrines" and it is necessary to unify the perspectives of the different parties so as to construct a "shared point of view" (2007, 226). Here Rawls seems to be suggesting that to achieve determinacy in the contract procedure it is necessary to "normalize" the perspectives of the parties.

The problem is this. Suppose that the parties to the contract closely model real agents, and so they have diverse bases for their deliberations—religious, secular, perfectionist, and so on. In this case, it is hard to see how the contract theorist can get a determinate result. Just as you and I disagree, so will the parties. Rawls (1999, 121) acknowledges that his restrictions on particular information in the original position are necessary to achieve a determinate result. If we exclude "knowledge of those contingencies which set men at odds…" then since "everyone is equally rational and similarly situated, each is convinced by the same arguments"(Rawls 1999, 17, 120). Gaus (2011a, 36–47) has argued that a determinative result can only be generated by an implausibly high degree of abstraction, in which the basic pluralism of evaluative standards—the core of our justificatory problem—is abstracted away. Thus, on Gaus's view, modelings of the parties that make them anything approaching representations of real people will only be able to generate a non-singleton set of eligible social contracts. The parties might agree that some social contracts are better than none, but they will disagree on their ordering of possible social contracts. This conclusion, refined and developed in (Gaus 2011a, Part Two) connects the traditional problem of indeterminacy in the contract procedure (see also Hardin 2003) with the contemporary, technical problem of equilibrium selection in games (see Vanderschraaf 2005). A topic we will explore more in §3 below.

It is possible, however, that determinacy may actually require diversity in the perspective of the deliberative parties in a way that Rawls and others like Harsanyi didn't expect. The reason for this is simple, though the proof is somewhat complex. Normalizing the perspectives of the parties assumes that there is one stable point of view that has all of the relevant information necessary for generating a stable and determinate set of social rules. There is no reason, antecedently, to think that such a perspective can be found, however. Instead, if we recognize that there are epistemic gains to be had from a "division of cognitive labor" there is good reason to prefer a diverse rather than normalized idealization of the parties to the contract (see: Weisberg and Muldoon 2009, Gaus 2016, Muldoon 2017, Muldoon 2017a, Muldoon 2018). There is reason to conclude that if we wish to discover social contracts that best achieve a set of interrelated normative desiderata (e.g., liberty, equality, welfare, etc.), a deliberative process that draws on a diversity of perspectives will outperform one based on a strict normalization of perspectives (Gaus 2011b, 2016; Thrasher 2020).

Doxastic vs. Evaluative

Any representation of the reasoning of the parties will have two elements that need to be specified: 1) doxastic and 2) evaluative. These elements, when combined, create a complete model that will specify how and why representatives in the contractual model choose or agree to some set of social rules. The first (doxastic) is the specification of everything the representatives in the original position know or at least believe. Choice in the contractual model in the broadest sense, is an attempt by the parties to choose a set of rules that they expect will be better than in some baseline condition, such as "generalized egoism" (Rawls, 1999: 127) a "state of nature" (Hobbes 1651) or the rules that they currently have (Binmore, 2005; Buchanan 2000 [1975]). To do this, they need representations of the baseline and of state of the world under candidate set of rules). Without either of these doxastic representations, the choice problem would be indeterminate. Rawls famously imposes severe doxastic constraints on his parties to the social contract by imposing a thick veil of ignorance that eliminates information about the specific details of each individual and the world they live in. James Buchanan imposes a similar, but less restrictive "veil of uncertainty" on his representative choosers (Buchanan and Tullock 1965 [1962]; Buchanan 1975; see also Rawls, 1958).

In addition to specifying what the representatives believe to be the case about the world and the results of their agreement, there must also be some standard by which the representative parties can evaluate different contractual possibilities. They must be able to rank the options on the basis of their values, whatever those may be. Rawls models parties to the contractual situation as, at least initially, having only one metric of value: primary goods. They choose the conception of justice they do insofar as they believe it will likely generate the most primary goods for them and their descendants. This specification of the evaluative parameter is uniform across choosers and therefore, choice in the original position can be modeled as the choice of one individual. Insofar as there is evaluative diversity between the representatives, more complex models of agreement will be needed (see §3). If we think in terms of decision theory, the doxastic specification individuates the initial state of affairs and the outcomes of the contractual model, while the specification of the evaluative elements gives each representative party a ranking of the outcomes expected to result from the choice of any given set of rules. Once these elements are specified, we have a model of the parties to the contract.

Modeling Agreement

Social contract theories fundamentally differ in whether the parties reason differently or the same. As we have seen (§2.3) in Rawls's Original Position, everyone reasons the same: the collective choice problem is reduced to the choice of one individual. Any one person's decision is a proxy for everyone else. In social contracts of this sort, the description of the parties (their motivation, the conditions under which they choose) does all the work: once we have fully specified the reasoning of one party, the contract has been identified.

The alternative view is that, even after we have specified the parties (including their rationality, values and information), they continue to disagree in their rankings of possible social contracts. On this view, the contract only has a determinate result if there is some way to commensurate the different rankings of each individual to yield an agreement (D'Agostino 2003). We can distinguish four basic agreement mechanisms of doing this.

Consent

The traditional social contract views of Hobbes, Locke, and Rousseau crucially relied on the idea of consent. For Locke only "consent of Free-men" could make them members of the government (Locke 1689, §117). In the hands of these theorists—and in much ordinary discourse—the idea of "consent" implies a normative power to bind oneself. When one reaches "the age of consent" one is empowered to make certain sorts of binding agreements—contracts. By putting consent at the center of their contracts these early modern contract theorists (1) were clearly supposing that individuals had basic normative powers over themselves (e.g. self-ownership) before they entered into the social contract (a point that Hume (1748) stressed), and (2) brought the question of political obligation to the fore. If the parties have the power to bind themselves by exercising this normative power, then the upshot of the social contract was *obligation*. As Hobbes (1651, 81 [chap xiv, ¶7) insisted, covenants bind; that is why they are "artificial chains" (1651, 138 [chap. xxi, ¶5).

Both of these considerations have come under attack in contemporary social contract theories, especially the second. According to Buchanan, the key development of recent social contract theory has been to distinguish the question of what generates political obligation (*the* key concern of the consent tradition in social contract thought) from the question of what constitutional orders or social institutions are mutually beneficial and stable over time (1965). The nature of a person's *duty* to abide by the law or social rules is a matter of morality as it pertains to individuals (Rawls 1999, 293ff), while the design and justification of political and social institutions is a question of public or social morality. Thus, in Buchanan's view, a crucial feature of more recent contractual thought has been to refocus political philosophy on public or social morality rather than individual obligation. In most modern social contract theories, including Rawls's, consent and obligation play almost no role whatsoever.

Although contemporary social contract theorists still sometimes employ the language of consent, the core idea of contemporary social contract theory is *agreement*. "Social contract views work from the intuitive idea of agreement" (Freeman 2007a, 17). One can endorse or agree to a principle without that act of endorsement in any way binding one to obey. Social contract theorists as diverse as Samuel Freeman and Jan Narveson (1988, 148) see the act of agreement as indicating what reasons we have; agreement is a "test" or a heuristic (see §5). The "role of unanimous collective agreement" is in showing "what we have reasons to do in our social and political relations" (Freeman 2007, 19).

Thus understood, the agreement is not itself a binding act—it is not a performative that somehow creates obligation—but is reason-revealing (Lessnoff 1986). If individuals are rational, what they agree to reflects the reasons they have. In contemporary contract theories such as Rawls's, the problem of justification takes center stage. Rawls's revival of social contract theory in *A Theory of Justice* thus did not base obligations on consent, though the apparatus of an "original agreement" persisted. Recall that for Rawls (1999, 16) the aim is to settle "the question of justification…by working out a problem of deliberation."

Given that the problem of justification has taken center stage, the second aspect of contemporary social contract thinking appears to fall into place: its reliance on models of counterfactual agreement. The aim is to model the reasons of citizens, and so we ask what they would agree to under conditions in which their agreements would be expected to track their reasons. Contemporary contract theory is, characteristically, *doubly* counterfactual. Certainly, no prominent theorist thinks that questions of justification are settled by an actual survey of attitudes towards existing social arrangements, and are not settled until such a survey has been carried out. The question, then, is *not* "Are these arrangements presently the object of an actual agreement among citizens?" (If this were the question, the answer would typically be "No".) The question, rather, is "*Would* these arrangements be the object of an agreement if citizens were surveyed?" Although both of the questions are, in some sense, susceptible to an empirical reading, only the latter is in play in present-day theorizing. The contract nowadays is always counterfactual in at least this first sense.

There is a reading of the (first-order) counterfactual question, "Would R be the object of agreement if___" which, as indicated, is still resolutely empirical in some sense. This is the reading where what is required of the theorist is that she try to determine what an actual survey of actual citizens would reveal about their actual attitudes towards their system of social arrangements. (This is seldom done, of course; the theorist does it in her imagination. See, though, Klosko 2000). But there is another interpretation that is more widely accepted in the contemporary context. On this reading, the question is no longer a counterfactual question about actual reactions; it is, rather, a *counterfactual* question about counterfactual reactions—it is, as we have said, *doubly* counterfactual. *Framing* the question is the first counterfactual element: "Would *R* be the object of agreement if they were surveyed?" *Framed* by this question is the second counterfactual element, one which involves the citizens, who are no longer treated empirically, i.e. taken as given, but are, instead, themselves considered from a counterfactual point of view—as they would be if (typically) they were better informed or more impartial, etc. The question for most contemporary contract theorists, then, is, roughly: "If we surveyed the idealized surrogates of the actual citizens in this polity, what social arrangements would be the object of an agreement among them?"

Famously, Ronald Dworkin (1975) has objected that a (doubly) hypothetical agreement cannot bind any actual person. For the hypothetical analysis to make sense, it must be shown that hypothetical persons in the contract can agree to endorse and comply with some principle regulating social arrangements. Suppose that it could be shown that your surrogate (a better informed, more impartial version of you) would agree to a principle. What has that to do with you? Where this second-stage hypothetical analysis is employed, it seems to be proposed that *you* can be bound by agreements that *others*, different from you, would have made. While it might (though it needn't) be reasonable to suppose that *you* can be bound by agreements that you would yourself have entered into if, given the opportunity, it seems crazy to think that you can be bound by agreements that, demonstrably, you wouldn't have made *even if* you had been asked.

This criticism is decisive, however, only if the hypothetical social contract is supposed to invoke your normative power to self-bind via consent. That your surrogate employs her power to self-bind would not mean that you had employed your power. Again, though, the power to obligate oneself is not typically invoked in the contemporary social contract: the problem of deliberation is supposed to help us make headway on the problem of justification. So the question for contemporary hypothetical contract theories is whether the hypothetical agreement of your surrogate tracks your reasons to accept social arrangements, a very different issue (Stark 2000).

This argument has been revived by Jussi Suikkanen (2014) as the claim that certain forms of contract theory, most notably Southwood's (2010) "deliberative" contractualism, commit the conditional fallacy. The conditional fallacy is a specific version of the problem we are considering here, namely that a conditional with counterfactual agents, will not necessarily apply if the counterfactual agents are sufficiently different from the real ones it is meant to apply to. In response, Southwood (2019) develops what he calls an "advice model" of contractualism wherein we take the counterfactual contractors to generate reasons that should appeal to us as advice from a more thoughtful, idealized version of ourselves, along lines similar to Michael Smith's (1994) ideal advisor theory of moral reasons. Thrasher (2019) raises a different but related concern that segmented choice in the model of agreement can create outcomes that are not rationalizable to the parties, since they are the result of path-dependent processes.

As we have argued, contemporary social contract theory rely on hypothetical or counterfactual agreement, rather than actual agreement. In one sense this is certainly the case. However, in many ways the "hypothetical/actual" divide is artificial: the counterfactual agreement is meant to model, and provide the basis for, actual agreement. All models are counterfactual Understanding contemporary social contract theory is best achieved, not through insisting on the distinction between actual and hypothetical contracts, but by grasping the interplay of the counterfactual and the actual in the model of agreement.

Rawls (1995) is especially clear on this point in his explication of his model of agreement in response to Habermas. There he distinguishes between three different perspectives relevant to the assessment of the model (1996, 28):

you and me

the parties to the deliberative model

persons in a well-ordered society

The agreement of the parties in the deliberative model is certainly counterfactual in the two-fold sense we have analyzed: a counterfactual agreement among counterfactual parties. But the point of the deliberative model is to help us (i.e., "you and me") solve *our* justificatory problem—what social arrangements we can all accept as "free persons who have no authority over one another" (Rawls 1958, 33). The parties' deliberations and the conditions under which they deliberate, then, model our actual convictions about justice and justification. As Rawls says (1999, 514), the reasoning of the counterfactual parties matters to us because "the conditions embodied in the description of this situation are ones that we do in fact accept." Unless the counterfactual models the actual, the upshot of the agreement could not provide *us* with reasons. Gaus describes this process as a "testing conception" of the social contract (2011a, 425). We use the counterfactual deliberative device of the contract to "test" our social institutions. In this way, the contemporary social contract is meant to be a model of the justificatory situation that all individuals face. The counterfactual and abstracted (see §2) nature of the contract is needed to highlight the relevant features of the parties to show what reasons they have.

Samuel Freeman has recently stressed the way in which focusing on the third perspective—of citizens in a well-ordered society—also shows the importance of counterfactual agreement in Rawls's contract theory. On Freeman's interpretation, the social contract must meet the condition of *publicity*. He (2007b:15) writes:

Rawls distinguishes three levels of publicity: first, the publicity of principles of justice; second, the publicity of the general beliefs in light of which first principles of justice can be accepted ("that is, the theory of human nature and of social institutions generally)"; and, third, the publicity of the complete justification of the public conception of justice as it would be on its own terms. All three levels, Rawls contends, are exemplified in a well-ordered society. This is the "full publicity" condition.

A justified contract must meet the full publicity condition: its complete justification must be capable of being actually accepted by members of a well-ordered society. The counterfactual agreement itself provides only what Rawls (1996, 386) calls a *"pro tanto"* or "so far as it goes" justification of the principles of justice. "Full justification" is achieved only when actual "people endorse and will liberal justice for the particular (and often conflicting) reasons implicit in the reasonable comprehensive doctrines they hold" (Freeman 2007b, 19). Thus understood, Rawls's concern with the stability of justice as fairness, which motivated the move to political liberalism, is itself a question of justification (Weithman, 2010). Only if the principles of justice are stable in this way are they fully justified. Rawls's concern with stability and publicity is not, however, idiosyncratic and is shared by all contemporary contract theorists. It is significant that even theorists such as Buchanan (2000 [1975], 26–27), Gauthier (1986, 348), and Binmore (2005, 5–7)—who are so different from Rawls in other respects—share his concern with stability.

Bargaining

It is perhaps no surprise that the renaissance in contemporary contact theory occurred at the same time as game-theoretic tools and especially bargaining theory began to be applied to philosophical problems. Bargaining theory, as it was developed by John Nash (1950) and John Harsanyi (1977) is a rigorous approach to modeling how rational individuals would agree to divide some good or surplus. In its most general form, the bargaining model of agreement specifies some set of individuals who have individual utility functions that can be represented in relation to one other without requiring interpersonal comparisons of utility directly. Some surplus is specified and if the individuals involved can agree on how to divide the good in question, they will get that division. If, however, they cannot agree they will instead get their disagreement result. This may be what they brought to the table or it could be some other specified amount. One example is a simple demand game where two people must write down how much of given pot of money they want. If the two "bids" amount to equal or less than the pot, each will get what he or she wrote down, otherwise each will get nothing.

As Rawls recognized in his 1958 essay "Justice as Fairness" one way for parties to resolve their disagreements is to employ bargaining solutions, such as that proposed by R.B. Braithwaite (1955). Rawls himself rejected bargaining solutions to the social contract since, in his opinion, such solutions rely on "threat advantage" (i.e., disagreement result) and "to each according to his threat advantage is hardly a principle of fairness" In addition to Rawls's concern about threat advantage, a drawback of all such approaches is the multiplicity of bargaining solutions, which can significantly differ. John Rawls, "Justice as Fairness.

The fundamental idea in the concept of justice is fairness. The paper will try to justify this claim. It is this aspect of justice, i.e. fairness, that classical utilitarianism[151] fails to account for.

Three things should be kept in mind. First, justice is considered as a virtue of social institutions (henceforth "practices") and its function is essentially distributive. Some clarifications. Justice considered only in its application to social institutions because its application to social institutions is "basic" and may be easily applied to other "subjects of justice" such as persons or particular actions once its principles are established. The word "practice" is used as a technical term meaning any form of activity specified by a system of rules which defines offices, roles, moves. penalties, defenses, and so on, and which gives the activity its structure

Second, justice is considered as only one of the many virtues of practices. Justice is just one aspect of any conception of a good society. Third, the principles of justice discussed below need not be seen as *the* principles of justice.

There are two principles of justice as fairness: (a) first, each person participating in a practice, or affected by it, has an equal right to the most extensive liberty compatible with a like liberty for all; (b) and second, inequalities are arbitrary unless it is reasonable to expect that they will work out for everyone's advantage, and provided the positions and offices to which they attach, or from which they may be gained, are open to all.

The term "person" could mean human individuals, nations, provinces, business firms, churches, teams, and so on. In any case, the principles apply to all. The use of the term is self-confessedly ambiguous.

The first principle expresses a presumption against "distinctions and classifications" created by practices. Put another way, the first principle presumes an original and equal liberty of all persons without ruling out deviations from this state of equality.

The second principle defines what sort of deviations from this original situation of equality — or inequalities — are permissible. These inequalities are not the differences in offices and positions and the differences in benefits and burden that ensue from them. First, only those inequalities are permitted which benefit *everyone*. This modification which requires that *everyone* must benefit from the inequality disallows utilitarian justifications that appeal to the greater magnitude of the benefits accruing to some compared to the burdens borne by others. Second, those offices and positions of practices that have benefits attached to them must be open for all to acquire through fair competition.

III

How are these two principles arrived at?

Imagine a society of persons where a system of practices is well in place. Now suppose that they are, *by and large*, mutually self-interested. This means that they are self-interested but not always so. They have loyalties to their families, nations, churches and the like whose interests they also pursue. This does not imply however that they are mutually self-interested under all circumstances. They are so only when they participate in "common practices".

Also, suppose also that they are rational meaning that (a) they know their own interests, (b) they can foresee the consequences of their actions, (c) they can adhere to their chosen course of action, (d) they can resist enticements for immediate gain, and (e) they are comfortable with certain limited differences in their condition and that of others. The last point is the only addition to usual definitions of rationality and it implies that the rational man in not greatly worried by seeing others in a better position unless that were the result of injustice. The rational man, in a word, is free from envy.

Finally, suppose that they have similar needs and interests which enables their fruitful cooperation and also that they are sufficiently equal in power and ability to guarantee that in normal circumstances none is able to dominate the others.

This society of mutually self-interested, rational, and similarly situated persons, since they *already* have a system of practices in place, can be imagined to regularly discuss complaints about the practices they have set up. They first establish the principles based on which their complaints will be judged by letting everyone propose the principles based on which he thinks complaints should be tried. This is done on the understanding that once the principles are adopted, they will be binding on everyone in all future cases. This provision disallows principles that may be peculiarly advantageous for a particular complaint as they will be, if adopted, imposed on everyone for every complaint that might arise.

The two parts of this conjectural story have definite significance. The first part reflects the typical circumstances in which questions of justice arise. Such circumstances are those where conflicting demands are brought to bear on the design of a practice by persons insisting on what they consider to be their rights. The second part represents the constraints under which persons are brought to act reasonably. The constraints are those of morality which, at the very least, imply acknowledgement (a) of principles that must be pursued even if they conflict with self-interest and (b) that principles must be applied impartially to all.

It is sufficient to remark here that having a morality is analogous to having made a firm commitment in advance; for one must acknowledge the principles of morality even when to one's disadvantage. A man whose moral judgments always coincided with his interests could be suspected of having no morality at all.

Given the circumstances and the constraints specified by the two parts, it can be seen how the two principles of justice put forth at the beginning of Section II might come about. This is not offered as proof that those two principles will necessarily be chosen but merely to show that those principles could be chosen.

IV

Justice on this account appears to be a sort of pact between rational and egoistic persons similar to the sort advanced by Glaucon at the beginning of Book II of Plato's *Republic*. However, this is not entirely so.

They say that to do injustice is naturally good and to suffer injustice bad, but that the badness of suffering it so far exceeds the goodness of doing it that those who have done and suffered injustice and tasted both, but who lack the power to do it and avoid suffering it, decide that it is profitable to come to an agreement with each other neither to do injustice nor to suffer it. As a result, they begin to make laws and covenants, and what the law commands they call lawful and just. This, they say, is the origin and essence of justice. It is intermediate between the best and the worst. The best is to do injustice without paying the penalty; the worst is to suffer it without being able to take revenge. Justice is a mean between these two extremes. People value it not as a good but because they are too weak to do injustice with impunity. Someone who has the power to do this, however, and is a true man wouldn't make an agreement with anyone not to do injustice in order not to suffer it. For him, that would be madness. This is the nature of justice, according to the argument, Socrates, and these are its natural origins.

The Republic, 358e–359b. from *Plato: Complete Works*, ed. John M. Cooper, (Indianapolis: Hackett, 1997) (See this if you don't know what the numbers mean.)

First, the conjectural account does not advance any theory of human motivation (or human nature) underlying the actions and decisions of persons. The account refers simply to the fact, in the circumstances of justice, the different parties *do* press their conflicting and competing claims on one another and *do* regard themselves as representing interests which need to be considered. Second, the account does not seek to explain the establishment of any particular society or practice as most social contract theories set out to do. The different parties "jointly acknowledge certain *principles of appraisal* relating to their practices [which are] either *already established* or *merely proposed*" (emphases added). Third, the account does not imply that the parties are coming together for the first time. It applies even when highly developed social institutions already exist. This means that the account is not fictitious. In any society where people reflect on their practices, there will be times when principles of justice would *actually* be discussed in the way sketched by the account.

V

Thinking about justice in the manner so described brings out the idea that fairness must be central to justice. Rules of a practice are fair if they are accepted as applicable by all concerned on the basis that they are legitimate. Similarly for principles of justice. It is this idea of mutual acceptance (or mutual acknowledgement) which makes fairness central to justice because when understood through the conjectural account, the principles of justice arrived at are what can be undoubtedly called as fair since they are premised on the notion of mutual acknowledgement brought about by the condition that these principles are binding on everyone. It is this notion of mutual acknowledgement that ensures a community between persons and their practices based not on force.

If the rules of a practice are correctly acknowledged as fair, duties on the part of the parties to act in accordance with those rules when it fall upon them to comply are born. This is the duty of "fair play". This obligation to abide by the rule does not depend on any explicit contract acknowledging the practice but merely requires knowing participation in and acceptance of the benefits of the practice.

The duty of fair play might enjoin upon the participants to sacrifice their self-interests in particular situations. This is the expected consequence of the strong commitment to the rules made in the *general position* (the situation described in the conjectural account, see Section III). The acceptance of the duty of fair play along with this constraint is recognition of the others as persons with similar interests and capacities, as specified in the general position.

These comments are made in order to anticipate and forestall the misinterpretation that the account presented of justice and fair play requires that there be *de facto* equality in the general position. Such equality is important but is *not* the basis. The recognition of one another as persons with similar interests and capacities involved in a common practice is enough basis for the acceptance of the principles of justice and the duty of fair play.

One consequence of the conception as explicated thus far is that there is no moral value in satisfying a claim that is incompatible with it. Put concretely, there is no moral value in the satisfaction derived out of something which one imposes on others but would not accept for himself, regardless of the pleasure it generates.

VI

For the classical utilitarians such as Jeremy Bentham and Henry Sidgwick, justice is a kind of efficiency. Justice is tied to benevolence and benevolence is brought about through the most efficient design of institutions to promote the general welfare.

…justice, in the only sense in which it has a meaning, is an imaginary personage, feigned for the convenience of discourse, whose dictates are the dictates of utility, applied to certain particular cases. Justice, then, is nothing more than an imaginary instrument, employed to forward on certain occasions, and by certain means, the purposes of benevolence. The dictates of justice are nothing more than a part of the dictates of benevolence, which, on certain occasions, are applied to certain subjects…

Jeremy Bentham, *An Introduction to the Principles of Morals and Legislation*, 1789, Ch. X, footnote 2 to section XL.

A common objection is that this would "justify institutions highly offensive to our ordinary sense of justice". This, of course, is the objection that the general welfare could be bought at great particular cost. The greatest happiness of the many, to use other words, could come at the expense of the greatest suffering of the few. However, classical utilitarianism can answer this objection. For one, individuals are considered as having roughly the same utility function and differences due to accidents of birth and upbringing are ignored. Hence the maxim that each counts for one and no more than one. For another, they accept the idea of marginal diminishing utility according to which satisfaction derived from additional units of a good diminishes. The implication here is that due to the operation of diminishing utility, fantastic differences in levels of satisfaction (or utility) are unlikely to occur. These two assumptions build a strong case for equality.

However, even if these assumptions actually operated and led to similar principles of justice as the ones presented here, they would still be fundamentally different from justice as fairness. Firstly, in the utilitarian conception, the principles of justice are the *contingent* result of a higher administrative decision similar, for instance, to that of an entrepreneur deciding how much to produce of this or that commodity in view of its marginal revenue. Second, the individuals receiving the benefits due to the utilitarian calculus represent so many different directions in which limited resources may be allocated. Their enjoyment of the benefits value irrespective of the moral relations between persons, say as members of a joint undertaking.

It is assumed that justice will prevail so long as the administrator makes the correct executive decisions based on utilitarian principles.

In this fact the principles of justice are said to have their derivation and explanation; they simply express the most important general features of social institutions in which the administrative problem is solved in the best way. These principles have, indeed, a special urgency because, given the facts of human nature, so much depends on them; and this explains the peculiar quality of the moral feelings associated with justice.

VII

Many social decisions are of course administrative decisions. And classical utilitarianism can properly account for many of these decisions about social utility. However, as an interpretation of the principles of justice, classical utilitarianism fails.

For one, it *allows* one to argue — this is not to say that any of the classical utilitarians ever did — that slavery is unjust because the disadvantage to the slaves outweighs the advantages to the slaveholder. Slavery is unjust, no doubt, but not for this reason. The point is not whether the disadvantages to one party can outweigh the advantage of the other, which is what utilitarianism considers, but simply that slavery is not in accordance with principles that can be mutually acknowledged, which is what justice as fairness says, and it is for this latter reason that slavery will *always* be unjust. For justice as fairness, slavery is unjust by definition.

The question whether these gains [accruing to the slaveholders] outweigh the disadvantages to the slave and to society cannot arise, since in considering the justice of slavery these gains have no weight at all which requires that they be overridden. Where the conception of justice as fairness applies, slavery is always unjust.

The classical utilitarian might retort that it is not always true that the disadvantage to the slaves outweighs the advantages to the slaveholder. He might insist that there could be, *in principle*, cases where the advantages to the slaveholders outweigh the disadvantages to the slaves and that in such case, slavery would not be wrong. Indeed, in such cases, slavery would be right. He would contend that utilitarianism is correct/justified in giving no special weight to justice above and beyond the basic concern with effectiveness. That's to say, if slavery is unjust, it should be for reasons of effectiveness only. That justice as fairness, in accordance with common moral opinion, finds slavery unjust is just a useful accident or error.

But reasons of justice do have a *special* weight which utilitarianism cannot account for but justice as fairness can. The defence of slavery is never that it is sufficiently advantageous to the slaveholder to outweigh the disadvantages to the slave. If someone does make this claim, he would be guilty of a moral fallacy. This is because slavery does not ensue from principles that could be accepted by the slaveholder anymore than it would be by the slave. As such, the advantages or disadvantages that result from slavery have no moral significance. That's to say, the slaveholder has no moral title to the advantages which he receives as a slaveholder. Such (morally arbitrary) advantages then cannot be grounds for defending any practice, slavery included, as just.

Amongst persons in a general position who are debating the form of their common practices, it cannot, therefore, be offered as a reason for a practice that, in conceding these very claims that ought to be denied, it nevertheless meets existing interests more effectively. By their very nature the satisfaction of these claims is without weight and cannot enter into any tabulation of advantages and disadvantages.

This criticism of utilitarianism does not depend upon whether or not the assumptions of similar utility functions for individuals and diminishing marginal utility (see Section V) are understood to be psychological/scientific or moral/political. However we consider them, the mistaken belief in the intrinsic value of satisfaction of (moral and psychological) desires which disregards the relations between persons still remains.

To see the error of this idea one must give up the conception of justice as an executive decision altogether and refer to the notion of justice as fairness: that participants in a common practice be regarded as having an original and equal liberty and that their common practices be considered unjust unless they accord with principles which persons so circumstanced and related could freely acknowledge before one another, and so could accept as fair.

VIII

"By way of conclusion I should like to make two remarks: first, the original modification of the utilitarian principle actually has a different conception of justice standing behind it. I have tried to show how this is so by developing the concept of justice... [which] involves the mutual acceptance, from a general position, of the principles on which a practice is founded, and how this in turn requires the exclusion from consideration of claims violating the principles of justice.

Second,...I have been dealing with the *concept* of justice.... Societies will differ from one another...in the range of cases to which they apply [the concept of justice as fairness] and in the emphasis which they give to it as compared with other moral concepts. A firm grasp of the concept of justice itself is necessary if these variations, and the reasons for them, are to be understood."

Section I claims that the fundamental idea for the concept of justice is fairness.

Section II introduces the two principles of this conception.

Section III explains how these two principles are arrived at.

Section IV pre-empts possible criticisms against justice as fairness as developed in Sections II and III.

Section V sketches why fairness should be central to any concept of justice.

Section VI characterises the utilitarian conception of justice as one concerned with efficacy.

Section VII discusses why such utilitarianism fails as a conception of justice.

I

The fundamental idea in the concept of justice is fairness. The paper will try to justify this claim. It is this aspect of justice, i.e. fairness, that classical utilitarianism fails to account for.

Three things should be kept in mind. First, justice is considered as a virtue of social institutions (henceforth "practices") and its function is essentially distributive. Some clarifications. Justice considered only in its application to social institutions because its application to social institutions is "basic" and may be easily applied to other "subjects of justice" such as persons or particular actions once its principles are established. The word "practice" is used as a technical term meaning any form of activity specified by a system of rules which defines offices, roles, moves. penalties, defenses, and so on, and which gives the activity its structure

Second, justice is considered as only one of the many virtues of practices. Justice is just one aspect of any conception of a good society. Third, the principles of justice discussed below need not be seen as *the* principles of justice.

II

There are two principles of justice as fairness:

(a) first, each person participating in a practice, or affected by it, has an equal right to the most extensive liberty compatible with a like liberty for all;

(b) and second, inequalities are arbitrary unless it is reasonable to expect that they will work out for everyone's advantage, and provided the positions and offices to which they attach, or from which they may be gained, are open to all.

The term "person" could mean human individuals, nations, provinces, business firms, churches, teams, and so on. In any case, the principles apply to all. The use of the term is self-confessedly ambiguous.

The first principle expresses a presumption against "distinctions and classifications" created by practices. Put another way, the first principle presumes an original and equal liberty of all persons without ruling out deviations from this state of equality.

The second principle defines what sort of deviations from this original situation of equality — or inequalities — are permissible. These inequalities are not the differences in offices and positions and the differences in benefits and burden that ensue from them. First, only those inequalities are permitted which benefit *everyone*. This modification which requires that *everyone* must benefit from the inequality disallows utilitarian justifications that appeal to the greater magnitude of the benefits accruing to some compared to the burdens borne by others. Second, those offices and positions of practices that have benefits attached to them must be open for all to acquire through fair competition.

III

How are these two principles arrived at?

Imagine a society of persons where a system of practices is well in place. Now suppose that they are, *by and large*, mutually self-interested.

This means that they are self-interested but not always so. They have loyalties to their families, nations, churches and the like whose interests they also pursue. This does not imply however that they are mutually self-interested under all circumstances. They are so only when they participate in "common practices".

Also, suppose also that they are rational meaning that (a) they know their own interests, (b) they can foresee the consequences of their actions, (c) they can adhere to their chosen course of action, (d) they can resist enticements for immediate gain, and (e) they are comfortable with certain limited differences in their condition and that of others. The last point is the only addition to usual definitions of rationality and it implies that the rational man in not greatly worried by seeing others in a better position unless that were the result of injustice. The rational man, in a word, is free from envy.

Finally, suppose that they have similar needs and interests which enables their fruitful cooperation and also that they are sufficiently equal in power and ability to guarantee that in normal circumstances none is able to dominate the others.

This society of mutually self-interested, rational, and similarly situated persons, since they *already* have a system of practices in place, can be imagined to regularly discuss complaints about the practices they have set up. They first establish the principles based on which their complaints will be judged by letting everyone propose the principles based on which he thinks complaints should be tried. This is done on the understanding that once the principles are adopted, they will be binding on everyone in all future cases. This provision disallows principles that may be peculiarly advantageous for a particular complaint as they will be, if adopted, imposed on everyone for every complaint that might arise.

The two parts of this conjectural story have definite significance. The first part reflects the typical circumstances in which questions of justice arise. Such circumstances are those where conflicting demands are brought to bear on the design of a practice by persons insisting on what they consider to be their rights. The second part represents the constraints under which persons are brought to act reasonably. The constraints are those of morality which, at the very least, imply acknowledgement (a) of principles that must be pursued even if they conflict with self-interest and (b) that principles must be applied impartially to all.

It is sufficient to remark here that having a morality is analogous to having made a firm commitment in advance; for one must acknowledge the principles of morality even when to one's disadvantage. A man whose moral judgments always coincided with his interests could be suspected of having no morality at all.

Given the circumstances and the constraints specified by the two parts, it can be seen how the two principles of justice put forth at the beginning of Section II might come about. This is not offered as proof that those two principles will necessarily be chosen but merely to show that those principles could be chosen.

IV

Justice on this account appears to be a sort of pact between rational and egoistic persons similar to the sort advanced by Glaucon at the beginning of Book II of Plato's *Republic*. However, this is not entirely so.

They say that to do injustice is naturally good and to suffer injustice bad, but that the badness of suffering it so far exceeds the goodness of doing it that those who have done and suffered injustice and tasted both, but who lack the power to do it and avoid suffering it, decide that it is profitable to come to an agreement with each other neither to do injustice nor to suffer it. As a result, they begin to make laws and covenants, and what the law commands they call lawful and just. This, they say, is the origin and essence of justice. It is intermediate between the best and the worst. The best is to do injustice without paying the penalty; the worst is to suffer it without being able to take revenge. Justice is a mean between these two extremes. People value it not as a good but because they are too weak to do injustice with impunity. Someone who has the power to do this, however, and is a true man wouldn't make an agreement with anyone not to do injustice in order not to suffer it. For him, that would be madness. This is the nature of justice, according to the argument, Socrates, and these are its natural origins.

The Republic, 358e–359b. from *Plato: Complete Works*, ed. John M. Cooper, (Indianapolis: Hackett, 1997) (See this if you don't know what the numbers mean.)

First, the conjectural account does not advance any theory of human motivation (or human nature) underlying the actions and decisions of persons. The account refers simply to the fact, in the circumstances of justice, the different parties *do* press their conflicting and competing claims on one another and *do* regard themselves as representing interests which need to be considered. Second, the account does not seek to explain the establishment of any particular society or practice as most social contract theories set out to do. The different parties "jointly acknowledge certain *principles of appraisal* relating to their practices [which are] either *already established* or *merely proposed*" (emphases added). Third, the account does not imply that the parties are coming together for the first time. It applies even when highly developed social institutions already exist. This means that the account is not fictitious. In any society where people reflect on their practices, there will be times when principles of justice would *actually* be discussed in the way sketched by the account.

V

Thinking about justice in the manner so described brings out the idea that fairness must be central to justice. Rules of a practice are fair if they are accepted as applicable by all concerned on the basis that they are legitimate. Similarly for principles of justice. It is this idea of mutual acceptance (or mutual acknowledgement) which makes fairness central to justice because when understood through the conjectural account, the principles of justice arrived at are what can be undoubtedly called as fair since they are premised on the notion of mutual acknowledgement brought about by the condition that these principles are binding on everyone. It is this notion of mutual acknowledgement that ensures a community between persons and their practices based not on force.

If the rules of a practice are correctly acknowledged as fair, duties on the part of the parties to act in accordance with those rules when it fall upon them to comply are born. This is the duty of "fair play". This obligation to abide by the rule does not depend on any explicit contract acknowledging the practice but merely requires knowing participation in and acceptance of the benefits of the practice.

The duty of fair play might enjoin upon the participants to sacrifice their self-interests in particular situations. This is the expected consequence of the strong commitment to the rules made in the *general position* (the situation described in the conjectural account, see Section III). The acceptance of the duty of fair play along with this constraint is recognition of the others as persons with similar interests and capacities, as specified in the general position.

These comments are made in order to anticipate and forestall the misinterpretation that the account presented of justice and fair play requires that there be *de facto* equality in the general position. Such equality is important but is *not* the basis. The recognition of one another as persons with similar interests and capacities involved in a common practice is enough basis for the acceptance of the principles of justice and the duty of fair play.

One consequence of the conception as explicated thus far is that there is no moral value in satisfying a claim that is incompatible with it. Put concretely, there is no moral value in the satisfaction derived out of something which one imposes on others but would not accept for himself, regardless of the pleasure it generates.

VI

For the classical utilitarians such as Jeremy Bentham and Henry Sidgwick, justice is a kind of efficiency. Justice is tied to benevolence and benevolence is brought about through the most efficient design of institutions to promote the general welfare.

…justice, in the only sense in which it has a meaning, is an imaginary personage, feigned for the convenience of discourse, whose dictates are the dictates of utility, applied to certain particular cases. Justice, then, is nothing more than an imaginary instrument, employed to forward on certain occasions, and by certain means, the purposes of benevolence. The dictates of justice are nothing more than a part of the dictates of benevolence, which, on certain occasions, are applied to certain subjects...

Jeremy Bentham, *An Introduction to the Principles of Morals and Legislation*, 1789, Ch. X, footnote 2 to section XL.

A common objection is that this would "justify institutions highly offensive to our ordinary sense of justice". This, of course, is the objection that the general welfare could be bought at great particular cost. The greatest happiness of the many, to use other words, could come at the expense of the greatest suffering of the few. However, classical utilitarianism can answer this objection. For one, individuals are considered as having roughly the same utility function and differences due to accidents of birth and upbringing are ignored. Hence the maxim that each counts for one and no more than one. For another, they accept the idea of marginal diminishing utility according to which satisfaction derived from additional units of a good diminishes. The implication here is that due to the operation of diminishing utility, fantastic differences in levels of satisfaction (or utility) are unlikely to occur. These two assumptions build a strong case for equality.

However, even if these assumptions actually operated and led to similar principles of justice as the ones presented here, they would still be fundamentally different from justice as fairness. Firstly, in the utilitarian conception, the principles of justice are the *contingent* result of a higher administrative decision similar, for instance, to that of an entrepreneur deciding how much to produce of this or that commodity in view of its marginal revenue. Second, the individuals receiving the benefits due to the utilitarian calculus represent so many different directions in which limited resources may be allocated. Their enjoyment of the benefits value irrespective of the moral relations between persons, say as members of a joint undertaking.

It is assumed that justice will prevail so long as the administrator makes the correct executive decisions based on utilitarian principles.

In this fact the principles of justice are said to have their derivation and explanation; they simply express the most important general features of social institutions in which the administrative problem is solved in the best way. These principles have, indeed, a special urgency because, given the facts of human nature, so much depends on them; and this explains the peculiar quality of the moral feelings associated with justice.

VII

Many social decisions are of course administrative decisions. And classical utilitarianism can properly account for many of these decisions about social utility. However, as an interpretation of the principles of justice, classical utilitarianism fails.

For one, it *allows* one to argue — this is not to say that any of the classical utilitarians ever did — that slavery is unjust because the disadvantage to the slaves outweighs the advantages to the slaveholder. Slavery is unjust, no doubt, but not for this reason. The point is not whether the disadvantages to one party can outweigh the advantage of the other, which is what utilitarianism considers, but simply that slavery is not in accordance with principles that can be mutually acknowledged, which is what justice as fairness says, and it is for this latter reason that slavery will *always* be unjust. For justice as fairness, slavery is unjust by definition.

The question whether these gains [accruing to the slaveholders] outweigh the disadvantages to the slave and to society cannot arise, since in considering the justice of slavery these gains have no weight at all which requires that they be overridden. Where the conception of justice as fairness applies, slavery is always unjust.

The classical utilitarian might retort that it is not always true that the disadvantage to the slaves outweighs the advantages to the slaveholder. He might insist that there could be, *in principle*, cases where the advantages to the slaveholders outweigh the disadvantages to the slaves and that in such case, slavery would not be wrong. Indeed, in such cases, slavery would be right. He would contend that utilitarianism is correct/justified in giving no special weight to justice above and beyond the basic concern with effectiveness. That's to say, if slavery is unjust, it should be for reasons of effectiveness only. That justice as fairness, in accordance with common moral opinion, finds slavery unjust is just a useful accident or error.

But reasons of justice do have a *special* weight which utilitarianism cannot account for but justice as fairness can. The defence of slavery is never that it is sufficiently advantageous to the slaveholder to outweigh the disadvantages to the slave. If someone does make this claim, he would be guilty of a moral fallacy. This is because slavery does not ensue from principles that could be accepted by the slaveholder anymore than it would be by the slave. As such, the advantages or disadvantages that result from slavery have no moral significance. That's to say, the slaveholder has no moral title to the advantages which he receives as a slaveholder. Such (morally arbitrary) advantages then cannot be grounds for defending any practice, slavery included, as just.

Amongst persons in a general position who are debating the form of their common practices, it cannot, therefore, be offered as a reason for a practice that, in conceding these very claims that ought to be denied, it nevertheless meets existing interests more effectively. By their very nature the satisfaction of these claims is without weight and cannot enter into any tabulation of advantages and disadvantages.

This criticism of utilitarianism does not depend upon whether or not the assumptions of similar utility functions for individuals and diminishing marginal utility (see Section V) are understood to be psychological/scientific or moral/political. However we consider them, the mistaken belief in the intrinsic value of satisfaction of (moral and psychological) desires which disregards the relations between persons still remains.

To see the error of this idea one must give up the conception of justice as an executive decision altogether and refer to the notion of justice as fairness: that participants in a common practice be regarded as having an original and equal liberty and that their common practices be considered unjust unless they accord with principles which persons so circumstanced and related could freely acknowledge before one another, and so could accept as fair.

VIII

"By way of conclusion I should like to make two remarks: first, the original modification of the utilitarian principle actually has a different conception of justice standing behind it. I have tried to show how this is so by developing the concept of justice…[which] involves the mutual acceptance, from a general position, of the principles on which a practice is founded, and how this in turn requires the exclusion from consideration of claims violating the principles of justice.

Second,…I have been dealing with the *concept* of justice…. Societies will differ from one another…in the range of cases to which they apply [the concept of justice as fairness] and in the emphasis which they give to it as compared with other moral concepts. A firm grasp of the concept of justice itself is necessary if these variations, and the reasons for them, are to be understood."

Although the Nash solution is most favored today, it can have counter-intuitive implications. Furthermore, there are many who argue that bargaining solutions are inherently indeterminate and so the only way to achieve determinacy is to introduce unrealistic or controversial assumptions Similar problems also exist for equilibrium selection in games.

Section 9 includes another often overlooked result that is pivotal to the evidential reasoning for universal gravity in Book 3. Proposition 45 applies the result on precessing orbits mentioned earlier to the special case of nearly circular orbits, that is, orbits like those of the then known planets and their satellites. This proposition establishes that such orbits, under purely centripetal forces, are stationary — that is, do not precess — if and only if the centripetal force governing them is *exactly* inverse-square. It does this by deriving a formula relating the exponent n in the force law to the angle θ between the point where the orbiting body is furthest from the force center to the point where it is nearest, that is, the apsidal angle: $n = (180/\theta)2-3$. (To illustrate, if the apsidal angle is 180 degrees, as in a Keplerian ellipse, then the exponent in the force law is -2, and if the apsidal angle is 90 degrees, as in an ellipse for which the force center is in the center, the exponent is +1.) This result is striking in three ways. First, insofar as the cumulative effect of even a very small precession is detectable after several revolutions, this formula turns the rate of precession (2θ per revolution) into a sensitive measure of the exponent in the force law. Second, it yields a conditional beyond *"If the orbit is stationary, then the centripetal force is inverse-square,"* namely, *"If the orbit is nearly stationary, then the centripetal force is nearly inverse-square."* Using Newton's preferred phrasing, *quam proxime* (literally, "most nearly as possible"), this latter conditional has an "If…*quam proxime*, then…*quam proxime*" form. Newton illustrates this by taking the mean precession rate of the lunar orbit, 3 degrees per revolution, to conclude that the exponent for the net centrifugal force acting on the Moon is -2 and 4/243. Third, even when an orbit does precess, once such a fractional departure of the exponent from -2 is shown to result from the perturbing effect of outside bodies, then one can still conclude that the force toward the central body is exactly -2. This is precisely the strategy Newton follows in concluding that the centripetal force on the Moon, once a correction is made for the perturbing effects of the Sun, is inverse-square.

This is not the only place in Book 1 where Newton takes the trouble to derive an "If…*quam proxime*, then…*quam proxime*" version of an exact "If…, then…" proposition. Propositions 1 and 2 establish that a motion is governed purely by centripetal forces if and only if equal areas are swept out in equal times. The second and third corollaries of Proposition 3 then yield the conclusion that a motion is *quam proxime* governed purely by centripetal forces if and only if equal areas are *quam proxime* swept out in equal times. Again, after establishing that Kepler's 3/2 power rule holds exactly for concentric uniform circular motions if and only if an exact inverse-square centripetal force holds across all the orbits, he adds the generalization, "And universally, if the periodic time is as any power R^n of the radius $R,...$ the centripetal force will be inversely as the power R^{2n-1} of the radius, and conversely." This result holds for non-integer values of n, and hence it yields the further result that the 3/2 power rule holds *quam proxime* for uniform circular orbits if and only if the centripetal force is *quam proxime* inverse-square. These propositions— which Newton has taken the trouble to show still hold in a *quam proxime* form — are the very ones he invokes in Book 3 to conclude that the forces retaining bodies in their orbits in our planetary system are all centripetal and inverse-square. (By contrast, as noted earlier, while the proposition, "if a Keplerian ellipse exactly, then inverse-square exactly," is true, the proposition, "if a Keplerian ellipse *quam proxime*, then inverse-square *quam proxime*," is not true when the eccentricity of the ellipse is not large, as explained in Smith, 2002.) A failure to notice these *quam proxime* forms in Book 1 blinds one to the subtlety of the approximative reasoning Newton employs in Book 3.

The purpose of Book 2 is to provide a conclusive refutation of the Cartesian idea, adopted as well by Leibniz, that the planets are carried around their orbits by fluid vortices. Newton's main argument, which extends from the beginning of Section 1 until the end of Section 7, occupies 80 percent of the Book. Section 9, which ends the Book, offers a further, parting argument. We best dispense with this second argument before turning to the first.

The thrust of the argument in Section 9 is that fluid vortices are incompatible with Kepler's area and 3/2 power rules. The argument has two shortcomings, both of them recognized by Newton's opponents at the time. First, the entire argument is predicated on a hypothesis: "The resistance that arises from want of slipperiness of the parts of the fluid is, *ceteris paribus*, proportional to the velocity with which the parts of the fluid are separated from one another." Fluids of this sort are now called "Newtonian." The absence of evidence for the hypothesis left Newton's opponents free to adopt other rules for the velocity gradient in a vortex generated around a rotating cylinder or sphere, rules that could undercut his conclusions. Second, his analysis of the vortex generated around a rotating cylinder or sphere involves fundamentally wrong physics: it defines steady state in terms of a balance of forces instead of torques across each shell element comprising the vortex. To use Johann Bernoulli's words from 1730, Newton "completely neglects to take into account the action of the lever, the consideration of which however is absolutely necessary here, it being obvious that the same force, applied along the tangent to the circumference of a large wheel, has a greater efficacity for making it turn than it has when applied to the circumference of a smaller radius." (This is not the only place in the *Principia* where it is clear that Newton had not thought through the mechanics of angular motion.)

The argument that carried much more weight at the time — it convinced Huygens, for example — is the one that extends across the first seven sections of the Book. The thrust of this argument is clear from its conclusion, as stated more forcefully in the second and third editions than in the first:

And even if air, water, quicksilver, and similar fluids, by some infinite division of their parts, could be subtilized and become infinitely fluid mediums, they would not resist projected balls any the less. For the resistance which is the subject of the preceding propositions arises from the inertia of matter; and the inertia of matter is essential to bodies and is always proportional to the quantity of matter. By the division of the parts of a fluid, the resistance that arises from the tenacity and friction of the parts can indeed be diminished, but the quantity of matter is not diminished by the division of its parts; and since the quantity of matter remains the same, its force of inertia — to which the resistance discussed here is always proportional — remains the same. For the resistance to be diminished, the quantity of matter in the spaces through which bodies move must be diminished. And therefore the celestial spaces, through which the globes of the planets and comets move continually in all directions freely and without any sensible diminution of motion, are devoid of any corporeal fluid, except perhaps the very rarest of vapors and rays of light transmitted through those spaces.

To reach this conclusion Newton had to show that (1) the inertia of the fluid does indeed produce a resistance force proportional to its density, a force that (2) is independent of the tenacity (that is, surface friction) and the friction of the parts (that is, viscosity) of the fluid. Perhaps in part in emulation of the approach to centripetal forces that appeared to have succeeded so well in Books 1 and 3, the approach Newton takes in Book 2 is to develop, so far as he can, a generic mathematical theory of motion under resistance forces and then turn to experimental phenomena so that, in the words of Book 1, "it may be found out which conditions of forces apply" to different kinds of fluids. The theory in Book 1 is generic in that it examines centripetal forces that vary as different functions of the distance from the force center. The theory in Book 2 is generic in that it examines motion under resistance forces that vary as the velocity, the velocity squared, the sum of these two, and ultimately even the sum of two or three independent contributions, each of which is allowed to vary as any power of velocity whatever. Because Newton's goal was to reach a conclusion about the contribution to the total resistance made by the inertia of the fluid, and he recognized that surface friction and viscosity can contribute to the resistance as well, his empirical problem became one of *disaggregating* the inertial contribution from the total resistance, that is, the contribution that alone varies with the density of the fluid. Fortunately, because gravitational forces so totally dominate celestial motions, this need to disaggregate different sorts of forces did not arise in Book 3.

From Newton's point of view, then, the basic problem — assuming that three independent mechanisms contribute to the total resistance forces, only one of which is proportional to the fluid density ρf — was to find an experimental phenomenon that would allow him to determine (1) the three exponents in the following schema, and (2) laws defining the three coefficients — or, more minimally, at least the variation of the coefficient of the last term for the specific case of spheres:

$$F_{resist} = a_0 v^n_0 + a_1 v^n_1 + b_2 \rho_f v^n_2$$

Some preliminary pendulum-decay experiments showed promise for doing this, leading him in the first edition to rely solely on this phenomenon. The idea was to start a pendulum from several different heights in order to cover a range of velocities and then to use simultaneous algebraic equations to fit a two or three term polynomial to two or three lost-arc data-points, changing the exponents until the polynomial achieved good agreement with the other lost-arc data points. The theoretical solutions for pendulum motion under resistance forces in Section 6 would then allow him to infer the forces from the rate of decay of the pendulum. These theoretical solutions covered resistance forces that vary not only as velocity to the powers 0, 1, and 2, but also as any power at all of velocity. In principle, therefore, he saw himself in a position to infer laws for resistance forces on spheres from the phenomenon of pendulum decay in full parallel with his deduction of the law of universal gravity from the phenomena of orbital motion in Book 3. And he could then conclude from the total absence of signs of resistance forces acting on the planets and, most especially, comets that the density of any fluid in the celestial regions must be exactly or very nearly zero.

Unfortunately, pendulum-decay turned out not to be as well behaved a phenomenon as Newton anticipated it was going to be while he was working on the first edition. The problem, as he later realized, was that he had to let the pendulum swing many times in order to measure the rate of decay, and in the process it gave rise to a "to and fro" motion in the surrounding fluid, so that the *relative* velocity between the bob and the fluid, which is the velocity that matters in resistance, could not be determined or controlled. The General Scholium following Section 6 reports detailed decay-rate data for an impressive range of experiments, including different size bobs in air and bobs moving as well in water and mercury. The reader is also shown in detail how to proceed from the data in each case to a polynomial as above defining the resistance force. Any reader who worked through the data discovered what Newton knew, but was less than candid about: no polynomial fit the data. The experiments did clearly indicate that resistance forces involve no power of velocity greater than 2, and they provided good evidence that a velocity squared effect was dominant, even to the extent of masking any effect involving some other power. Newton also managed to extract some highly qualified evidence that the velocity squared effect varies as the density of the fluid and the frontal area (that is, the square of the diameter) of spheres.

The approach to resistance in the first edition relied entirely on pendulum-decay experiments. The disappointing evidence they yielded led to a far weaker statement of the conclusion about the absence of fluid in the celestial regions in the first edition than the conclusion in the subsequent editions quoted above. Not long after the first edition was published, Newton initiated some vertical-fall experiments in water that persuaded him that the phenomenon of vertical-fall in resisting media would yield much better behaved data. In the second and third editions, therefore, even though the pendulum-decay experiments are still fully reported, the central argument in Book 2 relies on vertical-fall experiments (including ones from the top of the dome of the newly completed St. Paul's Cathedral) to establish a resistance effect on spheres that is proportional to the density of the fluid, the square of the diameter, and the square of the velocity. The data from these experiments were very good — indeed, even better than Newton realized, for small vagaries in them that he dismissed as experimental error were in fact not vagaries at all, but evidence that no polynomial of the sort he was seeking is adequate for resistance forces.

While the vertical-fall experiments put Newton in a position to make his concluding rejection of vortex theories more forceful, they also posed a methodological complication. The vertical-fall experiments offered no way of disaggregating the contribution to resistance made by the inertia of the medium from the total resistance. But the argument against vortices required him to show that, no matter how perfectly free of friction and viscosity the celestial fluid might be, its inertia would still give rise to resistance forces that would affect the motions of comets, if not planets as well. From the resistance measured in the pendulum-decay experiments, Newton could conclude that the forces in air and water are dominated by a contribution that varies as the velocity squared. In the vertical-fall experiments in air and water the measured forces varied to first approximation as the product of the density and the velocity squared, but only to a first approximation, leaving room to question whether a purely inertial contribution had been isolated. Newton dealt with this problem by offering a rather *ad hoc* theoretical derivation for the purely inertial contribution, showing how closely it agreed with the vertical-fall results, and proposing that the differences between the theoretical and the measured resistances could be used to investigate other contributions. Success of such a program in characterizing the contributions made by surface friction and the viscosity would have provided compelling support for Newton's theory of the inertial contribution. Still, the approach left Newton with not so straightforward a derivation of the laws of resistance forces from phenomena as he had hoped for in the first edition.

In fact, there is a deep mistake in Newton's approach to resistance forces that came to be understood only at the beginning of the twentieth century. Resistance forces do not arise from independent contributions made by such factors as the viscosity and inertia of the fluid. Consequently, no polynomial consisting of a few always positive terms in powers of velocity can ever be adequate for resistance forces. The first indication of this came when d'Alembert, unhappy with Newton's *ad hoc* theory for the inertial contribution, analyzed the flow of what we now call a perfect fluid about spheres and bodies of other shapes, discovering in all cases that the net force of the fluid is exactly zero. Consequently, contrary to Newton, there is no such thing as *the* contribution made to resistance purely by the inertia of the fluid. Resistance forces always arise from a combination of viscous and inertial effects, however low the viscosity of the fluid may be. Newton's assumption that resistance forces can be represented as a sum, one term of which gives the contribution made purely by the inertia of the fluid, was wrong empirically, much as his assumptions about simultaneity and space being Euclidean turned out to be wrong. Unlike the latter assumptions, however, the assumption about resistance amounted to a dead end. All Newton achieved in Book 2 with resistance forces was merely a curve-fit.

Save for the short opening sections, "*Regulae Philosophandi*" and "*Phenomena*," Book 3, in contrast to Books 1 and 2, is not marked off into sections. Nevertheless, the main body of it does consist of four clearly separate parts: (1) the derivation of the law of gravity (Props. 1-8); (2) implications of this law for orbital and rotating bodies (from the corollaries to Prop. 8 through Prop. 24); (3) a quantitative derivation of select lunar inequalities and the precession of the equinoxes from the law of gravity (Props. 25-39); and (4) a solution for comet trajectories, with examples and comments (Props. 40-42). These parts will be discussed in sequence below.

Newton's first two rules of reasoning appeared in the first edition (there labeled as hypotheses), the third rule was added in the second edition, and the fourth rule, in the third edition. These are rules intended to govern evidential reasoning in natural philosophy, akin to rules of deductive reasoning except for their very much not guaranteeing true conclusions from true premises. In particular, Rule 2 authorizes the inference from same effect to same cause, a notoriously invalid inference, and Rule 3 authorizes inductive generalization to all bodies universally of those qualities of bodies "that belong to all bodies on which experiments can be made." Newton's phrasing carries no suggestion that these rules yield truths or even a high probability of truth. The operative phrase in both Rules 3 and 4, for example, is properly translated "should be taken," and Rule 4 makes the provisional character of the authorized inferences explicit:

In experimental philosophy, propositions gathered from phenomena by induction should be taken to be either exactly or very nearly true notwithstanding any contrary hypotheses, until yet other phenomena make such propositions either more exact or liable to exceptions.

The philosophic question why Newton's rules are appropriate is best addressed not by asking how they increase the probability of truth, but by asking whether there is some strategy in ongoing research for which these rules will both promote further discoveries and safeguard against dead-end garden paths that ultimately require all the supposed discoveries to be discarded.

Six astronomical phenomena are listed and discussed in the section called "*Phenomena*" — most importantly, that Mercury, Venus, Mars, Jupiter, and Saturn, and the satellites of the latter two sweep out equal areas in equal times with respect to the central bodies of their respective orbits, and their periods vary as the 3/2 power of their mean distances from these bodies. The ellipse, by the way, is not one of the phenomena. In Phenomenon 3 Newton rules out the Ptolemaic system, just as Galileo had in his *Dialogue Concerning the Two Chief World Systems*, by appealing to the phases of Mercury and Venus and their absence in the case of Mars, Jupiter, and Saturn to conclude that these five orbits encircle the Sun. But this Phenomenon and all the others are carefully formulated to remain neutral between the Copernican and Tychonic systems. In Phenomenon 4 Boulliau's calculated orbits are treated on a par with Kepler's, indicating that the phenomena do not rule out the possibility that Boulliau's alternative to the area rule is correct. Phenomenon 6 explicitly grants that the area rule holds only approximately for the Moon, with a further remark indicating that none of the phenomena are being put forward as holding exactly. This points the way to the most reasonable reading of all of the phenomena: they describe to reasonably high approximation, but not more than that, the observations of the planets and their satellites made by Tycho and others over a finite period of time — roughly from 1570 to the time of Newton's writing. On this way of viewing the Phenomena, they are in no way contentious or problematic. They leave entirely open not only questions about whether any claims concerning the orbits made by Kepler and his contemporaries hold exactly, but also questions about whether any of these claims hold even remotely in other eras, past or future. The Phenomena are thus not inconsistent with Descartes' insistence that the motions are constantly changing.

The "deduction" of the law of universal gravity from the phenomena in the first eight propositions of Book 3 has provoked a great deal of controversy in the philosophical literature over the last century or so. At the heart of this controversy is the challenge posed by Pierre Duhem: how can a deduction proceed from premises (the planets sweep out equal areas in equal times and their orbits are stationary) to a conclusion, the law of gravity, that then implies that the premises are false (the planets do not sweep out equal areas in equal times and the orbits are not stationary, but instead precess)? The answer is simple: Newton's reasoning is approximative. He is using "if, then" statements that have been shown in Book 1 to hold in "if…*quam proxime*, then… *quam proxime*" form to infer conclusions from premises that hold at least *quam proxime* over a restricted period of time. Of course, this means that the deduction shows only that the conclusions, most notably the law of gravity, hold *quam proxime* over the restricted period of time for which the premises hold. The Rules of Reasoning then license the conclusion to be taken exactly, without restriction of space or time. The conclusions, so taken, do indeed then show that the premises hold only *quam proxime*, and not exactly. This conclusion in no way contradicts the premises.

Recognizing that Newton's reasoning is approximative answers another complaint about the "deduction" of universal gravity: Newton invokes the proposition, *if bodies move uniformly in concentric circular orbits whose periods vary as the 3/2 power of the radii, then the centripetal forces acting on these bodies vary as the inverse-square of the radii of the orbits*, knowing full well that observation had established for centuries that the planets do not move uniformly in circular orbits. Newton does indeed invoke this proposition first to conclude (in Prop. 1) that, in modern parlance, there is an inverse-square centripetal acceleration field around Jupiter and Saturn and next to conclude (in Prop. 2) that there is an inverse-square centripetal acceleration field around the Sun. The orbits of the satellites of Jupiter were then considered to be circular, and hence Newton's inference from their motion was not so problematic. While, however, the orbits of Venus, Jupiter, and Saturn were considered to be very nearly circular, the motion in them had been known from before Ptolemy not to be uniform. Newton expressly concedes that his inference of the inverse-square from the 3/2 power rule for the planets is only approximate when, in the very next sentence, he remarks, "But this second part of the proposition is proved with the greatest exactness from the fact that the aphelia are at rest." The absence of precession, however, can be used to infer the inverse-square only for each orbit individually, not a single, unified inverse-square centripetal acceleration field encompassing all of the orbits. Newton is accordingly using the 3/2 rule for circular orbits to establish that an inverse-square field holds around the Sun to at least a first approximation, and then using the absence of precession of the individual orbits to tighten the approximation.

Interpreting Newton's deduction of universal gravity as an exercise in approximative reasoning answers a further complaint of Duhem's: insofar as the area rule holds only to high approximation, so too do any number of alternatives to it, such as Boulliau's geometric construction, and hence Newton's "deduction" begs the question of why the area rule is to be preferred to these alternatives. This question, however, is irrelevant so long as the conclusion remains in the weak form, the law of gravity holds *quam proxime* for the planets and their satellites over the time period for which observations have shown the phenomena to hold *quam proxime*. The phenomena really are sufficient to reach the conclusion in this weak form. So, the complaint has bite only when the law of gravity is taken to be exact. But there, however, Newton does provide a response to it when he concludes in Propositions 13 and 14 that the planets *would* describe areas exactly proportional to the times in stationary orbits if "the Sun *were* at rest and the remaining planets did not act upon one another." The reason, then, why the phenomena from which Newton proceeded in the deduction have claim to being preferred to alternatives to them is that the theory deduced from them, when taken to hold exactly, identifies circumstances under which the phenomena would hold exactly, as well. That this be the case amounts to a requirement on the deduction from phenomena: the leap to taking the law of gravity as exact is justified only if it yields circumstances in which the phenomena from which it was inferred *would* hold exactly.

This analysis of the "deduction" of universal gravity does not answer two further complaints lodged against it. First, in concluding that the centripetal force acting on the Moon is inverse-square, Newton grants that the precession of the lunar orbit implies an exponent of -2 and 4/243 for the force rather than exactly -2, but then claims that the small fraction can be accounted for by the perturbing action of the Sun's gravity. But the magnitude for the action of the Sun that he gives in Proposition 3 is twice the value he later in Book 3 indicates is the correct value. This lacuna was not resolved by Alexis-Claude Clairaut until two decades after Newton died. Second, when Newton invokes the third law of motion in the corollaries to Proposition 5, he is tacitly assuming that, for example, Jupiter and the Sun are, in effect, directly interacting. In other words, he is ignoring the alternative favored by Huygens that some unseen medium is effecting the centripetal force on Jupiter, a medium that can in principle absorb the linear momentum which Newton is assuming is being transferred to the Sun. Huygens may well have perceived this lacuna, to which Cotes explicitly called Newton's attention while he was preparing the second edition.

The group of propositions following the deduction of universal gravity gives indications of the evidential strategy that lies behind the leap to taking this law to be exact. Immediately upon concluding first that the planets would sweep out equal areas in equal times in exact ellipses and then that the orbits would be exactly stationary were it not for the gravitational interactions among the planets, Newton calls attention to the easiest to observe deviations from this idealization, the then still mysterious vagaries in the motions of Jupiter and Saturn which Newton attributes to their gravitational interaction. Because, according to the theory, the idealization would hold exactly in the specified circumstances, these and all other deviations must result from further forces not taken into account in the idealized case. Identifying these forces and showing that, according to the theory, they do produce the deviations is a way for ongoing research to marshal continuing evidence to bear on the theory of gravity. To put the point differently, the initial idealizations that Newton identifies can serve as the starting point for a process of successive approximations that should yield increasingly close agreement with the complex true motions. These idealizations are especially well suited for this purpose precisely because, according to the theory, they would hold exactly were no other forces at work, and hence every deviation from them should be physically telling, and not just, for example, an accidental feature of a curve-fit. Pursuit of such a research program of successive approximations promises to yield either further evidence for the theory of gravity when the program is successful or the exceptions Newton speaks of in Rule 4 that require the theory to be revised.

Of the other results developed in the group of propositions following the deduction of universal gravity, the most heralded at the time were the defense of Copernicanism in Proposition 12 and the identification of the cause of the tides in Proposition 24 — two topics that Kepler, Galileo, and Descartes had all addressed. Nevertheless, the two Propositions that proved most important were 19 and 20, which respectively derive the non-spheroidal figure of the Earth and the variation of surface gravity with latitude under the assumption that the density of the Earth is uniform. This is the only passage in the *Principia* that Newton reworked extensively in both the second and then again in the third edition. As Newton was fully aware, and Huygens and a few others realized, these are the only results in the *Principia* that depend on *universal* gravity — that is, inverse-square gravity directed toward every particle of matter forming the Earth — and not merely macroscopic *celestial* gravity — inverse-square gravity directed toward celestial bodies. In his *Discourse on the Cause of Gravity*, Huygens offered an alternative theoretical account of the figure of the Earth and the variation of surface gravity, and he claimed to have evidence confirming it and hence refuting Newton's *universal* gravity. In part because evidence on the figure of the Earth and the variation of gravity with latitude were accessible in expeditions to the equator, these were the results in the *Principia* that were the first to receive concerted critical attention during the 1730s and 1740s. There was a complication in all this, however. The extremely precise results for both the figure of the Earth and the variation of gravity that Newton tabulated in the second and third editions were based on uniform density, and hence, just like Keplerian motion, represented an idealization, departures from which would point to non-uniformities of density. Not until Clairaut's *Theory of the Figure of the Earth* did means become available to calculate the effects of non-uniformities in the density.

Propositions 25 through 35 derive quantitative results for three lunar inequalities — the systematic departure from the area rule called the "the variation," the 18 year motion of the line of nodes, and the fluctuating inclination of the orbit — from the perturbing action of the Sun. For all three Newton starts with a circular orbit, so these too involve departures from an idealization. The values he obtained for the different components of the solar perturbing force in Proposition

25 and subsequently, as needed, were accurate to several significant figures. All three derivations, which are mathematically demanding, were successful in obtaining agreement with the values of the inequalities obtained from observation, especially so the derivation for the recession of the lunar nodes, for which he achieves agreement with the known value to better than 98 percent. (Newton must have been mystified by the failure of his seemingly parallel derivation of the 9 year precession of the line of apsides to achieve better than 50 percent agreement.)

The Scholium following Proposition 35 opens with the explanation for the preceding efforts on the lunar inequalities: "I wished to show by these computations of the lunar motions that the lunar motions can be computed from their causes by the theory of gravity". Newton never found a way of deriving the precession of the lunar apogee from the theory of gravity, and consequently he never succeeded with a complete, gravity-derived account of the lunar orbit. The mathematical treatment of the three lunar inequalities nevertheless did provide added support for his theory of gravity. It also introduced the idea of attacking the problem of the true orbit in a sequence of successive approximations by calculating perturbations in motion in an assumed orbit caused by the gravitational action of the Sun. This was not only an entirely new approach to the then unsolved problem of simply describing the motion of the Moon, an approach that proceeded from the physical cause to the motion; it was also the beginnings of the perturbational approach that dominated all of celestial mechanics from the middle of the eighteenth century until late in the twentieth. As difficult as Propositions 25 through 35 were for readers at the time — and still are for readers now — they crucially promoted the further research on the complicated orbital motions that ultimately supplied overwhelming support for Newton's theory of gravity.

It was a real breakthrough when Newton discovered that the gravitational forces of the Sun and Moon acting on an oblately spheroidal Earth would produce a wobble of the Earth that, at least qualitatively, could account for the precession of the Equinoxes. No physical explanation for this phenomenon had been proposed before.

Newton faced a problem, however, in trying to carry out a quantitative derivation of the precession: he knew the magnitude of the gravitational action of the Sun on the Earth but not that of the Moon, for he could not obtain the mass of the Moon in the way he had for the Sun, Jupiter, and Saturn insofar as no bodies orbit the Moon. Propositions 36 and 37 endeavor to infer the force of the Moon on the Earth from the difference in the heights of the tides when the Sun and Moon are in conjunction and in opposition. In the first edition Newton managed to derive a value for the rate of the precession in good agreement with the known value, but during the quarter century between the first and second editions he concluded that the value he had used for the Moon's force (6 and 1/3 times the Sun's force) was much too large. The derivation of the precession was therefore extensively revised in the second edition, using a new value for the Moon's force (4.4815 times the Sun's force, still more than a factor of 2 greater than the correct value). In all editions the derivation in Proposition 39 treated the wobble not directly as the motion of a rigid body, but by analogy with the motion of the lunar nodes. By the standards of our present physics, no part of Book 3 is further off-base than Newton's solution for the precession. The phenomenon, however, subsequently provided important evidence for Newton's theory of gravity when d'Alembert in 1749 carried out a successful derivation based on rigid body motion and a correct value of the Moon's force derived from the then recently discovered phenomenon of the nutation of the Earth.

Newton's account of the tides in Propositions 24, 36, and 37 was much heralded not only at the time, but still today. He is nevertheless receiving more credit for this than he is due. He did identify solar and lunar gravity as the forces driving the tides, but this is all he did. He ignored the rotation of the Earth, and worse he considered only the radial component of the solar and lunar gravitational forces in these three propositions. In fact, the radial component of these forces has a very small effect compared with the transradial component, that is, the component perpendicular to the radial component. All of this became clear in the 1770s when Laplace developed the mathematical theory of tidal motion from which all subsequent work has proceeded.

Book 3 ends with a revolutionary analysis of comet trajectories that occupies roughly one-third of the total length of the Book in all three editions. This analysis was slow in coming. As late as June 1686, Newton wrote: "the third [book] wants the Theory of Comets". What made the problem difficult, as compared to planet trajectories, was the need to work from a small number of imprecise one-shot observations made from a moving Earth. The method presented in the *Principia* fits a parabola iteratively to the observations, employing novel finite-difference methods that Newton later expanded into a full tract in mathematics, "Methodis Differentialis." The method presupposes the theory of gravity first in opting for a parabola and second in assuming that the inverse-square centripetal forces known from the planets act on comets along their entire trajectory. The text notes that the trajectories may well be ellipses, but the period of return in that case would be the best way of determining the ellipse. (The parabola approximates the high-curvature end of ellipses with high eccentricity.) The proposal that comets may return was novel, but even more revolutionary at the time was the claim that they button-hook around the Sun, implying that what had sometimes in the past been taken for two distinct comets were really one comet before and after perihelion.

In the first edition the method was applied only to the comet of 1680-81. The results are presented in a one-foot long diagram on the only fold-out page in the edition. Nothing like this diagram, shown in Figure 3, had ever appeared in print before. The diagram continued to appear in the next two editions, though in reduced form not requiring a fold-out in the third. In the second edition the method was refined and applied as well to the comets of 1664-65, 1683, and 1682 reflecting research Halley had carried out and published in his *Astronomiae Cometicae Synopsis* of 1705. The comet of 1682, now known as Halley's comet, was singled out as being sufficiently similar in trajectory to the comet of 1607 to warrant the proposal that it returns every 75 years.

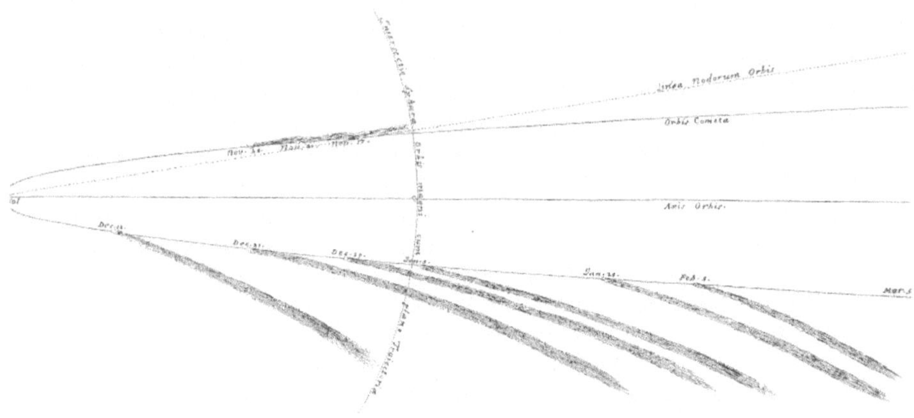

Figure 3

Added in the third edition was the retrograde comet of 1723, for which Bradley had supplied comparatively accurate observations and the method correspondingly displayed its most impressive success, with no discrepancies between the calculated and observed positions exceeding 1 minute of arc in either longitude or latitude. This suggested that the more exacting the observations entering into the calculation, the more accurate was the method.

Because Newton's theory of comet trajectories depended only on that part of the theory of gravity that was least controversial — inverse-square centripetal accelerations everywhere around the Sun — it did not provoke much philosophical resistance. The success of the method provided evidence that these centripetal forces act equally on comets, contrary to Hooke's proposal in his *Cometa* of 1678 that comets must consist of a fundamentally different kind of material from the planets insofar as they do not respond to the forces directed toward the Sun in the same way. The success of the method also provided strong evidence that inverse-square forces toward the Sun hold throughout the space surrounding it, for not only do comets traverse the spaces between the planet orbits, but also their trajectories, in contrast to those of the then known planets, are often highly inclined with respect to the plane of the ecliptic. Most of all, however, the success of the method provided the most compelling evidence against not only Cartesian vortices, but all theories claiming that the planets are carried around the Sun by fluid vortices. Corollary 3 to Proposition 39 in all three editions summarizes the argument:

Hence also it is manifest that the heavens are lacking in resistance. For the comets, following paths that are oblique and sometimes contrary to the course of the planets, move in all directions very freely and preserve their motions for a very long time even when these are contrary to the course of planets.

This was the argument that convinced Huygens when he read the first edition, and it became all the more compelling thereafter as the method was so successful with further comets.

The added evidence supplied by the theory of comets highlights a sometimes overlooked aspect of Book 3. The development of evidence for the theory of gravity in it does not end with the "deduction" of the law of universal gravity at the beginning, but continues all the way through the Book. During the eighteenth century attention focused overwhelmingly on the evidence supplied by Newton's theory of the figure of the Earth and the variation of surface gravity, the theory of the tides, the quantitative derivations of select lunar inequalities, the derivation of the precession of the equinoxes, and the theory of comets. This suggests that, both then and now, the "deduction" of universal gravity should not be read in isolation from the rest of Book 3, but instead the entire Book should be seen as offering a sustained evidential argument for the theory. Read this way in the context of the rest of the Book, the "deduction" is most appropriately viewed as intended to establish universal gravity, but only provisionally, as a theory on which further research is to be predicated, research that will continue to bring evidence to bear on the theory.

From Halley's anonymous review of the first edition of the *Principia* forward, there has been a marked tendency to overstate what the *Principia* achieved, glossing over the many loose ends it left for others to recognize and address. A consequence of this is an equal tendency to distort the context of the enormous advances made in both mechanics and orbital astronomy during the eighteenth century, diminishing the difficulties those following Newton faced and their accomplishments in resolving them. The *Principia* is peculiar in this regard, for a list of its achievements without mentioning their loose ends overstates what it accomplished, but a list of its loose ends risks understating its extraordinary achievements. In an effort to strike a balance we here list eleven major scientific issues of the time to which Book 3 supplied answers in the sequence listed, the answers, and the most important loose ends in the reasoning offered in the evidential arguments for those answers.

1. *What physically retains the planets in orbits around the Sun and their satellites in orbit around them?* Newton's answer — *inverse-square gravity, one in kind with everyday terrestrial gravity* — turned on a largely suppressed failure to account for more than half of the precession of the lunar orbit, it tacitly assumed interaction between the Sun and Jupiter and the other individual planets, and it raised unanswered questions about whether the perihelia of the planetary orbits do or do not precess.

2. *How does gravity vary, both below and above the surface of the Earth?* In the absence of confirming data, Newton's answer — *to a first approximation, linearly with distance to the center below the surface, and inversely with the square of the distance above it* — presupposed uniform density in the first part and a spherical Earth with spherically symmetric density in the second, and therefore left open the possibility that gravity is constant near the surface of the Earth, just as Huygens continued to claim in his response to the Principia, citing supporting evidence.

3. *What are the relative densities of the planets, with respect to one another and to the Sun?* Newton gives theory-dependent answers for Jupiter, Saturn, and the Earth in the corollaries to Proposition 8, but the one for the Earth, even in the third edition, depended on a still questionable value for the horizontal solar parallax (required to determine the distance of the Moon from the Earth in astronomical units), and no corroborating evidence

for these answers had emerged, such as from the actions of Jupiter and Saturn on one another.

4. *Is there some principled way to resolve the dispute between the Copernican and Tychonic systems and thereby settle the question of the proper center to which all the motions in our planetary system should be referred?* Newton's answer — *the center of gravity of the system, about which the Sun circulates at comparatively small distances* — depended on the assumed applicability of the third law of motion in claiming that the Sun is in motion, and the precise location of the center of gravity remained open in the absence of values for the relative masses of Mercury, Venus, and Mars.

5. *What are the true motions of the planets, and which, if any, of the schemes for calculating planet locations is to be preferred, Kepler's or one of the alternatives to it?* Newton's answer was not simple: "*If the sun were at rest and the remaining planets did not act upon one another, their orbits would be elliptical, having the sun in their common focus, and they would describe areas proportional to the times;*" *and the aphelia and nodes would be stationary. The Keplerian system, amended in the manner of Horrocks to infer mean distances from the periods, is therefore the preferred approximation to the true motions.* The main loose-end in this answer was whether the actual motions do deviate from the Keplerian ideal, and if so, whether all the deviations could be attributed to specific forces, gravitational or otherwise. A further loose-end, addressed in part in Book 3, was whether the non-Keplerian motion of the Moon can be shown not to be a counterexample to Newton's argument in the case of the planets.

6. *Is the motion of Jupiter and Saturn aberrant and, if so, what are the inequalities in it and what causes them?* Newton answered *yes, because they interact gravitationally, and the dominant inequality has a period corresponding to the 19 years between their consecutive conjunctions.* (The second part of this answer did not appear in the first edition.) By the

early 1720s it had become clear that the dominant period in the anomalies of motion of these two planets is not that of the time between conjunctions, but something of much longer duration, giving rise to the questions of what the vagaries actually are and whether they can truly be derived from Jupiter's and Saturn's gravitational forces.

7. *How, if at all, does the Earth's surface gravity vary with latitude, and how, if at all, does the Earth's figure differ from a sphere?* Newton's answer changes from the first to the second to the third edition, but in all cases vagaries in the cited data raise the question of what the actual variations are. Also, because his idealized theoretical calculation assumes uniform density, his answer raises the questions whether the density of the Earth is uniform and whether the true figure of the Earth and variation of surface gravity can be reconciled with non-uniformities in density.

8. *What precisely is the motion of the Moon, and what gives rise to the inequalities in it, inequalities not observed in the motions of the satellites of Jupiter and Saturn?* Newton's answer to the second part is the perturbing effect of the Sun's gravity, leaving the answer to the first in the form of a promissory note: work out all the perturbations from solar gravity, and you will have the answer. The major open question was whether the complex motion of the line of apsides and the inequality known as the evection — the two features for which the Horrocksian cinematic model that Newton had employed in the Scholium to Book 3, Proposition 35 had resorted to an old-fashoined epicycle — can be derived from the action of solar gravity.

9. *What causes the tides, and why do they vary in time as well as from place to place in the way they do?* Because Newton's answer — *the gravitational action of the Sun and the Moon* — was merely qualitative, it left room to question whether the Moon attracts the Earth and, if so, by how strong a force. Also left open was the question of how the inertia and viscosity of the seas and the rotation of the Earth affect the tides, a question

requiring a dynamic analysis of the motions of the seas in response to solar and lunar gravity.

10. *What physically produces the precession of the equinoxes?* Newton's derivation of the precession from the gravitational action of the Moon and Sun raised three unresolved questions: What are the correct values for the mass of the Moon and the oblateness of the Earth? Is the resulting motion of the Earth really analogous to that of the lunar nodes? How does the varying inclination of the Moon affect the calculated motion?

11. *What trajectories do comets describe?* Newton's answer — *conic-sections that can at least be approximated by parabolas in the region in which they are observable* — gave weight to the question whether the parabolic trajectory works for all comets, and not just the comet of 1680-81 in the case of the first edition, the three others analyzed in the second, and the additional one in the third. The *Principia* also left open questions about how the gravity of Jupiter and Saturn might affect comet motions, whether any significance should be attached to the residual discrepancies between theory and observation in Newton's results, and which, if any, comets do return in some regular fashion.

Careful reading of the *Principia* makes clear that, although unforthcoming about any of the loose ends, Newton was perfectly aware of them all, in one way or another flagging each for the benefit of the highly astute reader. An instructive way to present the history of eighteenth century research in the wake of the *Principia* is to trace how each of the loose ends became a prominent matter of concern and was then resolved, at least to the point of being removed as in any way a threat to Newton's theory of gravity. This process of addressing the loose ends in Book 3 did not get underway until the 1730s, after Newton had died. During his lifetime the most pressing complaint against the *Principia* was the absence of a mechanism to account for its action save for action at a distance, which Newton himself regarded as "so great an absurdity, that I believe no man who has in philosophical matters a competent faculty of thinking can ever fall into it." The absence of a mechanism, however, was not something that Newton himself regarded as a loose-end in the *Principia*, for he insisted that all the conclusions listed above could be established, and any loose ends in them resolved, through the law of universal gravity alone, independently of the mechanism responsible for it. Over the decades after he died, those engaged in research predicated on his theory of gravity came increasingly to this same view of the question of mechanism.

In two passages that remained word for word the same in all three editions Newton announced that the *Principia* was meant to illustrate a new approach to empirical inquiry. Neither the remark about deriving forces from phenomena of motion and then motions from these forces in the Preface to the first edition nor the remark about comparing a generic mathematical theory of centripetal forces with the phenomena in order to find out which conditions of force actually hold at the end of Book 1, Section 11, however, shed much light on just what this new approach is supposed to be. Other than these two passages, the only notable remark about methodology is the famous passage, quoted earlier, from the General Scholium added in the second edition as a final, parting statement:

I have not as yet been able to deduce from phenomena the reason for these properties of gravity, and I do not feign hypotheses. For whatever is not deduced from the phenomena must be called a hypothesis; and hypotheses, whether metaphysical or physical, or based on occult qualities, or mechanical, have no place in experimental philosophy. In this experimental philosophy, propositions are deduced from the phenomena and are made general by induction. The impenetrability, mobility, and impetus of bodies, and the laws of motion and law of gravity have been found by this method. And it is enough that gravity should really exist and should act according to the laws that we have set forth and should suffice for all the motions of the heavenly bodies and of our sea.

Much of the discussion of the methodology of the *Principia* in the philosophical literature, from the eighteenth century down to the present time, has taken this clearly polemical passage as the starting point, generating unfortunately more heat than light. This is not the place to grapple with all the controversies surrounding this passage. Some guarded comments about the methodology of the *Principia* may nevertheless prove helpful.

It is scarcely surprising that the unprecedented success of Newton's theory of gravity stimulated interest in the methodology of the *Principia*. The obvious thought was to emulate this success in other areas by following the same method. But then, even independently of questions about what the method was, one has to consider exactly how it contributed to the success. Viewed in retrospect, Book 2 makes clear that this question has no simple answer. If Newton followed the same method in Book 2, then the failure of his effort on resistance forces — even worse, the failure that he did not recognize — shows that the method was no guarantee of success. The empirical world must cooperate for it to succeed.

Two aspects of the general thrust of the method are perfectly clear. First, Newton viewed it as contrasting with what was then called the method of hypotheses — that is, the method of putting forward hypotheses that reached far beyond the available data and then marshalling evidence for them by deducing testable conclusions from them. Second, Newton viewed the method as requiring that questions be regarded as open when empirical considerations had not yet yielded answers to them. Whatever may have been required for empirical consideration to establish a theoretical conclusion, and whatever the status, provisional or otherwise, any such established conclusion was supposed to have, Newton viewed the method as allowing — even mandating — that theoretical answers to some questions could be established even while other closely related questions remained in abeyance. In particular, to use Newton's phrasing from the Scholium that ends Section 11, the physical species and physical proportions of forces could, in the appropriate sense, be established even though the question of their physical causes remained open. The clear aim of the method was accordingly to limit theoretical claims to "inductive generalizations," as specified by the Rules of Reasoning, of conclusions dictated by experiment and observation.

Newton's eschewing the method of hypotheses produced no controversy at the time. In a manuscript revision of his "Essay on the causes of celestial motions" Leibniz even adopted Newtonian phrasing: "What follows is not based on hypotheses but is deduced from phenomena by the laws of motion". A large fraction of those who had read at most small portions of the *Principia* and depended on others for their knowledge of it most likely saw Newton as having hypothesized inverse-square attraction and hence as in fact following the method of hypotheses. In the years after Newton died, the most celebrated issues receiving concentrated research arose not from how Newton had arrived at universal gravity, but from the claims he had derived from it concerning the figure of the Earth, the vagaries in the motions of Jupiter and Saturn, and the motion of the Moon. The individuals at the center of this research certainly saw these issues as a test of Newton's theory of gravity, but the distinction between taking the theory as a hypothesis and taking it as a provisionally established conclusion was a distinction without much difference for them. Still, it is worth noting that the conclusion Clairaut first drew from the factor of 2 discrepancy in the motion of the lunar apogee was not that Newton's theory of gravity was false, but that the inverse-square needed to be supplemented by a $1/r^4$ term — a response fully in keeping with Newton's fourth rule of reasoning.

The aspect of Newton's method that did produce controversy at the time was his insisting that he had established conclusions about the physical species and physical proportions of celestial forces while holding questions about their physical causes in abeyance. This was the core of the complaint by Cartesians that the *Principia* was a work of mathematics, not physics. For Newton's two most important critics, however, Huygens and Leibniz, the objection was not to holding the question of physical causes open, but to accepting certain conclusions that in their mind ruled out the very possibility of a proper answer to the question of physical cause. The defect in Newton's method lay in its not imposing the constraint on theory that all action be through contact, and not at a distance. The violation of this constraint lay behind Huygens's remarking,

Concerning the Cause of the tides given by M. Newton, I am by no means satisfied, nor by all the other Theories that he builds upon his Principle of Attraction, which seems to me absurd, as I have already mentioned in the addition to the *Discourse on Gravity*. And I have often wondered how he could have given himself all the trouble of making such a number of investigations and difficult calculations that have no other foundation than this very principle.

This, then, was the truly controversial aspect of Newton's method in the *Principia* with which the next generation had to come to some accommodation before research on its loose ends could become respectable.

The idea of developing a mathematical theory in order to enable experiment and observation to provide theory-mediated answers to questions did not originate with the *Principia*. In his *Horologium Oscillatorium*, the work the *Principia* most emulates, Huygens had developed a mathematical theory of pendulum motion that enabled measurement of the length and period of pendulums to provide a robust precise answer to the question, how far does an object fall in the absence of air resistance in the first second? — the measure then of the strength of surface gravity; and he had developed a mathematical theory of uniform circular motion that enabled measurement of the height and period of conical pendulums to provide a second answer to this question. By the time Newton started on the *Principia* pendulums had been used for more than a decade to answer questions about how surface gravity varies between Paris and other locations. The special problem Newton saw himself as having to face in using mathematical theory to a comparable end in the *Principia* stemmed from his realization, expressed in the "Copernican scholium," that the phenomena of orbital motions are inordinately complicated and hence open to multiple competing descriptions. The problem thus became one of finding a way to use mathematical theory to draw definite robust answers to questions about the physical species and proportions of forces from these phenomena. These answers opened the way to pursing the true motions in a sequence of successive approximations, in the process of which continuing evidence could be brought to bear on the theory, potentially delimiting its exactness and its universal applicability in the manner Newton had noted in his fourth rule of reasoning. Because the "Copernican scholium" was unknown at the time, the subtleties of the new method Newton followed to get around this problem went largely unnoticed.

Needless to say, these comments do not answer the philosophically most interesting question of how the method of the *Principia* contributed to the unprecedented success of its theory of gravity. Hopefully, however, they do remove some sources of confusion that have distorted so much of the philosophical discussion of the *Principia*.

Newton also made seminal contributions to optics, and shares credit with German mathematician Gottfried Wilhelm Leibniz for developing infinitesimal calculus[1]. In the Principia, Newton formulated the laws of motion and universal gravitation that formed the dominant scientific viewpoint for centuries until it was superseded by the theory of relativity Newton's calculus and optical theories provided the powerful Enlightenment metaphors for precisely measured change and illumination.

There was no single, unified Enlightenment. Instead, it is possible to speak of the French Enlightenment, the Scottish Enlightenment and the English, German, Swiss or American Enlightenment. Individual Enlightenment thinkers often had very different approaches. Locke differed from David Hume, Jean-Jacques Rousseau from Voltaire, Thomas Jefferson from Frederick the Great. Their differences and disagreements, though, emerged out of the common Enlightenment themes of rational questioning and belief in progress through dialogue.

Centered on the dialogues and publications of the French "philosophes" (Voltaire, Rousseau, Montesquieu, Buffon and Denis Diderot), the High Enlightenment might best be summed up by one historian's summary of Voltaire's "Philosophical Dictionary": "a chaos of clear ideas." Foremost among these was the notion that everything in the universe could be rationally demystified and cataloged. The signature publication of the period was Diderot's "Encyclopédie" (1751-

77), which brought together leading authors to produce an ambitious compilation of human knowledge.

Jefferson's Pursuit of Knowledge

It was an age of enlightened despots like Frederick the Great, who unified, rationalized and modernized Prussia in between brutal multi-year wars with Austria, and of enlightened would-be revolutionaries like Thomas Paine and Thomas Jefferson, whose "Declaration of Independence" (1776) framed the American Revolution in terms taken from of Locke's essays.

It was also a time of religious (and anti-religious) innovation, as Christians sought to reposition their faith along rational lines and deists and materialists argued that the universe seemed to determine its own course without God's intervention. Locke, along with French philosopher Pierre Bayle, began to champion the idea of the separation of Church and State. Secret societies—like the Freemasons, the Bavarian Illuminati and the Rosicrucians—flourished, offering European men (and a few women) new modes of fellowship, esoteric ritual and mutual assistance. Coffeehouses, newspapers and literary salons emerged as new venues for ideas to circulate

We quest as to what makes for the unity of such tremendously diverse thinkers under the idea or label of "Enlightenment". The Enlightenment is conceived broadly. D'Alembert, a leading figure of the French Enlightenment, characterizes his eighteenth century, in the midst of it, as "the century of philosophy par excellence", as because of the tremendous intellectual and scientific progress of the age, as well as because of the expectation of the age that philosophy (in the broad sense of the time, which includes the natural and social sciences) would dramatically improve human life. Guided by D'Alembert's characterization of his century, the Enlightenment is conceived here as having its primary origin in the scientific revolution of the 16th and 17th centuries. The rise of the new science progressively undermines not only the ancient geocentric conception of the cosmos, but also the set of presuppositions that had served to constrain and guide philosophical inquiry in the earlier times. The New Science (Italian: *La Scienza Nuova* pronounced is the major work of Italian philosopher Giambattista Vico. It was first published in 1725 to little success, but has gone on to be highly regarded and influential in the philosophy of history, sociology, and anthropology. The central concepts were highly original and prefigured the Age of Enlightenment.

The full title of the 1725 edition was *Principj di una Scienza Nuova Intorno alla Natura delle Nazioni per la Quale si Ritruovano i Principj di Altro Sistema del Diritto Naturale delle Genti*, ending with a dedication to Cardinal Lorenzo Corsini, the future Pope Clement XII. *Principj* and *ritruovano* being archaic spellings of *principi* and *ritrovano*, the title may be loosely translated "Principles of a New Science Concerning the Nature of Nations, through Which Are Recovered the Principles of Another System of the Natural Law of Peoples".

The 1730 edition was titled *Cinque Libri di Giambattista Vico de' Principj d' una Scienza Nuova d'Intorno alla Comune Natura della Nazion* ("Giambattista Vico's Five Books on the Principles of a New Science Concerning Nations' Shared Nature"), ending with a dedication to Clement XII.

The 1744 edition was slightly emended to *Principj di Scienza Nuova di Giambattista Vico d'Intorno alla Comune Natura delle Nazioni* ("Giambattista Vico's Principles of New Science Concerning Nations' Shared Nature"), without a title page dedication. Clement had died in 1740 and Vico in 1744, before the edition's publication.

Creation

In 1720, Vico began work on the *Scienza Nuova* as part of a treatise on universal rights. Although it was originally supposed to be sponsored by Cardinal Corsini, Vico was forced to finance the publication himself after the cardinal pleaded financial difficulty and withdrew his patronage. It was the first work by Vico to be written in Italian, since his previous ones had been in Latin.

The first edition of the *New Science* appeared in 1725. Vico worked on two heavily revised editions. The first was published in 1730, the second posthumously in 1744.

Approach, Style And Tone

In its first section, titled "Idea of the Work" (*Idea dell'Opera*), the 1730 and 1744 editions of *The New Science* explicitly present themselves as a "science of reasoning" (*scienza di ragionare*). The work (especially the section "Of the Elements") includes a dialectic between axioms (authoritative maxims or *degnità*) and "reasonings" (*ragionamenti*) linking and clarifying the axioms.

Vico began the third edition with a detailed close reading of a front piece portrait, examining the place of Gentile nations within the providential guidance of the Hebrew God. This portrait contains a number of images that are symbolically ascribed to the flow of human history. A triangle with the Eye of Providence appears in the top left. A beam of light from the eye shines upon a brooch attached to the breastplate of "the lady with the winged temples who surmounts the celestial globe or world of nature" (center right), which represents metaphysics. The beam reflects off the brooch onto the back of a robed character standing upon a pedestal (bottom left), representing the poet Homer. All around these main characters resides a variety of objects that represent the stages of human history which Vico categorizes into three epochs: the age of the gods "in which the gentiles believed they lived under divine governments, and everything was commanded them by auspices and oracles, which are the oldest institutions in profane history; the age of the heroes "in which they reigned everywhere in aristocratic commonwealths, on account of a certain superiority of nature which they held themselves to have over the plebs (or peasants);" and the age of men "in which all men recognized themselves as equal in human nature, and therefore there were established first the popular commonwealths and then the monarchies, both of which are forms of human government." By viewing these principles as universal phenomena which combined nature and government with language and philology, Vico could insert the history of the Gentile nations into the supreme guidance by divine providence. According to Vico, the proper end for government resulted with society entering into a state of universal equity: "The last type of jurisprudence was that of natural equity, which reigns naturally in the free commonwealths, in which the people, each for his own particular good (without understanding that it is the same for all), are led to command universal laws. They naturally desire these laws to bend benignly to the least details of matters calling for equal unity."

Vico specifies that his "science" reasons primarily about the function of religion in the human world ("Idea of the Work"), and in this respect the work "comes to be a civil theology reasoned from divine providence" (*vien ad essere una teologia civile ragionata della provvidenza divina*). Reconsidering divine providence within a human or political context, Vico unearths the "poetic theologians" (*poeti teologi*) of pagan antiquity, exposing the poetic character of theology independently of Christianity's sacred history and thus of Biblical authority. Vico's use of poetic theology, anticipated in his 1710 work *De Antiquissima Italorum Sapientia* ("On the Ancient Wisdom of the Italians"), confirms his ties to the Italian Renaissance and its own appeals to *theologia poetica*. With the early Renaissance, Vico shares the call for recovering a "pagan" or "vulgar" horizon for philosophy's providential agency or for recognizing the providence of our human "metaphysical" minds (*menti*) in the world of our "political" wills (*animi*). "Poetic theology" would serve as stage for an "ascent" to recognize the inherence or latency of rational agency in our actions, even when these are brutal. This way, the particular providence of the Bible's "true God" would not be required for the thriving of properly human life. All that would be needed was (A) false religions and gods and (B) the covert work of the *conatus* (the rational principle of a constitution of experience rooted in its proper infinite form), which was examined at length in *De Antiquissima Italorum Sapientia* and evoked again in the section "Of the Method" in the 1730 and 1744 editions of *The New Science*.

Vico is often seen as espousing a cyclical philosophy of history where human history is created by man, although Vico never speaks of "history without attributes" (Paolo Cristofolini, *Vice Pagano e Barbaro*), but of a "world of nations". Which is more, in the 1744 *Scienza Nuova* (esp. the "Conclusion of the Work") Vico stresses that "the world of nations" is made by men merely with respect to their sense of certainty (*certamente*), though not fundamentally, insofar as the world is guided by the human mind "metaphysically" independent of its makings (compare opening paragraph of the *Scienza Nuova*). Furthermore, although Vico is often attributed the expression "*corsi e ricorsi*" (cycles and counter cycles of growth and decay) of "history", he never speaks in the plural of "the cycle" or of "the counter-cycle" (*ricorso*) of "human things", suggesting that political life and order, or human creations, are oriented "backward," as it were, or called back to their constitutive "metaphysical" principle.

On present day "constructivist" readings, Vico is supposed to have promoted a vision of man and society as moving in parallel from barbarism to civilization.

As societies become more developed socially, human nature also develops, and both manifest their development in changes in language, myth, folklore, economy, etc.; in short, social change produces cultural change.

Vico would therefore be using an original organic idea that culture is a system of socially produced and structured elements. Hence, knowledge of any society would come from the social structure of that society, explicable, therefore, only in terms of its own language. As such, one may find a dialectical relationship between language, knowledge and social structure.

Relying on a complex etymology, Vico argues in the *Scienza Nuova* that civilization develops in a recurring cycle (*ricorso*) of three ages: the divine, the heroic, and the human. Each age exhibits distinct political and social features and can be characterized by master tropes or figures of language. The *giganti* of the divine age rely on metaphor to compare, and thus comprehend, human and natural phenomena.

In the heroic age, metonymy and synecdoche support the development of feudal or monarchic institutions embodied by idealized figures. The final age is characterized by popular democracy and reflection via irony; in this epoch, the rise of rationality leads to *barbarie della reflessione* or barbarism of reflection, and civilization descends once more into the poetic era. Taken together, the recurring cycle of three ages – common to every nation – constitutes for Vico a *storia ideale eterna* or ideal eternal history. Therefore, it can be said that all history is the history of the rise and fall of civilizations, for which Vico provides evidence (up until, and including the Graeco-Roman historians).

Endnotes

1   Post attending, a series of dialogue in Moscow, in 1986 on Perestroika, [restructure] and Glasnost, [transparence] the translation was as effective as ordering vegetarian dishes in a Moscow restaurant as complex garnish, to soon trigger the breakdown of the Soviet State, my desire was to research, as to whether our adopting constitutions and their relevancy in adopted countries is no assurance for its continuity or preventing its split into small countries, nor federated, and call it, The Cult of The Constitution, and was about to complete, when in November, 2019 I came across a book by the same name authored by an American author, Mary Ann Frank, but instead of quarreling about my right of earlier christening. I decided to alter it to replace the word 'of' with 'and', in reading and reflecting what Ann Frank's book, was about. On her culling the controversies drawn between the thin difference that lie between a fidelity [to follow faithfulness to either a person, or cause, or belief, demonstrate ones continuing loyalty and support.] to one's constitution and of its fundamentalism, [to commence with things like a religious connotation to indicate unwavering attachment as if, to one's irreducible beliefs, in a new avatar, in strict literalism applied to certain specific scriptures, dogmas, or ideologies, in strong sense of the importance of maintaining an, in and out or we and they' distinctions] in a relentless run of its deep abyss of fundamental strains in both conservative and liberal thought, anywhere press the Constitution in the service of its people require as commented, that it reads the Constitution selectively as self-serving sovereign, the fundamental interpretation of the Constitution, elevating certain interpreted constitutional rights above the rest others, in a binary, even to benefit sometimes the wrong like the most powerful members of society, undermine the integrity of the document as a whole, in a conservative fetish for the Second Amendment provides an obvious example of fundamentalism with a liberal fetish for the First Amendment is less obvious but no less influential. Economic and civil libertarianism increasingly merge to produce a deregulated free-market approach to constitutional rights that achieves fullest expression in the idealization of the Internet. The worship of guns, speech, and the Internet in the name of the Constitution blurs boundaries between conduct and speech and between veneration and violence, brought for free and open access reminded with each inauguration, when the President-elect places one hand on the Bible and raises the other before the Chief Justice of a country, that requires the President

"to solemnly swear" that he will "preserve, protect and defend the Constitution, a similar sworn duty is a universal feature of government service: have been used from 1787 to the present day, from the Chief Justiceship of John Marshall to John Roberts Jr. as embedded features of the interpretive process, to answer complex Constitutional questions, ignoring this reality consider only a narrow range of interpretive sources is frequently impossible and, indeed, absurd, when the Constitutions themselves contains the antidote to fundamentalism," which in layperson's terms means to reach the point in a lawsuit when it's clear to the parties involved what the exact nature of the dispute is. Lītem contestārī is the probable ultimate source of both contestation and contest.

2   The latin phrase litem contestari translated as to join issue in a legal suit, which in layperson's term means to reach the point in a lawsuit when it's clear to the parties involved what the exact nature of the dispute is litem contestari is the probabale ultimate source of both contestation and contest, the latter having first come to English as a meaning to make the subject of dispute, contention or battle. But while contest has gone on to have a life at home in another part of speech and in contexts ranging from sports to art, contestation continues to dwell mainly in serious speech and writing about adversarial dynamics between groups of people.

3   The title speaks of the theme, but the working of the cult of hundreds of constitutions except these causes consequences, difficult to have a right constitution to protect prevailing democracy.

4   Chat GPT

5   love bombing is an attempt to influence another person with over-the-top displays of attention and affection

6   An American religious leader who founded and led the Heaven's Gate new religious movement (often described as a cult), and organized their mass suicide in 1997.

7   An American cult leader and mass murderer who led the Peoples Temple between 1955 and 1978. In what Jones termed "revolutionary suicide", Jones and the members of his inner circle planned and orchestrated a mass murder-suicide in his remote jungle commune at Jonestown, Guyana, on November 18, 1978. Jones and the events that occurred at Jonestown have had a defining influence on society's perception of cults.

8   An American author and the founder of Scientology. A prolific writer of pulp science fiction and fantasy novels in his early career, in 1950 he authored Dianetics: The Modern Science of Mental Health and established organizations to promote and practice Dianetics techniques. Hubbard created Scientology in 1952 after losing the intellectual rights to his literature on Dianetics in bankruptcy. He would lead the Church of Scientology, variously described as a cult,[1] a new religious movement, or a business, until his death in 1986.

9   Article 25 guarantees the freedom of conscience, the freedom to profess, practice, and propagate religion to all citizens. Article 26 (Freedom to manage religious affairs)The right to form and maintain institutions for religious and charitable intents. Article 27 of the constitution provides that no person shall be compelled to pay any tax or fee for the promotion or maintenance of any particular religion or religious denomination. Article 28 talks about Freedom as to attendance at religious instruction or religious worship in certain educational institutions.

10   George Orwell's "1984" is a dystopian novel set in a totalitarian society ruled by the Party and its leader, Big Brother. The story follows Winston Smith, a low-ranking member of the Party who works at the Ministry of Truth, where his job is to alter historical records to fit the Party's propaganda. The novel explores themes of totalitarianism, surveillance, censorship, and individualism. In the oppressive world of Oceania, the Party exerts total control over every aspect of life, including thoughts, through the use of propaganda, language manipulation (Newspeak), and the omnipresent surveillance of the Thought Police. Winston becomes disillusioned with the Party and starts to rebel. He begins a forbidden love affair with Julia, a fellow Party member, and they seek ways to undermine the regime. They secretly meet and share their mutual hatred for Big Brother, hoping to find a way to resist the Party's control. Eventually, Winston and Julia are betrayed, arrested, and tortured by the Thought Police. Winston undergoes brutal psychological manipulation and physical torture at the Ministry of Love, particularly at the hands of O'Brien, a high-ranking Party official who initially seemed sympathetic to Winston's cause. O'Brien's purpose is to break Winston's spirit and force him to completely submit to the Party's ideology. In the end, after enduring severe torture and brainwashing, Winston is broken and comes to love Big Brother, losing his sense of individuality and resistance. The novel concludes with Winston's complete acceptance of the Party's dominance, illustrating the terrifying power of totalitarian regimes to crush human spirit and integrity.

11   Aldous Huxley's "Brave New World" is a dystopian novel set in a future society that is highly controlled and technologically advanced. The World State, as this society is known, prioritizes stability, consumerism, and superficial happiness over individuality and emotional depth. Human beings are genetically engineered and conditioned from birth to fit into predetermined roles within a rigid caste system. Key themes in the novel include the dangers of technological and scientific advancements when used for totalitarian control, the loss of individuality and personal freedom, and the consequences of a society driven by instant gratification and consumerism. The story follows several characters: Bernard Marx: An Alpha-plus who feels alienated due to his physical and intellectual differences from his peers. He is dissatisfied with the shallow pleasures of the World State. Lenina Crowne: A Beta who works in the Hatchery and Conditioning Centre and adheres to the norms of society, but becomes involved with Bernard. John the

Savage: Born naturally on the Savage Reservation, John is the son of two World State citizens. He is brought to London by Bernard and becomes a sensation due to his unique background and differing views on society. As the story progresses, John struggles to reconcile the values and freedoms he learned on the Savage Reservation with the oppressive and superficial culture of the World State. He becomes increasingly disillusioned by the lack of genuine human connection and the pervasive control over individuals' lives. Bernard initially enjoys the fame brought by John's presence but eventually faces repercussions for challenging societal norms. Lenina, attracted to John, is confused and hurt by his rejection of her advances, which are grounded in the promiscuity encouraged by the World State. The climax of the novel occurs when John incites a riot among the lower castes by trying to distribute soma, a drug used to pacify the population. He is arrested and, in a final confrontation with Mustapha Mond, one of the World Controllers, John debates the values of the World State. Mond defends the society's sacrifices of art, science, and religion for stability and happiness, while John argues for individual freedom and the right to experience suffering. In the end, unable to adapt to the World State's values and tormented by his own beliefs, John retreats to a lighthouse to live in isolation. However, he is pursued by curious citizens and ultimately succumbs to despair, taking his own life.

12 This quote emphasizes the importance of self-awareness and self-control in one's life. It suggests that one should observe their own actions and desires and give up those that are not beneficial to them. The quote also implies that true peace can only be achieved by giving up all desires and attachments. Astavakra Gita, a classic Hindu religious text, offers a radical version of dualism.

13 Sanātana Dharma is an alternative name for Hinduism used in Sanskrit and other Indian languages alongside the more common *Hindu Dharma*. The term denotes the "eternal" or absolute set of duties or religiously ordained practices incumbent upon all Hindus, regardless of class, caste, or sect.

14 Theory of Legislation Lexis Nexis by Upendra Baxi Principle of Legislation Chapter 1 The Principle of Utility

15 Doxography is a term describing the method of recording opinions (doxai) of philosophers frequently employed by ancient Greek writers on philosophy.

16 A good tenet should have a perfectly valid opposite tenet that would make sense in a different context.

17 Hermann Alexander Diels was a German classical scholar, who was influential in the area of early Greek philosophy and is known for his standard work Die Fragmente der Vorsokratiker. Diels helped to import the term Presocratic into classical scholarship and developed the Diels–Kranz numbering system for ancient Greek Pre-Socratic texts.

18 A Greek philosopher and the successor to Aristotle in the Peripatetic school. He was a native of Eresos in Lesbos.

19   A biographer of the Greek philosophers. Little is definitively known about his life, but his surviving *Lives and Opinions of Eminent Philosophers* is a principal source for the history of ancient Greek philosophy. His reputation is controversial among scholars because he often repeats information from his sources without critically evaluating it. He also frequently focuses on trivial or insignificant details of his subjects' lives while ignoring important details of their philosophical teachings and he sometimes fails to distinguish between earlier and later teachings of specific philosophical schools. However, unlike many other ancient secondary sources, Diogenes Laërtius generally reports philosophical teachings without attempting to reinterpret or expand on them, which means his accounts are often closer to the primary sources. Due to the loss of so many of the primary sources on which Diogenes relied, his work has become the foremost surviving source on the history of Greek philosophy.

20   A German scholar in the fields of philology and comparative religion.

21   A German classical scholar, who was influential in the area of early Greek philosophy and is known for his standard work *Die Fragmente der Vorsokratiker*. Diels helped to import the term Presocratic into classical scholarship and developed the Diels–Kranz numbering system for ancient Greek Pre-Socratic texts.

22   Simplicius of Cilicia (ca. 480–560 CE), roughly a contemporary of John Philoponus, is without doubt the most important Neoplatonic commentator on Aristotle and one of the two most influential exegetes within the Aristotelian tradition, along with Alexander of Aphrodisias (around 200 CE).

23   Neoplatonism is a version of Platonic philosophy that emerged in the 3rd century AD against the background of Hellenistic philosophy and religion. The term does not encapsulate a set of ideas as much as a series of thinkers. Among the common ideas it maintains is monism, the doctrine that all of reality can be derived from a single principle, "the One".

24   It would seem that, just as is the case for Aristotle, also in that of Theophrastus more than one treatise provided material that ultimately found a home in the *Placita*, namely at the very least the *Physikai Doxai*, the *Physics*, the *De sensibus*, and the *Metarsiology*.

25   A Greek philosopher and the successor to Aristotle in the Peripatetic school. He was a native of Eresos in Lesbos. His given name was (Túrtamos); his nickname (Theóphrastos) was given by Aristotle, his teacher, for his "divine style of expression."

26   Mansfeld & Runia 2020, 4.3.1135–37. The term 'doxography' has come to be applied in a much larger sense than seems to have been intended by its creator Hermann Diels. This name for the genre, if we may misleadingly call it that, derives from the Latin neologism 'doxographi' used by Diels to indicate the authors of a rather strictly specified type of literature studied and edited in his

monumental *Doxographi Graeci* ('Greek Doxographers') of 1879. His researches were focused on writings concerned with the *physical* part of philosophy (including principles, theology, cosmology, astronomy, meteorology, biology and part of medicine). But today overviews in the field of ethics are also called doxographical. And scholars speak of 'doxographies' to be found in the dialogues of Plato and the treatises of Aristotle, although these are works in which issues of philosophy are addressed, with only ancillary discussion of the views of others.

27 A supposition or proposed explanation made on the basis of limited evidence as a starting point for further investigation.

28 A Roman general and statesman of the closing period of the Western Roman Empire. He was a military commander and the most influential man in the Empire for two decades (433–454).

29 An influential theologian of the School of Antioch, biblical commentator. A Christian bishop of Cyrrhus (423–457). He played a pivotal role in several 5th-century Byzantine Church controversies that led to various ecumenical acts and schisms.

30 The compiler of a valuable series of extracts from Greek authors.

31 A Roman statesman, lawyer, scholar, philosopher, writer and Academic skeptic, who tried to uphold optimate principles during the political crises that led to the establishment of the Roman Empire. His extensive writings include treatises on rhetoric, philosophy and politics. He is considered one of Rome's greatest orators and prose stylists and the innovator of what became known as "Ciceronian rhetoric". Cicero was educated in Rome and in Greece. He came from a wealthy municipal family of the Roman equestrian order, and served as consul in 63 BC.

32 Marcus Terentius Varro (116–27 BC) was a Roman polymath and a prolific author. He is regarded as ancient Rome's greatest scholar, and was described by Petrarch as "the third great light of Rome" (after Virgil and Cicero).[1] He is sometimes called Varro Reatinus ("Varro of Rieti") to distinguish him from his younger contemporary Varro Atacinus.

33 Aetius was a Roman general and statesman of the closing period of the Western Roman Empire. He was a military commander and the most influential man in the Empire for two decades (433–454). He managed policy in regard to the attacks of barbarian federates settled throughout the West. Notably, he mustered a large Roman and allied (foederati) army in the Battle of the Catalaunian Plains, ending a devastating invasion of Gaul by Attila in 451, though the Hun and his subjugated allies still managed to invade Italy the following year, an incursion best remembered for the ruthless Sack of Aquileia and the intercession of Pope Leo I.

34 Pre-Socratic philosophy, also known as Early Greek Philosophy, is ancient Greek philosophy before Socrates. Pre-Socratic philosophers were mostly interested in

cosmology, the beginning and the substance of the universe, but the inquiries of these early philosophers spanned the workings of the natural world as well as human society, ethics, and religion.

35 A biographer of the Greek philosophers. Little is definitively known about his life, but his surviving Lives and Opinions of Eminent Philosophers is a principal source for the history of ancient Greek philosophy.

36 The study of the sources of, or influences upon, a literary work.

37 The method of reconstructing the text of a work based on the genealogical kinship of witnesses which was developed in the 19th century is often named after Karl Lachmann, although this scholar did not write any theoretical texts about it.

38 'Fragments of the Poet-Philosophers' of 1901, reprinted 2000- Epicureanism, which comes from ancient Greek philosophy, is a focus on the importance of pleasure. If you devote yourself to going to the symphony and eating fine foods, it's because of your epicureanism.

39 'Fragments of the Presocratics', abbreviated D.-K.'s, first published in 1903- Diels–Kranz (DK) numbering is the standard system for referencing the works of the ancient Greek pre-Socratic philosophers, based on the collection of quotations from and reports of their work, Die Fragmente der Vorsokratiker (The Fragments of the Pre-Socratics), by Hermann Alexander Diels.

40 A biographer of the Greek philosophers. Little is definitively known about his life, but his surviving Lives and Opinions of Eminent Philosophers is a principal source for the history of ancient Greek philosophy. His reputation is controversial among scholars because he often repeats information from his sources without critically evaluating it.

41 A German classical scholar and humanist. He served as rector of Heidelberg University in 1564.

42 Hermann Karl Usener, a German scholar in the fields of philology and comparative religion. He was influential most of all through his work on the formation of religious concepts, which influenced thinkers such as Albrecht Dieterich, Ludwig Radermacher, Aby Warburg, Walter F. Otto, and Ernst Cassirer. In his book "The Names of Gods" (Götternamen, 1896), Usener introduced the concept of a momentary god.

43 The Posterior Analytics; Latin: Analytica Posteriora) is a text from Aristotle's Organon that deals with demonstration, definition, and scientific knowledge. The demonstration is distinguished as a syllogism productive of scientific knowledge, while the definition marked as the statement of a thing's nature,…a statement of the meaning of the name, or of an equivalent nominal formula.

44 Inquiry into metaphysical contradictions and their solutions.

45 Nominative, accusative and vocative plural form of ἔνστασῃ (énstasi).

46 Mansfeld 1990, 1992, 1998, 2016a, Mansfeld & Runia 1997, Runia 1999a, Runia 2004, with criticism in Zhmud 2001 and rejoinder in Mansfeld 2002

47   Dialogue between people holding different points of view about a subject but wishing to arrive at the truth through reasoned argumentation.

48   An Ancient Greek pre-Socratic philosopher from Abdera, primarily remembered today for his formulation of an atomic theory of the universe

49   *Status quaestionis*, a Latin phrase translated roughly as "the state of investigation," is most commonly employed in scholarly literature to refer in a summary way to the accumulated results, scholarly consensus, and areas remaining to be developed on any given topic. The phrase is often used by ancient historians, classicists, theologians, philosophers, biblical scholars, and scholars in related fields, such as (Christian) church history.

50   An Epicurean philosopher and poet. He studied under Zeno of Sidon in Athens, before moving to Rome, and then to Herculaneum. He was once known chiefly for his poetry preserved in the *Greek Anthology*, but since the 18th century, many writings of his have been discovered among the charred papyrus rolls at the Villa of the Papyri at Herculaneum.

51   A Stoic philosopher and teacher of Augustus. Fragments of his handbooks summarizing Stoic and Peripatetic doctrines are preserved by Stobaeus and Eusebius.

52   (Mansfeld and Runia 2020)

53   Hindu philosophy is the longest surviving philosophical tradition in India. We can recognize several historical stages. The earliest, from around 700 bc, was the proto-philosophical period, when karma and liberation theories arose, and the proto-scientific ontological lists in the Upaniṣads were compiled.

54   The Iron Age ended around 600 or 500 B.C.E.

55   The Classical Period came after the Iron Age and lasted from around 600 B.C.E. to 600 C.E.

56   In Indian philosophy the term designates the distinctive way in which each philosophical system looks at things, including its exposition of sacred scriptures and authoritative knowledge. The six principal Hindu darshans are Samkhya, Yoga, Nyaya, Vaisheshika, Mimamsa, and Vedanta.

57   It is also the theory of creation recognized by both Yoga and Ayurveda. Sankhya means "empirical" or "number." It explains creation in a manner where the implicit becomes explicit and where there exists neither production nor destruction. All of creation stems from the two facets of Sankhya: Purusha and Prakriti.

58   Nyaya is a Sanskrit word which means justice, equality for all being, specially a collection of general or universal rules. In some contexts, it means model, axiom, plan, legal proceeding, judicial sentence, or judgment.

59   One of the six systems (darshans) of Indian philosophy, significant for its naturalism, a feature that is not characteristic of most Indian thought. The Sanskrit philosopher Kanada Kashyapa (2nd–3rd century ce?) expounded its theories and is credited with founding the school.

60   One of the six systems (darshans) of Indian philosophy. Mimamsa, probably the earliest of the six, is fundamental to Vedanta, another of the six systems, and has deeply influenced the formulation of Hindu law

61   Vedanta is an ancient school of Hindu philosophy that was based on three primary Hindu texts: the Upanishads, the Brahma Sutras, and the Bhagavad Gita. Vedanta teaches the concepts of the soul, known as atman, and its relationship with the Supreme God, known as Brahman. Vedanta is still studied today, with Advaita

62   including Buddhism, Jainism, Chārvāka, Ājīvik and others, which are thus classified under Indian but not Hindu philosophy.

63   The *Nyāya Sūtras* is an ancient Indian Sanskrit text composed by *Akṣapāda Gautama*, and the foundational text of the Nyaya school of Hindu philosophy.

64   A Sanskrit word that means "reflection" or "critical investigation" and thus refers to a tradition of contemplation which reflected on the meanings of certain Vedic texts.

65   Jaimini was an ancient Indian scholar who founded the Mīmāṃsā school of Hindu philosophy. He is considered to be a disciple of the *rishi* Vyasa, the son of Parāśara. Traditionally attributed to be the author of the *Mimamsa Sutras* and the *Jaimini Sutras*, he is estimated to have lived around 4th to 2nd century BCE. Some scholars place him between 250 BCE and 50 CE His school is considered non-theistic, but one that emphasized rituals parts of the *Vedas* as essential to *dharma*. Jaimini is known for his studies of the older Vedic rituals. Jaimini's *guru* was Badarayana who founded the Vedanta school of Hindu philosophy. He is also credited with authoring the *Brahma Sutras* Both Badarayana and Jaimini quoted each other as they analyzed each other's theories, Badarayana emphasising knowledge while Jaimini emphasises rituals, sometimes agreeing with each other, sometimes disagreeing, often anti-thesis of the other. Jaimini's contributions to textual analysis and exegesis influenced other schools of Indian philosophies. The most studied *bhashya* (reviews and commentaries) on Jaimini's texts were by scholars named Shabara, Kumarila, and Prabhakara

66   The *Yajnavalkya Smriti* is one of the many Dharma-related texts of Hinduism composed in Sanskrit. It is dated between the 3rd to 5th-century CE, and belongs to the Dharmashastra tradition. The text was composed after the Manusmriti, but like it and Naradasmriti, the text was composed in *shloka* (poetic meter) style. The legal theories within the *Yajnavalkya Smriti* are presented in three books, namely *achara-kanda* (customs), *vyavahara-kanda* (judicial process) and *prayascitta-kanda* (crime and punishment, penance).

67   The *Manusmṛiti* also known as the *Mānava-Dharmaśāstra* or Laws of Manu, is one of the many legal texts and constitutions among the many *Dharmaśāstras* of Hinduism. In ancient India, the sages often wrote their ideas on how society should run in the manuscripts. It is believed that the original form of *Manusmriti* was changed and interpolated with commentaries and opinions of the writers

rather than the original content, as many things written in the manuscript contradict each other.

68 Vijnaneshwara was a prominent jurist of the first millennium CE India. His treatise, the *Mitakshara,* dealt with inheritance, and is one of the most influential legal treatises in Hindu law. Mitakshara is the treatise on Yājñavalkya Smṛti, named after a sage of the same name.

69 Jīmūtavāhana (c. 12th century) was an Indian Sanskrit scholar and writer of legal and religious treatises on Vaishnavism of early medieval period. He was the earliest writer on *smriti* (law) from Bengal whose texts are extant.

70 The *Yajnavalkya Smriti* is one of the many Dharma-related texts of Hinduism composed in Sanskrit. It is dated between the 3rd to 5th-century CE, and belongs to the Dharmashastra tradition. The text was composed after the Manusmriti, but like it and Naradasmriti, the text was composed in *shloka* (poetic meter) style The legal theories within the *Yajnavalkya Smriti* are presented in three books, namely *achara-kanda* (customs), *vyavahara-kanda* (judicial process) and *prayascitta-kanda* (crime and punishment, penance). The text is the "best composed" and systematic specimen of this genre, with large sections on judicial process theories, one which had greater influence in medieval India's judiciary practice than Manusmriti. It later became influential in the studies of legal process in ancient and medieval India, during the colonial British India, with the first translation published in German in 1849. The text is notable for its differences in legal theories from Manusmriti, for being more liberal and humane, and for extensive discussions on evidence and judiciousness of legal documents.

71 The *Mitākṣarā* is a *vivṛti* (legal commentary) on the Yajnavalkya Smriti best known for its theory of "inheritance by birth." It was written by Vijñāneśvara, a scholar in the Western Chalukya court in the late eleventh and early twelfth century. Along with the Dāyabhāga, it was considered one of the main authorities on Hindu Law from the time the British began administering laws in India. The entire *Mitākṣarā*, along with the text of the *Yājñavalkya-smṛti*, is approximately 492 closely printed pages.

72 The *Dāyabhāga* is a Hindu law treatise written by Jīmūtavāhana which primarily focuses on inheritance procedure. The *Dāyabhāga* was the strongest authority in Modern British Indian courts in the Bengal region of India, although this has changed due to the passage of the Hindu Succession Act of 1956 and subsequent revisions to the act. Based on Jīmūtavāhana's criticisms of the *Mitākṣarā*, it is thought that his work is precluded by the *Mitākṣarā*. This has led many scholars to conclude that the *Mitākṣarā* represents the orthodox doctrine of Hindu law, while the *Dāyabhāga* represents the reformed version. The central difference between the texts is based upon when one becomes the owner of property. The *Dāyabhāga* does not give the sons a right to their father's ancestral property

until after his death, unlike *Mitākṣarā*, which gives the sons the right to ancestral property upon their birth. The digest has been commented on more than a dozen times.

73   Ur-Nammu (or Ur-Namma, Ur-Engur, Ur-Gur, Sumerian: ruled c. 2112 BC – 2094 BC middle chronology, or possibly c. 2048–2030 BC short chronology) founded the Sumerian Third Dynasty of Ur, in southern Mesopotamia, following several centuries of Akkadian and Gutian rule. His main achievement was state-building, and Ur-Nammu is chiefly remembered today for his legal code, the Code of Ur-Nammu, the oldest known surviving example in the world. He held the titles of "King of Ur, and King of Sumer and Akkad".

74   Eshnunna (modern Tell Asmar in Diyala Governorate, Iraq) was an ancient Sumerian (and later Akkadian) city and city-state in central Mesopotamia 12.6 miles northwest of Tell Agrab and 15 miles northwest of Tell Ishchali. Although situated in the Diyala Valley northwest of Sumer proper, the city nonetheless belonged securely within the Sumerian cultural milieu. It is sometimes, in archaeological papers, called Ashnunnak or Tuplias.

The tutelary deity of the city was Tishpak (Tišpak) though other gods, including Sin, Adad, and Inanna of Kititum were also worshiped there. The personal goddesses of the rulers were Belet-Šuḫnir and Belet-Terraban.

75   The Code of Lipit-Ishtar is a collection of laws promulgated by Lipit-Ishtar (r. 1934 – 1924 BCE (MC)), a ruler in Lower Mesopotamia. As cuneiform law, it is a legal code written in cuneiform script in the Sumerian language. It is the second-oldest known extant legal code after the Code of Ur-Nammu.

76   The Code of Hammurabi is a Babylonian legal text composed during 1755–1750 BC. It is the longest, best-organized, and best-preserved legal text from the ancient Near East. It is written in the Old Babylonian dialect of Akkadian, purportedly by Hammurabi, sixth king of the First Dynasty of Babylon. The primary copy of the text is inscribed on a basalt stele 2.25 m (7 ft 4+½ in) tall.

77   A Veda is a collection of poems or hymns composed in archaic Sanskrit by Indo-European-speaking peoples who lived in northwest India during the 2nd millennium BCE.

78   *Smriti* literally "that which is remembered" are a body of Hindu texts usually attributed to an author, traditionally written down, in contrast to Śrutis (the Vedic literature) considered authorless, that were transmitted verbally across the generations and fixed. *Smriti* is a derivative secondary work and is considered less authoritative than *Sruti* in Hinduism, except in the Mimamsa school of Hindu philosophy The authority of *smriti* accepted by orthodox schools is derived from that of *shruti*, on which it is based.

79   The Upanishads present a vision of an interconnected universe with a single, unifying principle behind the apparent diversity in the cosmos, any articulation of which is called brahman.

80 *Dharmaśāstra* Sanskrit texts on law and conduct, and refers to the treatises (śāstras) on Dharma. Unlike Dharmasūtra which are based upon Vedas, these texts are mainly based on Puranas. There are many Dharmashastras, variously estimated to be 18 to about 100, with different and conflicting points of view. Each of these texts exist in many different versions, and each is rooted in Dharmasutra texts dated to 1st millennium BCE that emerged from Kalpa (Vedanga) studies in the Vedic era.

81 The name given to a class of systematic 'digests' of dharma, compiled from a wide variety of Dharmaśāstra literature from about the 9th century ce onwards. They were the main source of the Indian legal system devised by the British in the 18th century. From: Nibandhas in A Dictionary of Hinduism.

82 Yajna (Sanskrit: यज्ञ, romanized: *yajña*, lit. 'sacrifice, devotion, worship, offering') refers in Hinduism to any ritual done in front of a sacred fire, often with mantras. [1] Yajna has been a Vedic tradition, described in a layer of Vedic literature called Brahmanas, as well as Yajurveda.[2] The tradition has evolved from offering oblations and libations into sacred fire to symbolic offerings in the presence of sacred fire (Agni).

83 The Arthashastra is an Ancient Indian Sanskrit treatise on statecraft, political science, economic policy and military strategy.

84 The Aṣṭādhyāyī employs a derivational system to describe the language, where real speech is derived from posited abstract utterances formed by means of affixes added to bases under certain conditions.

85 Jaimini was an ancient Indian scholar who founded the Mīmāṃsā school of Hindu philosophy. He is the son of Parāśara and is considered to be a disciple of sage Vyasa. Traditionally attributed to be the author of the Mimamsa Sutras and the Jaimini Sutras, he is estimated to have lived around 4th to 2nd century BCE. Some scholars place him between 250 BCE and 50 CE. His school is considered non-theistic, but emphasizes ritual parts of the Vedas as essential to dharma. Jaimini is known for his studies of the older Vedic rituals.

86 A pithy observation which contains a general truth.

87 Vijnaneshwara was a prominent jurist of the first millennium CE India. His treatise, the Mitakshara, dealt with inheritance, and is one of the most influential legal treatises in Hindu law. Mitakshara is the treatise on Yājñavalkya Smṛti, named after a sage of the same name. Vijnaneshwara was born in the village of Masimadu, near Basavakalyan in Karnataka. He lived in the court of king Vikramaditya VI (1076-1126), the Western Chalukya Empire monarch.

88 Jīmūtavāhana (c. 12th century) was an Indian Sanskrit scholar and writer of legal and religious treatises on Vaishnavism of early medieval period. He was the earliest writer on *smriti* (law) from Bengal whose texts are extant.

89 Usually the word mina referred to a mina of silver, but Plautus also twice mentions a mina of gold.

90 The term proportionality describes any relationship that is always in the same ratio.

91 The Purva Mimamsa sutras of Jaimini is one of the most important ancient Hindu philosophical texts. it forms the basis of Mimamsa, the earliest of the six orthodox schools (Darsanas) of Indian Philosophy. The complete work is divided into twelve adhyayas (chapters) which are further divided into sixty padas (sections).

92 Rudrapatna Shamasastry FRAS (1868–1944) was a Sanskrit scholar and librarian at the Oriental Research Institute Mysore.

93 The Mitākṣarā is a vivṛti (legal commentary) on the Yajnavalkya Smriti best known for its theory of "inheritance by birth.

94 The Dāyabhāga is a Hindu law treatise written by Jīmūtavāhana which primarily focuses on inheritance procedure.

95 An Indian philosopher, logician and mathematician from the kingdom of Mithila. He established the Navya-Nyāya ("New Logic") school. His *Tattvachintāmaṇi* (The Jewel of Thought on the Nature of Things), also known as *Pramāṇacintāmaṇi* (The Jewel of Thought on the Means of Valid Knowledge), is the basic text for all later developments. The logicians of this school were primarily interested in defining their terms and concepts related to non-binary logical categories.

96 The Mimamsa Sutra or the Purva Mimamsa Sutras (ca. 300–200 BCE), written by Rishi Jaimini is one of the most important ancient Hindu philosophical texts.

97 observation which contains a general truth.

98 1992 A.L.R. 921

99 This is laid down in Book 1 Chapter II, Sutra 9 of Jaimini's Sutras. This principle is illustrated in the Dayabhaga by Jimutavahana. In the context of rule relating to succession on which there are inconsistent texts regarding the right of a son born after partition, Manu says "A son, born after division, shall alone take the paternal wealth", and this is also the view of Narada and Gautam. However, Vishnu says "Sons, with whom the father has made a partition, should give a share to the son born after the distribution". This is also the view of Yajnavalkya. Jimutvahana reconciles these texts by applying samanjasya principle holding that the former text applies to the self acquired property of the father, while the latter applies to property which is descended from the grand-father.

100 *Badha principle* signifies exclusion by repugnancy. For example, a special law prevails over a general law, a higher law prevails over a lower law, a clear law prevails over an unclear law, a law which serves a purpose immediately prevails over that which is of remote service, a manifest sense prevails over a sense by context, etc. See Shree Bhatt Sankar's *Mimansa Valaprakash*. Jaimini has described this principle in the tenth chapter of his work.

101 (1988) 4 SCC 274

102 Lord Denning: *The Discipline of Law*, (1979) Butterworth, London.

103 (1990) 1 SCC 613

104 See Jaimini: 2, 1, 48

105 The uha principle, referred to in the ninth chapter of Jaimini's sutras, originally meant only adaptation. However, Kumarila Bhatta considerably widened its import, and made it equivalent to the use of reason for various purposes in interpretation.

106 (1991) 2 SCC 87

107 Also see P.V. Kane: *History of the Dharmashastras*, Vol. 5 Pt. II, pp. 1339-51.

108 For example Nanda Pandit in his *Dattak Mimansa* has used the pranabhrit maxim to show that although the word 'substitute' was initially applied only to 5 descriptions of sons, later by general use it became applicable to all 12 descriptions.

109 (1990) 2 SCC 231

110 1993 ALR 89

111 AIR 1992 All 351

112 1993 ALR 1

113 Sāmkhya is an enumerationist philosophy whose epistemology accepted three of six *pramāṇas* as the only reliable means of gaining knowledge.

114 A group of physical, mental, and spiritual practices or disciplines which originated in ancient India and aim to control (yoke) and still the mind, recognizing a detached witness-consciousness untouched by the mind (*Chitta*) and mundane suffering (*Duḥkha*). There is a wide variety of schools of yoga, practices, and goals in Hinduism, Buddhism, and Jainism, and traditional and modern yoga is practiced worldwide.

115 Vaisesika is one of the six systems of Hindu philosophy. It represents a pluralistic realism and is usually held to be an atomistic, metaphysical theory.

116 Also called *Kanada sutra*, is an ancient Sanskrit text at the foundation of the Vaisheshika school of Hindu philosophy.

117 while atoms are invisible. The Vaiśeṣikas stated that size, form, truths and everything that human beings experience as a whole is a function of atoms, their number and their spatial arrangements, their *guṇa* (quality), *karma* (activity), *sāmānya* (commonness), *viśeṣa* (particularity) and *amavāya* (inherence, inseparable connectedness of everything)

118 One of the six systems (darshans) of Indian philosophy, important for its analysis of logic and epistemology.

119 The epistemology of the Vedantins included, depending on the sub-school, five or six methods as proper and reliable means of gaining any form of knowledge.

120 A school of Vedanta representing the philosophy of *inconceivable one-ness and difference*.[1] In Sanskrit *achintya* means 'inconceivable', *bheda* translates as 'difference', and *abheda* translates as 'non-difference'

121 Akshar-Purushottam Darshan (*Akṣara-Puruṣottama Darśana*) or Aksarabrahma-Parabrahma-Darsanam, "Akshar-Purushottam philosophy," is a designation used

by BAPS as an alternative name for the Swaminarayan Darshana, Swaminarayan's view or teachings, to distinguish it from other Vedanta-traditions. It is based on Swaminarayan's distinction between Parabrahman (Purushottam, Narayana) and Aksharbrahman as two distinct eternal realities, which in this view sets Swaminarayan's teachings apart from other Vedanta-traditions. It is an essential element for the BAPS and its *Akṣara-Puruṣottama Upāsanā* ("worship"), in which Purushottam c.q. Parabrahman is present in a lineage of Aksharbrahman guru's, who are the abode (*akshar*) of God.

122 Shaivism is an ancient form of Hinduism that focuses on the worship and veneration of the god Lord Shiva. The term has been derived from the Sanskrit word shiva, which refers to the god of destruction and transformation.

123 Pashupata Shaivism (Pāśupata) is one of the oldest major Shaivite Hindu schools.

124 Shaiva Siddhanta is a form of Shaivism popular in South India and Sri Lanka which propounds a devotional philosophy with the ultimate goal of experiencing union with Shiva. It draws primarily on the Tamil devotional hymns written by Shaiva saints from the 5th to the 9th century CE, known in their collected form as *Tirumurai*.

125 Kashmir Shaivism or Trika Shaivism, is a nondualist Hindu tradition of Shaiva-Shakta Tantra which originated in Kashmir sometime after 850 CE.

126 Writes Barbara O'Brien is a Zen Buddhist practitioner who studied at Zen Mountain Monastery. She is the author of "Rethinking Religion" and has covered religion for The Guardian, Tricycle.org, and other outlets.

127 Internet Encyclopedia of Philosophy

128 A dialogue that was written by the ancient Greek philosopher Plato. It depicts a conversation between Socrates and his wealthy friend Crito of Alopece regarding justice, injustice, and the appropriate response to injustice after Socrates's imprisonment, which is chronicled in the Apology. In Crito, Socrates believes injustice may not be answered with injustice, personifies the Laws of Athens to prove this, and refuses Crito's offer to finance his escape from prison. The dialogue contains an ancient statement of the social contract theory of government.

129 An English philosopher. Hobbes is best known for his 1651 book Leviathan, in which he expounds an influential formulation of social contract theory. He is considered to be one of the founders of modern political philosophy.

130 An English philosopher and physician, widely regarded as one of the most influential of Enlightenment thinkers and commonly known as the "father of liberalism".

131 A Genevan philosopher (philosophe), writer, and composer. His political philosophy influenced the progress of the Age of Enlightenment throughout Europe, as well as aspects of the French Revolution and the development of modern political, economic, and educational thought.

132 Although it is one of the many elements of his political philosophy, we could consider it among the most important ones. For Kant, social contract is the glue that holds the state together. Kant says: The act by which a people forms itself into a state is the original contract.

133 A Canadian philosopher best known for his neo-Hobbesian or contractarian theory of morality, as developed in his 1986 book Morals by Agreement.

134 Feminism is a range of socio-political movements and ideologies that aim to define and establish the political, economic, personal, and social equality of the sexes. Feminism holds the position that societies prioritize the male point of view and that women are treated unjustly in these societies. Efforts to change this include fighting against gender stereotypes and improving educational, professional, and interpersonal opportunities and outcomes for women.

135 In general, Critical Philosophers of Race focus on how race operates in societies, the effects of race at both the structural and phenomenological levels, and the ways in which some forms of resistance to racial systems can be recuperated into sustaining the status quo.

136 A Greek philosopher from Athens who is credited as the founder of Western philosophy and among the first moral philosophers of the ethical tradition of thought. An enigmatic figure, Socrates authored no texts and is known mainly through the posthumous accounts of classical writers, particularly his students Plato and Xenophon.

137 The Law of Athens was known for its strict punishments, which included the death penalty for even minor crimes. The impact of Draco's laws was significant, as they marked a shift in the legal system of ancient Greece from reliance on oral tradition and custom to a more organized and formalized system of written laws.

138 He divides good things into three classes: things good in themselves, things good both in themselves and for their consequences, and things good only for their consequences.

139 In Plato's Republic, Gyges was a shepherd who discovered a magic ring of invisibility, by means of which he murdered the king and won the affection of the queen.

140 Oliver Cromwell was an English statesman, politician, and soldier, widely regarded as one of the most important figures in the history of the British Isles.

141 An English political theorist who defended the divine right of kings. His best known work, Patriarcha, published posthumously in 1680, was the target of numerous Whig attempts at rebuttal, including Algernon Sidney's Discourses Concerning Government, James Tyrrell's Patriarcha Non Monarcha and John Locke's Two Treatises of Government. Filmer also wrote critiques of Thomas Hobbes, John Milton, Hugo Grotius and Aristotle.

142 "Leviathan" has four main parts that serve to highlight his belief in a monarchy as the most ideal form of government. He believed people should give up

some of their personal liberties for the greater good, protection, and rule by a powerful sovereign- these beliefs constituted Hobbes' ideas about the social contract. A metaphor for the state, the Leviathan is described as an artificial person whose body is made up of all the bodies of its citizens, who are the literal members of the Leviathan's body. The head of the Leviathan is the sovereign.

143 Ludwig Wittgenstein was one of the most important philosophers of the 20th century. There were few philosophical fields left untouched by the British-Austrian genius; he worked with logic, mathematics, ethics, the mind, and most notably, revolutionized the way that we understand language.

144 Norman Malcolm, American Philosopher, who believe that If God does not exist, then He cannot come into existence. Therefore, if God does not exist, His existence is impossible. Therefore, God's existence is either necessary or impossible. However, God's existence is only impossible if the concept of God is self-contradictory.

145 Herbert Lionel Adolphus Hart was an English legal philosopher. He was the Professor of Jurisprudence at Oxford University and the Principal of Brasenose College, Oxford. His most famous work is The Concept of Law, which has been hailed as "the most important work of legal philosophy written in the twentieth century". He is considered one of the world's foremost legal philosophers in the twentieth century.

146 Isaiah Berlin is renowned for his defence of liberalism and most notably, for his two concepts of liberty: positive and negative liberty. He puts forth these two concepts in defence of liberalism, to articulate the boundaries of legitimate state interference.

147 An English philosopher, literary critic and university administrator. He was one of the antirationalist Oxford thinkers who gave a new direction to moral and political thought in the post-World War II era.

148 *Political Liberalism* is a 1993 book by the American philosopher John Rawls,[1] an update to his earlier *A Theory of Justice* (1971). In it, he attempts to show that his theory of justice is not a "comprehensive conception of the good" but is instead compatible with a liberal conception of the role of justice, namely, that government should be neutral between competing conceptions of the good. Rawls tries to show that his two principles of justice, properly understood, form a "theory of the right" (as opposed to a theory of the good) which would be supported by all reasonable individuals, even under conditions of reasonable pluralism. The mechanism by which he demonstrates this is called "overlapping consensus". Here he also develops his idea of public reason. An expanded edition of the book was published in 2005. It includes an added introduction, the essay "The Idea of Public Reason Revisited" (1997) – some 60 pages – and an index to the new material.

149 "The Law of Peoples" extends the idea of a social contract to the Society of Peoples and lays out the general principles that can and should be accepted by both liberal and non-liberal societies as the standard for regulating their behavior toward one another.

150 Rawls argued that only under a "veil of ignorance" could human beings reach a fair and impartial agreement (contract) as true equals not biased by their place in society. They would have to rely only on the human powers of reason to choose principles of social justice for their society.

151 Utilitarianism is a moral philosophy that advocates for actions that promote happiness and well-being for the greatest number of people. It's based on the idea that the best action is the one that produces the most good and the least harm. It's a type of consequentialism, meaning it judges the morality of an action based on its consequences.